HISTORY AND SOCIAL THEORY

HISTORY AND SOCIAL THEORY

Peter Burke

Cornell University Press
Ithaca, New York

First published 1993 by Cornell University Press.

International Standard Book Number 0–8014–2861–0 (cloth)
International Standard Book Number 0–8014–8100–7 (paper)
Library of Congress Catalog Card Number 92–054434

Printed in Great Britain

Librarians: A CIP catalog record for this book is available from the Library of Congress.

This book is printed on acid-free paper.

CONTENTS

PREFACE

At the beginning of my academic career, at the University of Sussex in the early 1960s, I volunteered to teach a course on 'Social Structure and Social Change' on the grounds that it was a good idea to know what 'society' was before writing its history and that the best way to learn a subject is to teach it. Involvement with the course led to an invitation from Tom Bottomore to write a book on 'Sociology and History', published by Allen and Unwin in 1980, attempting to introduce students of each discipline to what they might find most valuable in the other. Over a decade later, Polity Press has given me the opportunity to revise, enlarge and rewrite that book.

This second version appears under a new title which represents more accurately what the book is about. The original preface explained that social anthropology 'plays a more important role in this essay than the title suggests', while there was also some discussion of economics and politics. In the 1990s, however, a discussion of social theory might reasonably be expected to include much more, including such disciplines or sub-disciplines as communications, geography, international relations, law, linguistics (especially sociolinguistics), psychology (especially social psychology) and religious studies. It is also virtually impossible to exclude interdisciplinary enterprises such as critical, cultural and feminist theory, or indeed philosophy (which might be defined as the theory of theory).

Broadening the scope of the essay in this way raises a number of problems. The field is too large for a single individual to master. Although I have been reading reasonably widely in social theory for the past thirty years, and thinking about its possible uses in the writing of history, my own historical experience is obviously limited. I have always worked on the cultural and social history of Europe in the sixteenth and seventeenth centuries, and have at best a patchy knowledge of other continents, other periods and other disciplines. Hence I have tended to choose concrete examples which are familiar to me from research and teaching, even at the price of a certain lack of balance.

To view what is going on in all these areas the writer cannot avoid a personal standpoint. The perspective from which this essay is written is that of what the late Fernand Braudel used to call 'total history' – not an account of the past including every detail, but one which emphasizes the connections between different fields of human endeavour.

There is also a linguistic problem. What term should replace 'sociology' now that the discussion has widened? To write 'sociology, anthropology etc.' is cumbrous. To speak of the 'social sciences', as used to be customary, is also awkward for anyone who does not believe that the model of the physical sciences (if there is such a unified model) is one to be followed by students of society. 'History and Theory' is an appealing title, but is likely to arouse false expectations of a rather more philosophical book than this one happens to be.

I have therefore decided to use the term 'social theory' (which should be understood as including 'cultural theory'). As the reader will soon discover, this choice does not imply the assumption that general theories are all that historians are likely to find interesting in sociology and other disciplines. Some of the concepts, models and methods employed in these disciplines also have their uses in the study of the past, while case-studies of contemporary societies may suggest fruitful comparisons and contrasts with earlier centuries.

The decision to extend the book in this way was rather like the decision to enlarge a house. It has involved a great deal of reconstruction. Indeed, it might be more exact to say that a few fragments of the first edition have been incorporated into what is essentially a new structure. There are many references to studies published in the 1980s. All the same, I have done my best not to be too up-to-date. I continue to believe that Marx and Durkheim, Weber and Malinowski – to name no more – still have much to teach us.

The first version of the book was written in the interdisciplinary atmosphere of the University of Sussex. The new version is the fruit of more than a decade at Cambridge, and it too owes much to colleagues. Ernest Gellner, Alan Macfarlane, Gwyn Prins and the Historical Geography group which meets in Emmanuel College will all recognize what I have learned from their stimulus, their criticisms and their suggestions for further reading. So will a number of colleagues outside Britain, among them Antonio Augusto Arantes, Anton Blok, Ulf Hannerz, Tamás Hofer, Vittorio Lanternari and Orvar Löfgren. The rewriting was begun at the Wissenschaftskolleg at Berlin, and the book owes much to the historians and anthropologists there, especially to André Béteille for his constructive comments on the draft. John Thompson, who has been responsible for my continuing education in sociology over the past few years, and my wife Maria Lúcia both read the penultimate version with care. Without their help I might still have meant what I said, but I would not always have been able to say what I meant.

Peter Burke

1
THEORISTS AND HISTORIANS

This book is an attempt to answer two deceptively simple questions. What is the use of social theory to historians, and what is the use of history to social theorists? I call these questions 'deceptively simple' because the formulation hides certain important distinctions. Different historians or kinds of historian have found different theories useful in different ways, some as an over-arching framework and others as a means to crack a particular problem. Others have shown and still show a strong resistance to theory.[1] It may also be useful to distinguish theories from models and concepts. Relatively few historians utilize theory in the strict sense of the term, but larger numbers employ models, while concepts are virtually indispensable.[2]

The distinction between practice and theory is not identical with the distinction between history and sociology – or other disciplines such as social anthropology, geography, politics or economics. Some students of these disciplines produce case-studies in which theory plays only a small role. On the other side some historians, notably the Marxists, discuss theoretical issues with vigour, even when they complain, as Edward Thompson did, in a famous polemical essay, of what he called 'the poverty of theory'.[3]

After all, two concepts which have been extremely influential in sociology, anthropology and political studies in the past few years were originally launched by British Marxist historians; Edward Thompson's

[1] Man (1986).
[2] Leys (1959).
[3] Thompson (1978b).

'moral economy' and Eric Hobsbawm's 'invention of tradition'.[4] Generally speaking, however, workers in these other disciplines use concepts and theories more often, more explicitly, more seriously and more proudly than historians do. It is this difference in attitudes to theory which accounts for most of the conflicts and misunderstandings between historians and the rest.

A Dialogue of the Deaf

Historians and sociologists (in particular) have not always been the best of neighbours. Intellectual neighbours they certainly are, in the sense that practitioners of both disciplines are concerned (like social anthropologists) with society viewed as a whole and with the whole range of human behaviour. In these respects they differ from economists, geographers, or specialists in political or religious studies.

Sociology may be defined as the study of human society, with an emphasis on generalizations about its structure and development. History is better defined as the study of human societies in the plural, placing the emphasis on the differences between them and also on the changes which have taken place in each one over time. The two approaches have sometimes been viewed as contradictory, but it is more useful to treat them as complementary. It is only by comparing it with others that we can discover in what respects a given society is unique. Change is structured, and structures change. Indeed, the process of 'structuration', as some sociologists call it, has become a focus of attention in recent years (below, p. 161).[5]

Historians and social theorists have the opportunity to free each other from different kinds of parochialism. Historians run the risk of parochialism in an almost literal sense of the term. Specializing as they usually do in a particular region, they may come to regard their 'parish' as completely unique, rather than as a unique combination of elements each one of which has parallels elsewhere. Social theorists display parochialism in a more metaphorical sense, a parochialism of time rather than place, whenever they generalize about 'society' on the basis of contemporary experience alone, or discuss social change without taking long-term processes into account.

Sociologists and historians each see the mote in their neighbour's eye.

---

[4] Thompson (1971); Hobsbawm and Ranger (1983).
[5] Giddens (1979, 1984).

Unfortunately, each group tends to perceive the other in terms of a rather crude stereotype. In Britain, at least, many historians still regard sociologists as people who state the obvious in a barbarous and abstract jargon, lack any sense of place and time, squeeze individuals without mercy into rigid categories and, to cap it all, describe these activities as 'scientific'. Sociologists, for their part, have long viewed historians as amateurish, myopic fact-collectors without system or method, the imprecision of their 'data base' matched only by their incapacity to analyse it. In short, despite the existence of an increasing number of bilinguals, whose work will be discussed in the pages which follow, sociologists and historians still do not speak the same language. Their dialogue, as the French historian Fernand Braudel once put it, is usually 'a dialogue of the deaf'.[6]

To understand this situation it may be helpful to view the different disciplines as distinct professions and even subcultures, with their own languages, values and mentalities or styles of thought, reinforced by their respective processes of training or 'socialization'. Sociologists, for example, are trained to notice or formulate general rules and often screen out the exceptions. Historians learn to attend to concrete detail at the expense of general patterns.[7]

From a historical point of view, it is clear that both parties are guilty of anachronism. Until relatively recently, many social theorists regarded historians as if they were still concerned with little more than the narrative of political events, as if the approach associated with the great nineteenth-century historian Leopold von Ranke were still dominant. In similar fashion some historians still speak of sociology as if it were stuck in the age of Auguste Comte, in the mid-nineteenth-century phase of grand generalizations without systematic empirical research. How and why did the opposition between history and sociology – or more generally, between history and theory – develop? How, why and to what extent has this opposition been overcome? These questions are historical ones, and I shall try to give them historical answers in the next section, focusing on three moments in the history of Western thought about society: the mid-eighteenth century, the mid-nineteenth century and the 1920s or thereabouts.

[6] Braudel (1958).
[7] Cohn (1962); K. Erikson (1970); Dening (1971–3).

The Differentiation of History and Theory

In the eighteenth century there were no disputes between sociologists and historians for a simple and obvious reason. Sociology did not exist as a separate discipline. The French legal theorist Charles de Montesquieu and the Scottish moral philosophers Adam Ferguson and John Millar have since been claimed by sociologists and anthropologists.[8] Indeed, they are sometimes described as 'founding fathers' of sociology. However, such a label gives the misleading impression that these men set out to found a new discipline, an intention they never expressed. A similar point might be made about the so-called founder of economics, Adam Smith, who moved in the same circles as Ferguson and Millar.

It might be better to describe all four men as social theorists, discussing what was called 'civil society' in the systematic way in which earlier thinkers, from Plato to Locke, had discussed the state. Montesquieu's *Spirit of the Laws* (1748), Ferguson's *Essay on the History of Civil Society* (1767), Millar's *Observations on the Distinction of Ranks* (1771) and Smith's *Wealth of Nations* (1776) were all concerned with general theory, with 'the philosophy of society' as Millar called it. The authors discussed economic and social systems, such as the 'feudal system' in medieval Europe (a 'species of government' characterized by decentralization) or the 'mercantile system' (contrasted with the 'system of agriculture') in the work of Smith. They commonly distinguished four main types of society, on the criterion of their principal mode of subsistence: hunting, the raising of animals, agriculture and commerce. The same key concept can be found in the *Essay on the Principle of Population* (1798) by Thomas Malthus, with its famous proposition that population tends to increase up to the limits of the means of subsistence.

One might equally well describe these social theorists as analytical, or to use the eighteenth-century term, as 'philosophical' historians. The third book of Smith's *Wealth of Nations*, which deals with the 'progress of opulence', is in effect a brief economic history of Europe. Montesquieu wrote a historical monograph on the greatness and decline of Rome, Ferguson wrote on the 'progress and termination of the Roman Republic', and Millar on the relation between government and society from the age of the Anglo-Saxons to the reign of Queen Elizabeth.

---

[8] Aron (1965), 17–62; Hawthorn (1976); Meek (1976).

Malthus, like Montesquieu and Hume before him, was concerned with the history of world population.

At this time, scholars less concerned with theory were also turning from the traditional subject-matter of history, politics and war, to the study of social history in the sense of developments in commerce, the arts, law, customs and 'manners'. For example, Voltaire's *Essay on Manners* (1756) dealt with social life in Europe from the time of Charlemagne. The essay was not based directly on the sources, but it was a bold and original synthesis, and a contribution to what Voltaire was the first to call the 'philosophy of history'. Justus Möser's *History of Osnabrück* (1768), on the other hand, was a local history written from the original documents, but it was also an early example of the contribution of social theory to historical analysis. Möser had surely read his Montesquieu and his reading encouraged him to discuss the relation between Westphalian institutions and their environment.[9]

Again, Gibbon's famous *Decline and Fall of the Roman Empire* (1776–88) was a social as well as a political history. His chapters on the Huns and other barbarian invaders, emphasizing general features of the manners of 'pastoral nations', reveal the author's debt to the ideas of Ferguson and Smith.[10] The capacity to see the general in the particular was for Gibbon a characteristic of the work of what he called the 'philosophical' historian.

A hundred years later, the relation betwen history and social theory was rather less symmetrical than it had been during the Enlightenment. Historians were moving away not only from social theory but from social history as well. In the later nineteenth century, the historian most revered in the West was Leopold von Ranke. Ranke did not reject social history outright, but his books were generally focused on the state. In his time and that of his followers, who were more extreme than their leader – as followers often are – political history recovered its old position of dominance.[11]

This retreat from the social may be explained in various ways. In the first place, it was in this period that European governments were coming to view history as a means of promoting national unity, as a means of education for citizenship, or, as a less sympathetic observer might have put it, a means of nationalist propaganda. At a time when the new states of Germany and Italy, and older states such as France

---

[9] Contrast Knudsen (1986), 94–111.
[10] Pocock (1981).
[11] Burke (1988).

and Spain, were still divided by their regional traditions, the teaching of national history in schools and universities encouraged political integration. The kind of history for which governments were prepared to pay was, naturally enough, the history of the state. The links between historians and the government were particularly strong in Germany.[12]

A second explanation for the return to politics is an intellectual one. The historical revolution associated with Ranke was above all a revolution in sources and methods, a shift away from the use of earlier histories or 'chronicles' to the use of the official records of governments. Historians began to work regularly in archives and they elaborated a set of increasingly sophisticated techniques for assessing the reliability of these documents. They argued that their own histories were therefore more objective and more 'scientific' than those of their predecessors. The spread of the new intellectual ideals was associated with the professionalization of the discipline in the nineteenth century, when the first research institutes, specialist journals and university departments were founded.[13]

The work of social historians looked unprofessional when compared with that of Rankean historians of the state. 'Social history' is really too precise a term for what was still treated in practice as a residual category. G. M. Trevelyan's notorious definition of social history as 'the history of a people with the politics left out' did no more than turn an implicit assumption into an explicit statement.[14] The famous chapter on society in the late seventeenth century in T. B. Macaulay's *History of England* (1848) was described by a contemporary reviewer, cruelly but not altogether unjustly, as an 'old curiosity shop' because the different topics – roads, marriage, newspapers and so on – followed one another in no apparent order. In any case, political history was regarded (at least within the profession) as more real, or more serious, than the study of society or culture. When J. R. Green published his *Short History of the English People* (1874), a book which concentrated on everyday life at the expense of battles and treaties, his former tutor E. A. Freeman is said to have remarked that if only Green had left out all that 'social stuff' he might have written a good history of England.[15]

These prejudices were not peculiarly British. In the German-speaking world, Jacob Burckhardt's essay on *The Civilization of the Renaissance*

[12] Moses (1975).
[13] Gilbert (1965).
[14] Trevelyan (1942), vii.
[15] Cf. Burrow (1981), 179–80.

in Italy (1860), later recognized as a classic, was not a success at the time of publication, probably because it was based on literary sources rather than official records. The French historian Numa Denis Fustel de Coulanges, whose masterpiece *The Ancient City* (1860) was largely concerned with the family in ancient Greece and Rome, was relatively exceptional in being taken seriously by his professional colleagues while at the same time insisting that history was the science of social facts, the true sociology.

In short, Ranke's historical revolution had an unintended but extremely important consequence. Since the new 'documents' approach worked best for traditional political history, its adoption made nineteenth-century historians narrower and even in a sense more old-fashioned in their choice of subject than their eighteenth-century predecessors. Some of them rejected social history because it could not be studied 'scientifically'. Other historians rejected sociology for the opposite reason, because it was too scientific, in the sense that it was abstract and general and failed to allow for the uniqueness of individuals and events.

This rejection of sociology was made most articulate in the work of some late nineteenth-century philosophers, notably Wilhelm Dilthey. Dilthey, who wrote cultural history (*Geistesgeschichte*) as well as philosophy, argued that the sociology of Comte and Spencer (like the experimental psychology of Hermann Ebbinghaus), was pseudo-scientific because it offered causal explanations. He drew a famous distinction between the sciences, in which the aim is to explain from outside (*erklären*), and the humanities, including history, in which the aim is to understand from within (*verstehen*). Students of the natural sciences (*Naturwissenschaften*) employ the vocabulary of causality, but students of the humanities (*Geisteswissenschaften*) should speak the language of 'experience'.[16]

A similar position was taken by Benedetto Croce, best known as a philosopher but also one of the outstanding Italian historians of his time. In 1906 he refused a request to support the foundation of a chair of sociology at the University of Naples. He believed that sociology was only a pseudo-science.

For their part, social theorists became increasingly critical of historians, although they continued to study history. Alexis de Tocqueville's *The Old Regime and the French Revolution* (1856) was a seminal work of history, based on original documents, as well as a milestone in social

---

[16] Dilthey (1883).

and political theory. Marx's *Capital* (1867) – like Smith's *Wealth of Nations* – is a path-breaking contribution to economic history as well as economic theory, discussing labour legislation, the shift from handicrafts to manufactures, the expropriation of the peasantry and so on.[17] Although it attracted relatively little attention from historians in the nineteenth century, Marx's work has been a powerful influence on the practice of history in our own time. As for Gustav Schmoller, a leading figure in the so-called 'historical school' of political economy, he is better known as a historian than as an economist.

Tocqueville, Marx and Schmoller were relatively unusual in combining theory with an interest in the details of concrete historical situations. What was much more common in the later nineteenth century, in a number of emerging academic disciplines, was a concern with long-term trends, and in particular with what contemporaries called social 'evolution'. Again, Comte believed that social history, or, as he called it, 'history without the names of individuals or even the names of peoples', was indispensable to the work of theory, which he was the first to call 'sociology'. His life work might be described as 'philosophy of history' in the sense that it was fundamentally a division of the past into three ages: the age of religion, the age of metaphysics and the age of science. The 'comparative method' – another slogan of the time – was historical in the sense that it involved placing every society (indeed, every custom or artifact) on an evolutionary ladder.[18]

The model of laws of evolution linked the different disciplines. Economists described the shift from a 'natural economy' to a money economy. Lawyers, such as Sir Henry Maine, in his *Ancient Law* (1861), discussed the move from 'status' to 'contract'. Ethnologists such as Edward Tylor in his *Primitive Culture* (1871) or Lewis Henry Morgan in his *Ancient Society* (1872), presented social change as an evolution from 'savagery' (otherwise known as the 'wild' or 'natural' state of mankind) to 'civilization'. The sociologist Herbert Spencer used historical examples, from ancient Egypt to the Russia of Peter the Great, to illustrate the development from 'military' to 'industrial' societies, as he called them.[19]

Again, the geographer Friedrich Ratzel and the psychologist Wilhelm Wundt produced remarkably similar studies of the so-called 'people of nature' (*Naturvölker*), the first concentrating on their adaptation to the

[17] Cohen (1978).
[18] Aron (1965), 63–110; Burrow (1965); Nisbet (1969) ch. 6.
[19] Peel (1971).

physical environment, the second on their collective mentalities. The evolution of thought from magic to religion and from 'primitive' to civilized was the major theme in Sir James Frazer's *Golden Bough* (1890), as it was in Lucien Lévy-Bruhl's *Primitive Mentality* (1922). For all his emphasis on the 'primitive' elements surviving in the psyche of civilized men, and women, Sigmund Freud is a late example of this evolutionary tradition, as is apparent from such essays as *Totem and Taboo* (1913), and *The Future of an Illusion* (1927), in which the ideas of Frazer (for example) play a significant role.

Evolution was generally viewed as change for the better – but not always. The famous book by the German sociologist Ferdinand Tönnies, *Community and Society* (1887), in which he described with nostalgia the transition from the traditional face-to-face community (*Gemeinschaft*) to a modern anonymous society (*Gesellschaft*), is only the most explicit of a number of studies expressing nostalgia for the old order as well as analysing the reasons for its disappearance.[20]

The theorists took the past seriously, but they often showed little respect for historians. Comte, for instance, referred with contempt to what he called the 'insignificant details so childishly collected by the irrational curiosity of the blind compilers of sterile anecdotes'.[21] Spencer declared that sociology stood to history 'much as a vast building stands related to the heaps of stones and bricks around it', and that 'The highest office which the historian can discharge is that of so narrating the lives of nations, as to furnish materials for a Comparative Sociology'. At best, the historians were collectors of raw material for sociologists. At worst, they were totally irrelevant because they did not even provide the right kind of material for the master builders. To quote Spencer once more, 'The biographies of monarchs (and our children learn little else) throw scarcely any light upon the science of society'.[22]

A few historians were exempted from the general condemnation, notably Fustel de Coulanges, whose study of the ancient city has already been mentioned, and F. W. Maitland, the historian of English law, whose view of social structure as a set of relations between individuals and between groups, regulated by rights and obligations, has had considerable influence on British social anthropology.[23]

---

[20] Nisbet (1966); cf. Hawthorn (1976).
[21] Comte (1864), lecture 52.
[22] Spencer (1904), 26–9; cf. Peel (1971), 158–63.
[23] Pollock and Maitland (1895).

However, the combination of an interest in history with a dismissal of what most historians were writing was characteristic of the majority of social theorists in the early twentieth century. A number of them – the French geographer Paul Vidal de la Blache, the German sociologist Ferdinand Tönnies and the Scottish anthropologist James Frazer, for instance – had begun their careers as historians, especially as historians of the ancient world. Others tried to combine the study of the past and the present of a particular culture. The anthropologist Franz Boas did this in the case of the Kwakiutl Indians in the Vancouver area, while the geographer André Siegfried did something similar in his famous 'political picture' (*tableau politique*) of western France, in which he studied the relation between the local environment and the religious and political opinions of its inhabitants, arguing that 'there are political regions just as there are geological or economic ones' and comparing voting patterns with religious affiliation and the ownership of land.[24]

The three most famous sociologists of this period – Pareto, Durkheim and Weber – were all well read in history. Vilfredo Pareto's *Treatise on General Sociology* (1916) discussed classical Athens, Sparta and Rome at considerable length and also took examples from the history of Italy in the Middle Ages. Emile Durkheim, who was bent on carving out a territory for the new discipline of sociology by distinguishing it from history, philosophy and psychology, had himself studied history under Fustel de Coulanges. He dedicated one of his books to Fustel. He wrote a monograph on the history of education in France. He also made it the policy of his journal, the *Année Sociologique*, to review books on history, provided they were concerned with something less 'superficial' than the history of events.[25]

As for Max Weber, both the breadth and the depth of his historical knowledge were truly phenomenal. He wrote books on the trading companies of the Middle Ages and the agrarian history of ancient Rome before making his famous study of *The Protestant Ethic and the Spirit of Capitalism* (1904–5). The great classical scholar Theodor Mommsen considered Weber a worthy successor. When he came to concentrate his attention on social theory, Weber did not abandon the study of the past. As well as drawing on history for material, he drew on historians for concepts. His famous idea of 'charisma', for example (below, p. 89), was derived from a discussion of the 'charismatic organization' of the

[24] Boas (1966); Siegfried (1913), v.
[25] Bellah (1959); Momigliano (1970); Lukes (1973), ch. 2.

early church by an ecclesiastical historian, Rudolf Sohm.[26] What Weber did was to secularize the concept, to give it a more general application. It was appropriate that the most historically minded of the great twentieth-century sociologists should have come from what was then the most historically minded culture in Europe. Indeed, Weber scarcely thought of himself as a sociologist. At the end of his life, when he had accepted a chair in the subject at Munich, he made the dry comment, 'I now happen to be a sociologist according to my appointment papers'. He viewed himself either as a political economist or a comparative historian.[27]

The Dismissal of the Past

Durkheim died in 1917, Weber in 1920. For various reasons, the next generation of social theorists turned away from the past.

The economists were pulled in two opposite directions. Some of them, such as François Simiand in France, Joseph Schumpeter in Austria, and Nikolai Kondratieff in Russia, collected statistical data about the past in order to study economic development, especially trade cycles. This interest in the past was sometimes combined with contempt for historians of the kind already noted in the case of Herbert Spencer. François Simiand, for instance, published a famous polemical article against what he called the three 'idols' of the tribe of historians, the idol of politics, the idol of the individual and the idol of chronology, rejecting what he was one of the first to call 'event-centred history' (*histoire événementielle*) and deploring the tendency to try to fit studies of the economy into a political framework, as in the case of a study of French industry during the reign of Henri IV.[28]

Other economists were increasingly drawn away from the past and towards a 'pure' economic theory on the model of pure mathematics. The theorists of marginal utility and economic equilibrium had less and less time for the historical approach of Gustav Schmoller and his school. A celebrated 'conflict over method' (*Methodenstreit*) polarized the profession into historicists and theorists.

Psychologists as diverse as Jean Piaget, author of *The Language and Thought of the Child* (1923), and Wolfgang Köhler, author of *Gestalt*

---

[26] Weber (1920), 3, 1111–57; Bühler (1965), 150ff.
[27] Bendix (1960); Mommsen (1974); Roth (1976).
[28] Simiand (1903).

Psychology (1929), were turning towards experimental methods which could not be applied to the past. They abandoned the library for the laboratory. In similar fashion, social anthropologists discovered the value of 'fieldwork' in other cultures as opposed to reading accounts of them by travellers, missionaries and historians. Franz Boas, for example, made protracted visits to the Kwakiutl, a tribe of Indians on the Pacific coast of Canada. A. R. Radcliffe-Brown lived in the Andaman Islands (in the Bay of Bengal) from 1906 to 1908 in order to study the local social structure. Bronislaw Malinowski spent most of the years 1915–18 in the Trobriand Islands (near New Guinea). It was Malinowski who insisted most vigorously that fieldwork was the anthropological method *par excellence*. 'The anthropologist,' he declared, 'must relinquish his comfortable position in the long chair on the verandah of the missionary compound, Government station or Planter's bungalow.' Only by going out into the villages, the 'field', would he be able 'to grasp the native's point of view'. Following Malinowski's example, fieldwork became a necessary stage in the training of every anthropologist.[29]

Sociologists also abandoned the armchair in the study (rather than the long chair on the verandah) and began to take more and more of their data from contemporary society. For a dramatic example of the shift towards the present – 'the retreat of sociology into the present', as Norbert Elias has called it – one might take the first sociology department in the United States, founded at the University of Chicago in 1892.[30] Its first chairman, Albion Small, was an ex-historian. In the 1920s, however, under the leadership of Robert E. Park, the Chicago sociologists turned to the study of contemporary society, especially their own city, its slums, ghettos, immigrants, gangs, hobos and so on. 'The same patient methods of observation,' wrote Park, 'which anthropologists like Boas and Lowie have expended on the study of the life and manners of the American Indian might be even more fruitfully employed in the investigation of the customs, beliefs, social practice and general conceptions of life prevalent in Little Italy or the Lower North Side in Chicago.'[31] An alternative strategy was to base social analyses on responses to questionnaires, together with interviews of selected respondents. Survey research became the backbone of American sociology. Sociologists generated their own data and treated the past as

[29]   Discussed by Jarvie (1964), 2; cf. Stocking (1983).
[30]   Elias (1987).
[31]   Park (1916), 15; cf. Matthews (1977).

'largely irrelevant to an understanding of how people came to do what they did'.[32]

Several different explanations might be given for this shift to the study of the present at the expense of the past. The centre of gravity of sociology was itself shifting from Europe to America, and in the American case (more especially that of Chicago) the past was less important and also less visible in everyday life than it was in Europe. A sociologist might argue that the rejection of the past is related to the increasing independence and the increasing professionalization of economics, anthropology, geography, psychology and sociology. Like the historians, workers in these fields were founding their own professional associations and specialized journals at this time. Independence from history and historians was necessary to the formation of the new disciplinary identities.

A historian of ideas, on the other hand, might stress an intellectual trend, the rise of 'functionalism'. In the eighteenth and nineteenth centuries, explanations of customs or social institutions were generally given in historical terms, using concepts like 'diffusion', 'imitation', or 'evolution'. Much of the history was speculative or 'conjectural'. What was the alternative?

The alternative, inspired by physics and biology, was to explain these customs and institutions by their social function in the present, by the contribution of each element to the maintenance of the whole structure. On the model of the physical universe, or the human body, society was perceived as a system in equilibrium (a favourite term of Pareto's). In anthropology, this functionalist position was adopted by Radcliffe-Brown and by Malinowski, who dismissed the past as 'dead and buried', irrelevant to the actual working of societies.[33] It is hard to say whether it was the spread of fieldwork which led to the rise of functionalism or vice versa. Slipping into the idiom of the functionalists themselves, one might say that the new explanation and the new method of research 'fitted' each other. Unfortunately, they reinforced the tendency of social theorists to lose interest in the past.

It is certainly not my intention to dismiss such formidable intellectual achievements as functionalist anthropology, experimental psychology, or mathematical economics. These developments in the study of human behaviour may well have been necessary in their day. They were reactions against genuine weaknesses in earlier theories and methods.

---

[32] Hawthorn (1976), 209.
[33] Malinowski (1945), 31.

Fieldwork, for example, provided a far more reliable factual basis for the study of contemporary tribal societies than the speculative evolutionary history which had preceded it.

What I do want to suggest, however, is that all these developments – like the style of history associated with Ranke – had their price. Neo-Rankean historians and functionalist anthropologists were more rigorous in their methods than their predecessors, but they were also narrower. They omitted, or rather deliberately excluded from their enterprise whatever they were not able to handle in a way compatible with the new professional standards. Sooner or later, however, there was bound to be what a psychoanalyst might call a 'return of the repressed'.

The Rise of Social History

Ironically enough, social anthropologists and sociologists were losing interest in the past at just the time that historians were beginning to produce something like an answer to Spencer's demand for a 'natural history of society'. At the end of the nineteenth century, some professional historians were becoming increasingly unhappy with neo-Rankean history. One of the most vocal of the critics was Karl Lamprecht, who denounced the German historical establishment for its emphasis on political history and great men.[34] He called instead for a 'collective history' which would draw on other disciplines for its concepts. The other disciplines included the social psychology of Wilhelm Wundt and the 'human geography' of Friedrich Ratzel, both colleagues of Lamprecht's at the University of Leipzig. 'History,' Lamprecht declared with characteristic boldness, 'is primarily a socio-psychological science.' He put this socio-psychological approach into practice in his multivolume *History of Germany* (1891–1909), a study which was favourably reviewed in Durkheim's *Année Sociologique* but was not so much criticized as mocked by more orthodox German historians, not only for its inaccuracies (which were in fact numerous) but for its so-called 'materialism' and 'reductionism'.

However, the violence of the 'Lamprecht controversy', as it came to be called, suggests that his real sin was to have called Rankean or neo-Rankean orthodoxy into question. Otto Hintze, later a follower of Max Weber, was one of the few historians to treat the kind of history advocated by Lamprecht as 'progress beyond Ranke' and Ranke's

[34] Steinberg (1971).

concern with the mountain-peaks of history, the great men. 'We want,' wrote Hintze, 'to know not only the ranges and the summits but also the base of the mountains, not merely the heights and the depths of the surface but the whole continental mass.'[35]

Around 1900 most German historians did not think in terms of going beyond Ranke. When Max Weber was making his famous studies of the relation between Protestantism and capitalism, he was able to draw on the work of a few colleagues who were interested in similar problems, but it may be significant that the most important of them, Werner Sombart and Ernst Troeltsch, occupied chairs in economics and theology respectively, not in history.

Lamprecht's attempts to break the monopoly of political history was a failure, but in the United States and France, in particular, the campaign for social history met with more favourable responses. In the 1890s, the American historian Frederick Jackson Turner launched an attack on traditional history which was similar to Lamprecht's. 'All the spheres of man's activity must be considered,' he wrote. 'No one department of social life can be understood in isolation from the others.' Like Lamprecht, Turner was impressed by Ratzel's historical geography. His essay, 'The Significance of the Frontier in American History', was a controversial but epoch-making interpretation of American institutions as a response to a particular geographical and social environment. Elsewhere he discussed the importance in American history of what he called 'sections', in other words regions, like New England or the Middle West, which had their own economic interests and their own resources.[36] Turner's contemporary, James Harvey Robinson, was another eloquent preacher of what he called 'the new history', a history which would be concerned with all human activities and draw on ideas from anthropology, economics, psychology and sociology.[37]

In France, the 1920s were the years of a movement for a 'new kind of history', led by two professors at the University of Strasbourg, Marc Bloch and Lucien Febvre. The journal they founded, *Annales d'histoire économique et sociale*, was relentless in its criticisms of traditional historians. Like Lamprecht, Turner and Robinson, Febvre and Bloch were opposed to the dominance of political history. Their ambition was to replace it with what they called a 'wider and more human history', a

[35] Quoted in Gilbert (1975), 9.
[36] Turner (1893).
[37] Robinson (1912).

history which would include all human activities and which would be less concerned with the narrative of events than with the analysis of 'structures', a term which has since become a favourite with French historians of the so-called '*Annales* school'.[38]

Febvre and Bloch both wanted historians to learn from neighbouring disciplines, although they differed in their preferences. Both men were interested in linguistics, both of them read the studies of 'primitive mentality' by the philosopher-anthropologist Lucien Lévy-Bruhl. Febvre was particularly interested in geography and psychology. So far as psychological theory was concerned, he followed his friend Charles Blondel and rejected Freud. He studied the 'anthropogeography' of Ratzel, but rejected his determinism, preferring the 'possibilist' approach of the great French geographer Vidal de la Blache, which stressed what the environment enabled men to do rather than what it prevented them from doing. Bloch was closer to the sociology of Emile Durkheim and his school (notably Maurice Halbwachs, the author of a famous study on the social framework of memory). He shared Durkheim's interest in social cohesion and collective representations (below, p. 92) and also his commitment to the comparative method.

Bloch was shot by a German firing-squad in 1944, but Febvre survived the Second World War to take over the French historical establishment. Indeed, as president of the reconstructed Ecole des Hautes Etudes en Sciences Sociales, he was able both to encourage interdisciplinary cooperation and to give history a position of hegemony among the social sciences. Febvre's policies were continued by his successor Fernand Braudel. Besides being the author of a book with a good claim to be regarded as the most important historical work of the century (below, pp. 151–3), Braudel was well-read in economics and geography and a firm believer in a common market of the social sciences. He believed that history and sociology should be particularly close because the practitioners of both disciplines try, or ought to try to see human experience as a whole.[39]

France and the United States are two countries in which social history has been taken seriously for a relatively long time and in which the relations between social history and social theory have been particularly close. This is not to say that nothing of the kind was going on elsewhere in the first half of the twentieth century. It would not

[38] Burke (1990).
[39] Braudel (1958).

be difficult to find social historians oriented by theory in Japan, for example, in this period, or in the USSR, or in Brazil.

The late Gilberto Freyre, for example, who studied in the United States with the anthropologist Franz Boas, might equally well be described as a sociologist or a social historian. He is best known for his trilogy on the social history of Brazil, *The Masters and the Slaves* (1933); *The Mansions and the Shanties* (1936); and *Order and Progress* (1955). Freyre's work is controversial, and he has often been criticized for his tendency to identify the history of his own region, Pernambuco, with the history of the whole country, for viewing the whole society from the point of view of the 'great house' (more precisely, the males in the great house), and for underestimating the degree of conflict in race relations in Brazil.

On the other hand, Freyre's originality of approach puts him in the same class as Braudel (with whom he had many discussions when Braudel was teaching at the University of São Paulo in the 1930s). He was one of the first to discuss such topics as the history of language, the history of food, the history of the body, the history of childhood and the history of housing as part of an integrated account of a past society. He was also a pioneer in his use of sources, using newspapers to write social history and adapting the social survey to historical purposes. For his third volume on the history of Brazil, concerned with the nineteenth and twentieth centuries, he focused on a thousand individuals born between 1850 and 1900 who would represent the main social groups within the nation, and sent them questionnaires.[40]

The Convergence of Theory and History

There was no period when historians and social theorists lost touch with one another completely, as a few examples will show. In 1919 the great Dutch historian Johan Huizinga published his *Waning of the Middle Ages*, a study of fourteenth- and fifteenth-century culture which draws on the ideas of social anthropologists.[41] In 1929, the new journal *Annales d'histoire économique et sociale* included the political geographer André Siegfried and the sociologist Maurice Halbwachs on its editorial board, alongside the historians. In 1939, the economist Joseph Schumpeter published his historically informed study of business cycles,

[40] Freyre (1959).
[41] Bulhof (1975).

and the sociologist Norbert Elias his book on *The Civilizing Process*, which has since been recognized as a classic (below, pp. 148–50). In 1949, the anthropologist Edward Evans-Pritchard, a lifelong advocate of close relations between anthropology and history, published a history of the Sanusi of Cyrenaica.

In the 1960s, however, the trickle became a stream. Such books as Shmuel N. Eisenstadt's *The Political Systems of Empires* (1963), Seymour M. Lipset's *The First New Nation* (1963), Charles Tilly's *The Vendée* (1964), Barrington Moore's *Social Origins of Dictatorship and Democracy* (1966) and Eric Wolf's *Peasant Wars* (1969) – to quote only a few of the best-known examples – all expressed and encouraged a sense of common purpose among social theorists and social historians.[42]

In the past twenty years, the trend has continued. An increasing number of social anthropologists, notably Clifford Geertz and Marshall Sahlins, give their studies a historical dimension.[43] A group of British sociologists, notably Ernest Gellner, John Hall and Michael Mann, have revived the eighteenth-century project for a 'philosophical history', in the sense of a study of world history in the tradition of Adam Smith, Karl Marx and Max Weber, aimed at 'distinguishing different types of society and explaining the transitions from one type to another'.[44] On a similar scale is the anthropologist Eric Wolf's *Europe and the Peoples without History*, a study of the relationship between Europe and the rest of the world since 1500.[45] The terms 'historical sociology', 'historical anthropology', 'historical geography', and (rather less frequently) 'historical economics' have come into use to describe both the incorporation of history into these disciplines and their incorporation into history.[46] Convergence on the same intellectual territory occasionally leads to border disputes (where does historical geography end, for instance, and social history begin?) and sometimes to the coining of different terms to describe the same phenomena, but it also allows different skills and points of view to be exploited in a common enterprise.

There are obvious reasons for the increasingly close relation between history and social theory. Accelerating social change virtually forced

---

[42] Hamilton (1984); Hunt (1984a); Smith (1991), 22–5, 59–61.

[43] Geertz (1980); Sahlins (1985).

[44] Hall (1985), 3; cf. Abrams (1982).

[45] Wolf (1982).

[46] Ohnuki-Tierney (1990), 1–25; Smith (1991); Baker and Gregory (1984); Kindleberger (1990).

itself on the attention of sociologists and anthropologists (some of whom returned to the areas of their original fieldwork to find them transformed by their incorporation into a world economic system). Demographers studying the world population explosion and economists or sociologists analysing conditions for the development of the agriculture and industry of the so-called 'underdeveloped' countries found themselves studying change over time, in other words history, and some of them – the French demographer Louis Henry, for example, or the American sociologist Immanuel Wallerstein – were tempted to extend their investigations to the more remote past.[47]

Meanwhile there has been a massive shift of interest on the part of historians all over the world away from traditional political history (the narrative of the actions and policies of rulers) and towards social history. As one critic of the trend puts it, 'What was at the centre of the profession is now at the periphery.'[48] Why? A sociological explanation may be in order. In order to orient themselves in a period of rapid social change, many people find it increasingly necessary to find their roots and to renew their links with the past, particularly the past of their own community – their family, their town or village, their occupation, their ethnic or religious group.

I believe that the 'theoretical turn' on the part of some social historians and the 'historical turn' of some theorists are very much to be welcomed. In a famous passage, Francis Bacon formulated equally pungent criticisms of the antlike empiricists, who simply collected data, and of the pure theorists, spiders whose webs originated within themselves. Bacon recommended the example of the bee, who searches for raw material but also transforms it. His parable is as applicable to the history of historical and social research as it is to the history of the natural sciences. Without the combination of history and theory we are unlikely to understand either the past or the present.

There is, of course, more than one way in which history and theory can be combined. Some historians have accepted a particular theory and attempted to follow it in their work, as in the case of many Marxists. For an example of the – sometimes fruitful – tensions inherent in such an enterprise, one might examine the intellectual itinerary of Edward Thompson, who has described himself as a 'Marxist empiricist'.[49] Other historians are interested in theories rather than committed to them.

---

[47] Henry (1956); Wallerstein (1974).
[48] Himmelfarb (1987), 4.
[49] Trimberger (1984); Kaye and McClelland (1990).

They use them to become aware of problems, in other words to find questions rather than answers. Reading Malthus, for example, has encouraged some historians who do not accept his views to examine the changing relation between population and the means of subsistence. This kind of interest in theory has enriched the practice of history, especially in the course of the last generation.

All the same, it is only fair to add that we are not living in an intellectual golden age. As often happens in the history of intellectual endeavour, new problems have been generated by the attempts to solve old ones. Indeed, it has been argued that 'convergence' is the wrong word to use about the changing relation between history and sociology, that it is 'too simple and too bland to do justice to a tangled, difficult relationship'.[50] To this objection one might reply that convergence is actually a rather modest term which suggests only that the two parties are approaching each other. It says nothing about meeting, let alone agreement.

At times, indeed, rapprochement has led to conflict. When the American sociologist Neil Smelser turned towards history and published a study of social change in the industrial revolution, analysing the family structure and working conditions of Lancashire weavers in the early nineteenth century (and in the process offering a veiled critique of Marxism), he provoked the wrath of the English historian Edward Thompson, who denounced the inability of 'sociology' to comprehend that 'class' is a term referring to process rather than structure.[51]

There have also been moments in the past few years when historians and anthropologists, rather than converging, appear to have been rushing past one another, like two trains on parallel lines. For example, historians discovered functional explanations at about the time that anthropologists were becoming dissatisfied with them.[52] Conversely, anthropologists have been discovering the importance of events at a time when many historians have abandoned *histoire événementielle* for the study of underlying structures.[53]

To complicate the situation still further, more kinds of theory are competing for attention than ever before. Social historians, for example, cannot afford to confine their attention to sociology and social anthropology. They need at the very least to consider the possibility that other

---

[50] Abrams (1980), 4.
[51] Smelser (1959); E. P. Thompson (1963), 10; cf. Smith (1991), 14–16, 162.
[52] Thomas (1971) and the review by Geertz (1975).
[53] Sahlins (1985), 72.

forms of theory are relevant to their work. From geography, an old ally but also a discipline which has been changing rapidly in the past few years, historians may learn to consider central-place theory, or the theory of the spatial diffusion of innovations, or that of 'social space'.[54] Literary theory now impinges upon historians as it does upon sociologists and social anthropologists, all of whom are increasingly aware of the existence of literary conventions in their own texts, rules which they have been following without realizing that they were doing so.[55]

We are living in an age of blurred lines and open intellectual frontiers, an age which is at once exciting and confusing. References to Mikhail Bakhtin, to Pierre Bourdieu, to Fernand Braudel, to Norbert Elias, to Michel Foucault, to Clifford Geertz, can be found in the work of archaeologists, geographers and literary critics, as well as in that of sociologists and historians. The rise of a discourse shared between some historians and sociologists, some archaeologists and anthropologists, and so on, coincides with a decline of shared discourse within the social sciences and humanities, and indeed within each discipline. Even a subdiscipline such as social history is now in danger of fragmenting into two groups, one of them concerned with major trends, the other with case-studies on a small scale. In Germany in particular, the two groups are in conflict, with the so-called 'societal historians' (*Gesellschaftshistoriker*) on one side, and the practitioners of 'microhistory' on the other.[56]

Despite this tendency to fragment, it is striking how many of the fundamental debates about models and methods are common to more than one discipline. To discuss these debates is the aim of the following chapter.

[54] Christaller (1933); Hägerstrand (1953); Buttimer (1969).
[55] Brown (1977); White (1976); Clifford and Marcus (1986).
[56] Kocka (1984); Medick (1987).

2

MODELS AND METHODS

This chapter is concerned with four general approaches which are common to various disciplines, but highly controversial in some of them. Its four sections deal in turn with comparison, with the use of models, with quantitative methods and, finally, with the employment of the social 'microscope'.

Comparison

Comparison has always had a central place in social theory. Indeed, Durkheim declared that, 'Comparative sociology is not a special branch of sociology; it is sociology itself.' He emphasized the value of the study of 'concomitant variation' in particular as a kind of 'indirect experiment' which allowed the sociologist to move from the description of a society to an analysis of why it takes a particular form. He distinguished two kinds of comparison, both of which he advocated. In the first place, comparisons between societies which are fundamentally the same in structure, or, as he put it in a revealing biological metaphor, 'of the same species', and in the second place, comparisons between societies which are fundamentally different.[1] The influence of Durkheim on comparative linguistics and comparative literature, especially in France, is obvious enough.

Historians, on the other hand, tended to reject comparison, on the grounds that they are concerned with the particular, the unique, the

---

[1] Durkheim (1895), ch. 6; cf. Béteille (1991).

unrepeatable.[2] To this classic objection there is, however, an equally classic answer, given by Max Weber in 1914 to the historian Georg von Below, in the course of a debate on urban history. 'We are absolutely in accord that history should establish what is specific, say, to the medieval city; but this is possible only if we first find what is missing in other cities (ancient, Chinese, Islamic).'[3] It is only thanks to comparison that we are able to see what is not there, in other words to understand the significance of a particular absence.

This was the point of Werner Sombart's famous essay, *Why is there no socialism in the United States?* It was also the strategy underlying Weber's own essay on the city, which argued that the truly autonomous city could only be found in the West.[4] Indeed, Weber spent much of his working life in the attempt to define the distinctive characteristics of Western civilization (notably what he called its institutionalized 'rationality'), by means of systematic comparisons between Europe and Asia in the economic, political and religious spheres and even in that of music. He paid particular attention to the rise of Protestantism, capitalism and bureaucracy in the West, arguing that the three phenomena were at once similar and connected, and contrasting them with phenomena elsewhere (what Reinhard Bendix calls 'contrast-conceptions' are fundamental to the comparative approach).[5]

The implication of these examples is that the two approaches, particularizing and generalizing (or historical and theoretical), complement each other, and that both of them depend on comparison, whether explicit or implicit. The American historian Jack Hexter once divided intellectuals into 'lumpers' and 'splitters', arguing that the discriminating splitters are superior to those who regard diverse phenomena as a single lump.[6] Of course no one wants to be a coarse lumper, incapable of making fine distinctions. However, to see what apparently diverse phenomena have in common is surely as valuable an intellectual quality as to see how apparently similar phenomena differ. In any case, splitting too depends on a prior act of comparison.

Among the first historians to follow the lead of Durkheim and Weber were Marc Bloch and Otto Hintze. Hintze learned the comparative method from Weber, though he confined his analysis to Europe. He concentrated on the development in different European states of what

[2] Windelband (1894); Collingwood (1935); Elton (1967), 23ff.
[3] Quoted in Roth (1976), 307.
[4] Sombart (1906); Weber (1920), 3, 1212–1374; cf. Milo (1990).
[5] Bendix (1967).
[6] Hexter (1979), 242.

Weber called 'legal-rational' or 'bureaucratic' forms of government, noting, for example, the significance of the rise of the *commissarius*, an official who had not bought his office (as was customary in early modern Europe) and was therefore removable at the king's will.[7]

For his part, Marc Bloch learned the comparative method from Durkheim and his followers, notably the linguist Antoine Meillet.[8] He defined it in a similar way to them, distinguishing comparisons between 'neighbours' from those between societies remote from each other in place and time. He advocated the method on similar grounds, because it allowed the historian 'to take a real step forward in the exciting search for causes'.[9] Two of Bloch's comparative studies are particularly famous. *The Royal Touch* (1924) developed a comparison between neighbours, England and France, the two countries whose rulers were believed to possess the power to cure scrofula by touching the sufferer. *Feudal Society* (1939–40) surveyed medieval Europe, but also included a section on Japan, noting the similarities in the position of knights and samurai but also emphasizing the difference between the unilateral obligation which bound the samurai to his master and the bilateral obligation between lord and vassal in Europe, where the junior partner had the right of rebellion if the senior partner did not keep his share of the bargain.

After the Second World War, comparative studies gained momentum, especially in the United States, with the rise of sub-disciplines such as development economics, comparative literature and comparative politics. The foundation of the journal *Comparative Studies in Society and History* in 1958 was part of the same trend.[10] Although many professional historians remain suspicious of comparison, it is possible to point to a few areas where the method has proved to be extremely fruitful.

In economic history, for example, the process of industrialization is often viewed in a comparative perspective. Following the sociologist Thorstein Veblen, who published an essay on Germany and the industrial revolution, historians have asked whether other industrializing nations followed or diverged from the English model, and whether latecomers, like Germany and Japan, enjoyed advantages over their predecessors.[11]

[7] Hintze (1975).
[8] Sewell (1967); Rhodes (1978).
[9] Bloch (1928).
[10] Grew (1990).
[11] Veblen (1915); Rostow (1958); Gershenkron (1962); Kemp (1978).

In the case of political history, it is the comparative study of revolutions which has attracted most interest. Among the best-known works in this genre are Barrington Moore's analysis of the 'social origins of dictatorship and democracy', which ranges from seventeenth-century England to nineteenth-century Japan; Lawrence Stone's essay on 'The Causes of the English Revolution'; and Theda Skocpol's study of France in 1789, Russia in 1917 and China in 1911, as cases which 'reveal similar causal patterns'.[12] Moore makes particularly effective use of comparison as a means of testing general explanations (he is interested in what does not fit, as Weber was interested in what is not there). In his own words

> Comparisons can serve as a rough negative check on accepted historical explanations ... after learning about the disastrous consequences for democracy of a coalition between agrarian and industrial elites in nine-teenth- and early twentieth-century Germany, the much discussed marriage of iron and rye – one wonders why a similar marriage between iron and cotton did not prevent the coming of the Civil War in the United States.[13]

In social history, the comparative study of feudalism, inspired by Marc Bloch, continues to flourish, with discussions of India and Africa as well as Europe and Japan. The suggestion that it was the tsetse fly which – by attacking horses – prevented the development of anything like feudalism in West Africa is one of the most fascinating studies of 'what is missing', as Weber called it.[14] Comparative marriage patterns are the subject of a famous study by John Hajnal which contrasts the West European system of late marriage linked to the establishment of an independent household for the newly-weds, with the practices prevalent in the rest of the world. In his turn Hajnal has stimulated other comparative studies, notably an essay by Jack Goody arguing that the West European system was the creation of the medieval Church, which discouraged marriages between relatives in order to increase its chances of inheriting from the unmarried.[15] Using a strategy much like Weber's, the historical anthropologist Alan Macfarlane has published a series of studies which attempt to define the Englishness of English society (individualism, a low propensity to violence, a culture par-

[12] Moore (1966); Stone (1972); Skocpol (1979).
[13] Moore (1966); xiii–xiv.
[14] Goody (1969).
[15] Hajnal (1965); Goody (1983).

ticularly compatible with capitalism, and so on), by means of comparisons and contrasts with other parts of Europe, from Poland to Sicily.[16]

It would not be difficult to add to this brief list of examples, but they are perhaps sufficient to show that comparative history has a number of substantial achievements to its credit. It also has its dangers, two in particular.

In the first place, there is the danger of accepting too easily the assumption that societies 'evolve' through an inevitable sequence of stages. The comparative method of Marx, Comte, Spencer, Durkheim and other nineteenth-century scholars consisted essentially in identifying the stage which a particular society had reached, in placing it on the ladder of social evolution. To many scholars today, this assumption no longer seems tenable (below, p. 134). The problem is then to make comparative analyses which are neither evolutionist nor static – as Weber's tended to be – but take account of the different paths along which a society may travel.[17]

In the second place, there is the danger of ethnocentrism. It may well seem odd to point out such a danger, since comparative analysis has long been associated with the increasing awareness of non-Western cultures on the part of Western scholars. All the same, these scholars have often treated the West as a norm from which other cultures diverge. 'Feudalism', for example, like 'capitalism', is a concept originally formulated on the basis of Western experience. There is an obvious danger of trying to force other people's history into Western categories of this kind.

The case of 'feudalism' in the Indian kingdom of Rajasthan, for example, is a cautionary tale which would-be comparative historians might do well to bear in mind. In 1829, James Tod presented to the public what he called a 'Sketch of a Feudal System in Rajasthan'. Relying on Henry Hallam's recent *View of the State of Europe during the Middle Ages* (1818), Tod emphasized relatively superficial analogies between the two societies. With Hallam in his head, he failed to notice the greater importance of family relationships between 'lords' and 'vassals' in the Indian case.[18]

Another problem is that of deciding what exactly to compare with what. The comparatists of the nineteenth century, such as Sir James

---

[16] Macfarlane (1979, 1986, 1987).
[17] Anderson (1974a,b).
[18] Thorner (1956); cf. Mukhia (1980–1).

Frazer, concentrated attention on similarities between specific cultural traits or customs, ignoring the social context of those customs, which was often quite different. For this their analyses have been criticized, like Tod's, as superficial.[19] What is the alternative? The functionalists (below, p. 104) would say that the true objects of study are the 'functional equivalents' in different societies. Robert Bellah, for example, noting the discrepancy between the Japanese economic achievement (as early as the seventeenth century) and Weber's hypothesis about the connection between capitalism and Protestantism, suggested that a certain type of Japanese Buddhism was functionally analogous in the sense of encouraging an ethos of hard work and thrift similar to the 'Protestant ethic'.[20]

In the course of solving one problem, however, we find ourselves faced with others. The concept of a 'functional equivalent' forms part of an intellectual package, 'functionalism', which is open to criticism (below, p. 104). In any case, examples of functional equivalents are not always as clear as Bellah's. How do we decide what counts as an analogue? Comparatists face a dilemma. If we compare specific cultural traits, we have fixed on something precise, and can note its presence or absence, but we risk superficiality. The search for analogues, on the other hand, leads towards comparisons between whole societies. Yet how can one usefully compare or contrast societies which differ from each other in so many different ways?

The problems of comparison on the grand scale become apparent if we look at a famous example, Arnold Toynbee's massive *Study of History*.[21] Toynbee's unit of comparison was a 'civilization', and he distinguished some twenty such civilizations in world history. He had of course to reduce each civilization to a small bundle of traits in order to make comparison possible. As his critics were quick to point out, he also had to create artificial barriers between civilizations. To make matters still more difficult, Toynbee lacked an adequate conceptual apparatus for such an ambitious work. Like Pascal discovering geometry for himself as a child, Toynbee created his own concepts, such as 'challenge and response', 'withdrawal and return', or 'external proletariat' – an ingenious adaptation of Marx in order to explain the incursions of 'barbarians' into empires – but they were not sufficient for his enormous task. It is difficult to resist the conclusion that a wider

---

[19] Leach (1965).
[20] Bellah (1957).
[21] Toynbee (1935–61).

acquaintance with the social theory of his day would have assisted Toynbee with his analysis. Durkheim might have introduced him to the problems of comparison, for example, Norbert Elias (below, pp. 148– 50) to the idea of civilization as process, and Weber to the use of models and types.

Models and Types

A preliminary definition of a 'model' might be an intellectual construct which simplifies reality in order to understand it. Like a map, its usefulness depends on omitting some elements of reality altogether. It also makes its limited elements or 'variables' into an internally con- sistent system of interdependent parts. So far, 'model' has been de- scribed in such a way that it would be true to say that even historians, with their commitment to the particular, use models all the time. A narrative account of the French Revolution, for example, is a model in the sense that it is bound to simplify events and also to stress their coherence in order to tell an intelligible story.

However, it is probably more useful to use the term 'model' more strictly. Let us add one more element to this model of a model and say that it is an intellectual construct which simplifies reality in order to emphasize the recurrent, the general and the typical, which it presents in the form of clusters of traits or attributes. Models and 'types' then become synonyms – which is perhaps appropriate, since *typos* is Greek for mould or 'model' and Max Weber wrote of 'ideal types' (*Ideal-typen*) where modern sociologists would write 'models'.[22] Not 'French Revolution' but 'revolution' makes an example of a model in the sense in which that term will be used from now on.

An example which will recur in these pages is that of two contrasting models of society, the 'consensual' and the 'conflictual'. The 'consensual model', associated with Emile Durkheim, emphasizes the importance of social bonding, social solidarity, social cohesion. The 'conflictual model', associated with Karl Marx, emphasizes the ubiquity of social 'contradiction and social conflict'. Both models are obviously simpli- fications. It seems equally obvious, at least to the present writer, that both models contain important insights. It is impossible to find a society from which conflict is absent, while without solidarities there would be no society at all. All the same, as I shall try to show in later sections, it

[22] Weber (1920), 1, 212–301.

is not difficult to find sociologists and historians who work with one of these models and apparently forget about the other.

Some historians deny having anything to do with models and assert, as we have seen, that it is their job to study the particular, especially the unique event, not to generalize. In practice, however, most of them use models as Molière's Monsieur Jourdain used prose, without realizing that they do so. They commonly make general statements about particular societies. Burckhardt's famous essay on the Italian Renaissance was explicitly concerned with 'the recurrent, the constant, the typical'. Sir Lewis Namier studied 'why men went into Parliament' in eighteenth-century England. Marc Bloch wrote a general study of 'feudal society' in which he specified the main features of a society of this type (a subject peasantry, the dominance of warriors, personal ties between superiors and inferiors, political decentralization, and so on).[23] For the past century or so, historians have found it difficult to avoid such general terms as 'feudalism' and 'capitalism', 'Renaissance' or 'Enlightenment'. Avoiding the word 'model', they often allow themselves to speak about a system – the phrase 'the feudal system' goes back to the eighteenth century – or about the 'classic' or 'textbook' form of the medieval manor.

In a famous polemical essay, the German economic historian Werner Sombart told economic historians that they needed to be aware of economic theory, on the grounds that this was the way in which they could move from the study of isolated facts to the study of systems.[24] These systems are generally discussed in the form of simplified models. Thus economic historians use the term 'mercantilism', although, as Eli Heckscher put it, 'Mercantilism never existed in the sense that Colbert or Cromwell existed.' It is a model, one of the two models used by Adam Smith in his famous contrasts between the 'system of agriculture' and the 'mercantile system'.[25] 'Capitalism' is another model which it is extremely difficult to manage without. So is the 'peasant economy', analysed in a classic study by Alexander Chayanov.[26] The city-state is yet another type of economic organization which has been helpfully described in the form of a model emphasizing recurrent features. For example, the political dominance of the city over the countryside around it is often combined with the exaction of a quota of food at a

[23] Burckhardt (1860); Namier (1928); Bloch (1939–40).
[24] Sombart (1929); cf. Hicks (1969), ch. 1.
[25] Heckscher (1931), 1
[26] Chayanov (1925); cf. Kerblay (1970).

low price, because the city government is more afraid of urban food riots than of peasant revolt.[27]

Political historians of many regions and periods find the model of 'revolution' indispensable, and sometimes contrast it with that of 'revolt' (defined as a protest against individuals or abuses, rather than an attempt to change a whole system). They have offered similar explanations for revolutions extremely distant in space and time. Lawrence Stone, for example, in his study of the English revolution, makes use of the famous sociological hypothesis of 'relative deprivation', according to which revolutions occur not so much when times are bad as when they get worse; or more precisely, when there is a discrepancy between the expectations of a group and their perception of reality.[28] Again, Theda Skocpol has argued that what was common to the French, Russian and Chinese revolutions (but distinguishes them from less successful revolts) was the combination of two factors, 'intensified pressures' on the state from 'more developed countries abroad' and agrarian structures which 'facilitated widespread peasant revolts against landlords'. These states were caught between 'cross-pressures', with increasing international competition for power on one side and on the other the constraints imposed on the government's response by the economic political structure of the society.[29]

To return to neighbourly comparisons. Historians have often tried to generalize about institutional changes in neighbouring countries in a particular period, coining such phrases as 'the new monarchies', 'the Tudor revolution in government', 'the rise of absolutism', 'the nineteenth-century revolution in government', and so on. From a comparative point of view, all these changes look rather like local examples of stages of transition from the type of government Max Weber called 'patrimonial' to the kind he called 'bureaucratic'.[30] This distinction of Weber's has inspired a considerable amount of historical research on different regions, from Latin America to Russia.[31] It may be formulated in terms of five contrasted attributes, as follows:

patrimonial system	bureaucratic system
1 undefined areas of jurisdiction	fixed areas
2 informal hierarchy	formal hierarchy

---

[27] Hicks (1969), 42ff; cf. Burke (1986a), 140–2.
[28] Stone (1972), 18–20, 134; cf. Gurr (1970) and the criticisms of Aya (1990), 30ff.
[29] Skocpol (1979); some criticisms in Aya (1990), 73–5, 90–2.
[30] Weber (1920), 3, 956–1005.
[31] Phelan (1967); Pintner and Rowney (1980); cf. Litchfield (1986).

3	informal training and testing	formal training and testing
4	part-time officials	full-time officials
5	oral commands	written orders

Social and cultural historians also use models. Social historians, for example, often use the term 'class', or compare 'class societies' with 'societies of estates' (below, p. 61). Cultural history is at first sight the least promising terrain for the employment of models. And yet ... what are terms such as 'Renaissance' or 'Baroque' or 'Romantic' if they are not the names of clusters of traits? And what about 'Puritanism'?

Paraphrasing Heckscher, one might say that Puritanism never existed in the sense that Richard Sibbes or John Bunyan existed, but that it might be useful to use the term to refer to a constellation of traits such as a stress on original sin, an arbitrary God, predestination, an ascetic morality and a fundamentalist reading of the Bible. In the case of early modern England, this precise definition is extremely useful. On the other hand, anyone interested in cross-cultural comparison (between Christianity and Islam, for instance) would be well advised to follow the example of Ernest Gellner and operate with a broader concept of 'generic puritanism'.[32] In a similar manner, historians are coming to use terms such as 'Renaissance' or 'Reformation' in the plural, identifying a 'renaissance' in twelfth-century France, a 'reformation' in tenth-century Europe, and so on.

One reason for suspicion of models on the part of historians is the belief that using them leads to indifference to change over time. This has sometimes been the case. Weber, for example, was justly criticized for ignoring change when he wrote about 'puritanism' as if this system of values had remained uniform from Jean Calvin in the sixteenth century to Benjamin Franklin in the eighteenth. However, models can incorporate change. Antithetical models may be a useful way of characterizing complex processes of change, from feudalism (say) to capitalism, or from preindustrial to industrial society ('agraria' to 'industria').[33] These labels are of course descriptive and do not say how change occurs. However, attempts have been made to identify typical sequences of change, as in the case of the model or theory of 'modernization' which will be discussed in detail below (p. 132).

Using models without admitting that they are doing so or without being aware of their logical status has sometimes landed historians in

[32] Gellner (1981), 149–73.
[33] Riggs (1959).

needless difficulties. Some well-known controversies have turned on one historian's misunderstanding of another historian's model; the celebrated controversy between Sir Paul Vinogradoff and F. W. Maitland about the medieval manor provides an example. Vinogradoff suggested that

> The structure of the ordinary manor is always the same. Under the headship of the lord we find two layers of population – the villeins and the freeholders, and the territory occupied divides itself accordingly into demesne land [the produce of which went directly to the lord] and 'tributary land' . . . The entire population is grouped into a village community which centres round the manorial court or halimote, which is both council and tribunal. My investigation will necessarily conform to this typical arrangement.[34]

This is the 'classic' medieval manor as it has been drawn on innumerable blackboards. However, Maitland argued – in an equally classic critique – that 'to describe a typical *manerium* is an impossible feat'. He showed that each of the traits in the cluster identified by Vinogradoff was lacking in some instances. Some manors had no villeins, others no freeholders, others no demesne, others no court.[35] Maitland was absolutely right in these respects. Vinogradoff seems to have been uncertain about the logical status of his generalizations (note the shift from 'always' in the first sentence of the quotation to 'typical' in the last). If he had been aware that he was using a model, however, he might have been able to make an effective reply to Maitland's criticisms.

It is useful to distinguish two kinds of model according to the criteria for membership in the group of entities – in this case manors – to which the model applies. Technical terms are unavoidable at this point, since we need to distinguish a 'monothetic' group of entities from a 'polythetic' group. A monothetic group is one 'so defined that the possession of a unique set of attributes is both sufficient and necessary for membership'. A polythetic group, on the other hand, is a group in which membership does not depend on a single attribute. The group is defined in terms of a set of attributes such that each entity possesses most of the attributes and each attribute is shared by most of the entities.[36] This is the situation described by Ludwig Wittgenstein in a famous passage on

---

[34] Vinogradoff (1892), 223–4.
[35] Maitland (1897).
[36] Clarke (1968) 37; cf. Needham (1975).

'family resemblances'. Mothers and sons, brothers and sisters resemble one another, yet these resemblances may not be reducible to any one essential feature.

It should be clear that Maitland's critique of Vinogradoff assumed that he was talking about all manors or defining the 'typical' manor with reference to a monothetic group. Vinogradoff could have answered this critique by saying that his model was polythetic – had the concept been available. The onus would then have been on him to show that each of the attributes in his cluster was shared by most manors. It is interesting to learn that when a Soviet historian used quantitative methods to study thirteenth-century manors in the Cambridge area, he discovered that more than 50 per cent of them were of Vinogradoff's type, with demesne, villein land and freeholds.[37] It is to the strengths and weaknesses of quantitative methods that we must now turn.

Quantitative Methods

Quantitative methods of research have a long history. Regular censuses of the empire were taken in ancient Rome, while grain prices in different cities were published in eighteenth-century France. Economists have long based their analyses on statistics dealing with prices, production and so on, and economic historians were already following their example in the nineteenth century.

What is relatively new, and remains controversial, is the idea that quantitative methods can be useful in the study of other forms of human behaviour and even attitudes. Sociologists, for example, conduct what they call 'survey analysis' by issuing questionnaires, or conducting interviews with a group of people large enough for the answers to be analysed statistically. Psychologists too make use of questionnaires and interviews. Students of politics study voting statistics – 'psephology', as this approach has been called – and public opinion 'polls', which are a kind of social survey. Demographers study variations in the rates of birth, marriage and death in different societies. Students of communication practise what is called 'content analysis', which often takes the form of a quantitative study of newspapers, journals, books or television programmes, examining how much space is allotted to a particular topic, how often certain keywords occur, and so on.[38]

[37] Kosminsky (1935).
[38] Carney (1972).

A number of historians have followed these paths. When Gilberto Freyre was writing his history of nineteenth-century Brazil, he sent a questionnaire to survivors of the period (including President Getulio Vargas, who failed to reply).[39] Specialists in 'contemporary history' often interview informants, and sometimes analyse these interviews statistically. The methods of content analysis or 'lexicometry' have been applied to historical documents, such as newspapers or the lists of grievances produced by towns and villages at the beginning of the French Revolution.[40] The study of historical demography has developed in France and elsewhere as an enterprise in which demographers and historians have collaborated. Needless to say, the rise of the personal computer has done a great deal to encourage historians to use quantitative methods, freeing them from the need to punch cards, consult programmers and so on.[41]

There is more than one quantitative method, however, and some are more suitable for historians than others. Tailor-made for the needs of historians is the statistical analysis of a series, showing changes over time in the price of grain, for example, the average age of women at their first marriage, the percentage of votes cast for the Communist Party in Italian elections, the number of Latin books offered for sale at the annual book fair in Leipzig, or the proportion of the population of Bordeaux going to communion on Easter Sunday. This is what the French describe as 'serial history' (*histoire sérielle*).

However, 'quanto-history', or 'Cliometrics' as it is variously called, takes a number of forms. In the case of historical survey analysis, there is an obvious distinction to be made between total and sample surveys. The Roman Senate and the English Parliament have been studied through the biographies of all their members, a method known as 'prosopography'.[42] In these cases the whole group, the 'total population' as statisticians would say, has been studied. This method is appropriate for the study of relatively small elites or for societies in which information is sparse, so that historians in these fields are well advised to collect all the data they can find.

Historians of industrial societies, on the other hand, tend to have access to more information than they can handle, so that they have to proceed by sampling. The technique of sampling was developed by

[39] Freyre (1959).
[40] Robin (1970).
[41] For developments in this fast-changing field, see recent issues of the journal *History and Computing*.
[42] Stone (1971).

statisticians from the late seventeenth century onwards in order to estimate the population of London, say, or France, without going to the trouble and expense of a complete survey. The problem is choosing a small group which 'represents' the total population. Gilberto Freyre, for example, tried to find a thousand Brazilians born between 1850 and 1900 who would represent the main regional and social groups within the nation, although he did not explain by what method this sample was selected. Paul Thompson picked 500 surviving Edwardians for interview on the basis of a 'quota sample' which provided a balance between men and women, town and country, north and south, and so on, similar to the balance prevailing in the whole country at the time (which can be calculated from the census).[43]

Other quantitative methods are more complex. The so-called 'new economic history', for example, differs from the old in its emphasis on the measurement of the performance of whole economies, the calculation of the Gross National Product in the past, especially for Western countries since 1800, when statistics become relatively plentiful and less unreliable than they had been.[44] The conclusions of these historians are often presented in the form of a 'model' of the economy.

For a simple example, one may turn to Fernand Braudel, who described the Mediterranean economy of the later sixteenth century as follows. Population: 60 million. Urban population: 6 million, or 10 per cent. Gross product: 1,200 million ducats a year, or 20 ducats per head. Cereal consumption: 600 million ducats, half of the gross product. The poor (defined as those with an income below 20 ducats a year): 20–25 per cent of the population. Government taxes: 48 million ducats, in other words below 5 per cent of the average income.[45]

This general description is a model in the sense that (as he admits) Braudel did not have statistics for the whole region but had to extrapolate from partial data which did not form a sample in the strict sense of the term. Historians of industrial economies, working with relatively rich and precise data, construct mathematical models which can be expressed in the form of equations, models which are rather like recipes in the sense that it is possible to specify the amount of input (labour, capital and so on) for a given output. The models can be tested by means of computer simulation, a kind of experiment. Historical demographers have also made use of computer simulation, in which 'a series

[43] Freyre (1959); Thompson (1975), 5–8.
[44] Temin (1972).
[45] Braudel (1949), part 2, ch. 1, section 3.

of hypothetical events is constructed by the computer in a random fashion but in accordance with specified probabilities'.[46]

Without quantitative methods, certain kinds of history would be impossible, most obviously the study of price and population movements. The use of these methods in some parts of the discipline encourages other historians to pause before they use terms like 'more' or 'less', 'rise' and 'fall', and to ask themselves whether there is quantitative evidence for what are implicitly quantitative statements. This approach gives a sharper edge to comparison, making apparent the similarities and differences between two societies and also the possible correlations between (say) the degree of urbanization and literacy in each.

All the same, these methods are far from uncontroversial. In the 1950s and 1960s, their supporters were self-confident and aggressive, criticizing other approaches as 'merely impressionistic', using the language of science (a room used for the content analysis of texts might be described as a 'laboratory'), and claiming that historians had no choice but to learn to program computers. This mood has changed, as the limitations of various quantitative methods have become more apparent.

In the first place, the sources are not as accurate or as objective as used to be assumed. It is not difficult to show that a particular census contains mistakes and omissions, and more generally that many of its basic categories ('servants', 'citizens', 'the poor' and so on), however useful at a particular moment, are imprecise.[47] Social classes, for example, are not as objective as the various species of plants. They have much to do with the stereotyped ways in which groups see themselves or others (below, p. 58).

The great difficulty for the user of quantitative methods, however, is the well-known one of the difference between 'hard' data, which are measurable, and 'soft' data, which are not. 'All too often,' as a veteran of social surveys sadly remarked, 'it is the soft data which are valuable, and the hard which are relatively easy to get.' Hence the problem is to find 'hard facts which can be relied upon to serve as good indices of soft ones'.[48]

An index may be defined as something measurable which is related to or varies together with something which is not ('correlation' and 'co-

[46] Wachter, Hammel and Laslett (1978), 1–2.
[47] Burke (1987), 27–39.
[48] Wootton (1959).

variance' are the technical terms). Sociologists have shown themselves to be extremely ingenious in their search for indices. In the 1930s, for example, an American sociologist claimed that the furniture in the living room of a given family normally correlated well with income and occupation, so that it could be taken as an index of that family's social status. On the 'living room scale', a telephone or a radio, for example, scored high (+8), while an alarm clock scored very low (−2).[49] There remains the problem whether income and occupation are exact indices (rather than vague indicators) of 'status', which is itself a somewhat imprecise concept.

Again, what looks at first sight like an index may turn out to have its own rules of variation. For some time, historians of literacy believed that a signature on a marriage register, for example, was a good index of the capacity to read, though not of the capacity to write anything else. More recently, doubts have been raised. It has been pointed out that some people who were able to read were unable to sign (because certain schools taught reading but not writing), and even that some people who were able to write may have made a cross in the marriage register rather than signing in order not to embarrass an illiterate spouse. These objections are not insuperable, but once again they do highlight the difficulties of moving from hard to soft data.[50]

Sociologists of religion have to deal with an even more acute problem, that of finding indices to measure the intensity or the orthodoxy of religious belief. In the Christian world they have tended to fasten on church or chapel attendance figures, or in Catholic countries such as France or Italy, the number of Easter communicants. An ingenious French historian even tried to calculate the decline of devotion in eighteenth-century Provence from the falling weight of candles burned before images of the saints.[51] There can be little doubt that statistics of this kind have a story to tell, since they vary so much between regions and change so much, sometimes quite suddenly, over time.

Whether historians are able to decipher that story is another matter. The rise of 'history from below', an enterprise devoted to the recovery of the viewpoint of ordinary people in the past, has cast some doubt on the utility of indices based on official criteria. If we are going to use the communion statistics to study the intensity of devotion in a particular region, then we need to know (among other things) what the practice of

---

[49] Chapin (1935).
[50] Schofield (1968); Furet and Ozouf (1977).
[51] Le Bras (1955−6); Vovelle (1973).

Easter communion meant to the people involved. It is difficult to be sure whether or not the peasants of the Orléans region in the nineteenth century, say, shared orthodox clerical views of the importance of making one's 'Easter duties'. If they did not share these views, then absences from communion cannot be taken as an index of dechristianization. To take the religious temperature of a community, whether it is hot, cold or lukewarm, is no simple matter. The problems of inferring political attitudes from voting figures are of the same order. The very notion of a 'series' is problematic, since it depends on the assumption that the object of study (wills, grain prices, church attendance, or whatever) does not change over time in form, meaning and so on. How could these documents or practices fail to change over the long term? But how can one measure change if the instrument of measurement is itself changing?

For this kind of reason, among others, there has been something of a reaction in the past twenty years or so against quantitative methods in the study of human behaviour, and still more against the grand claims which used to be made for such methods. The intensity of this reaction should not be exaggerated. The use of prosopography by historians is probably more widespread than ever before. It is difficult to deny the value of family reconstitution or the attempt to compare the Gross National Product in different periods in the past. All the same, a search for alternative approaches is under way. It is partly for this reason that ethnography, in which the use of quantitative methods was always minimal, has become a model which some sociologists and historians aspire to follow. This ethnographic approach is associated with the study in depth of the small-scale.

The Social Microscope

Like sociologists, the social historians of the 1950s and 1960s generally employed quantitative methods, concerned themselves with the lives of millions of people and concentrated on the analysis of general trends, viewing social life 'from the twelfth floor'.[52] In the 1970s, however, some of them turned from the telescope to the microscope. Following the lead of social anthropologists, sociologists paid more attention to microsocial analysis and historians to what has come to be known as 'microhistory'.

[52] Erikson (1989), 532.

Two famous studies did much to put microhistory on the map: *Montaillou*, but the French historian Emmanuel Le Roy Ladurie and *The Cheese and the Worms*, by the Italian historian Carlo Ginzburg.[53] Both studies are based essentially on registers describing the interrogation of suspected heretics by the inquisition, documents which Ginzburg has compared to videotapes on the grounds that great care was taken to record not only the exact words of the accused but also their gestures and even their groans under torture. Another comparison which has sometimes been made is that between inquisitor and anthropologist, both of them outsiders of high status asking ordinary people questions the point of which they often find hard to grasp.[54]

Ginzburg's book might be taken as an extreme case of the microhistorical method, since it is concerned to reconstruct the ideas, the vision of the cosmos of a single individual, a sixteenth-century miller from north-east Italy known as 'Menocchio'. Le Roy Ladurie, for his part, described a village in south-west France at the beginning of the fourteenth century. He noticed that no fewer than twenty-five suspect heretics summoned before the inquisition came from the village of Montaillou, and decided to use their testimonies to write a study of the village itself, discussing the pastoral economy of the region, the structure of the family, the position of women, and the local conceptions of time, space, religion and so on.

Since these famous and controversial studies by Le Roy Ladurie and Ginzburg, a whole shelf of microhistories have been produced. Some of the most interesting of them focus on what may be called a 'social drama' such as a trial or an act of violence. For example, the American historian Natalie Davis has written about a *cause célèbre* in sixteenth-century France, in which a peasant was accused of the impersonation of another man (below, p. 164). Another American historian, Wyatt-Brown, inspired by Geertz, has described a lynching in Natchez, Mississippi, in 1834, where an act of 'popular justice' against a man who had murdered his wife is analysed as 'a moral scenario in which actions spoke a language that revealed inner passions and intensely felt social values', notably the local sense of honour.[55]

Another well-known example of the approach is a study of the small town of Santena in Piedmont in the late seventeenth century by Giovanni Levi. Levi analyses the trial of the local parish priest, Giovan

---

[53] Le Roy Ladurie (1975); Ginzburg (1976).
[54] Rosaldo (1986).
[55] Wyatt-Brown (1982), 462–96; quotation from 463.

Battista Chiesa (charged with unorthodox methods of exorcism) as a social drama revealing the conflicts which divided the community, notably the struggle between two families and their followers. He stresses the importance of what he calls 'non-material inheritance', arguing that Chiesa's spiritual power was another form of the dominance exercised by his family.[56]

The turn towards microhistory has been closely associated with the discovery by historians of the work of social anthropologists. Le Roy Ladurie, Ginzburg, Davis and Levi are all well-read in anthropology. The microhistorical method has much in common with the community studies undertaken by anthropologists such as Robert Redfield in the 1930s, or the 'extended case-study' developed by Max Gluckman and others a little later. The first historical community study of the Montaillou type was made by a Swedish ethnologist, Borje Hansen, in the 1950s.[57] *Montaillou* itself consciously follows the model of community studies of Andalusia, Provence and East Anglia.[58]

As for the term 'social drama', it was coined by the British anthropologist Victor Turner to refer to a small-scale conflict which reveals latent tensions in the society at large and goes through a sequence of four phases – breach, crisis, redressive action and reintegration.[59] An essay which has exerted even more influence on historians is Clifford Geertz's study of a cockfight in Bali. Using Jeremy Bentham's concept of 'deep play' (in other words betting for high stakes), Geertz analyses the cockfight as 'fundamentally a dramatization of status concerns'. In this way he moves from what he calls a 'microscopic example' to the interpretation of a whole culture.[60]

Although his own work was mainly concerned with social trends on a grand scale, Michel Foucault encouraged micro-studies by his discussion of power not only at the level of the state but also at the level of the factory, the school, the family and the prison – the 'microphysics of power' as he sometimes called it, picturing power in 'capillary forms', as it 'reaches into the very grain of individuals, touches their bodies and inserts itself into their actions and attitudes, their discourses, learning processes and everyday lives'.[61] 'Micropolitics' is probably the best term

[56] Levi (1985).
[57] Hansen (1952).
[58] Pitt-Rivers (1954).
[59] Turner (1974).
[60] Geertz (1973), 412–54, esp. 432, 437; cf. Geertz (1973), 21, 146.
[61] Foucault (1980), 39; cf. Foucault (1975), *passim*.

to describe this approach, although the word is sometimes used in political studies with a somewhat different meaning.

It was in the 1970s that the microhistorical approach attracted serious attention, favourable and unfavourable alike. Some studies of this type, notably those of Le Roy Ladurie and Ginzburg, have appealed very strongly to the general public. Professional historians have been rather less enthusiastic. Curiously enough, however, there has been relatively little discussion until now of the fundamental issues raised by the shift from large-scale to small-scale studies. It will therefore be necessary to generalize from some of the criticisms made of certain well-known contributions to microhistory, and the replies to these criticisms.[62]

One might begin with the charge that the microhistorians trivialize history by studying the biographies of unimportant people or the difficulties of small communities. Some contributions to the genre have indeed done little more than tell what journalists call 'human interest stories' about the past. However, the aim of microhistorians is generally more intellectually ambitious than that. If they do not aspire to show the world in a grain of sand, these historians do claim to draw general conclusions from local data. According to Ginzburg, Menocchio the miller is a spokesman for traditional oral popular culture. Le Roy Ladurie presents the world of the medieval village through his monograph on Montaillou, which he calls a drop in the ocean.

These claims of course raise the problem of typicality. Of what larger group is the case-study supposed to be typical, and on what grounds is the claim supported? Is Montaillou typical of a Mediterranean village, a French village, or simply a village of the Ariège? Can a village containing so many suspect heretics be regarded as typical at all? As for Menocchio, he was very much his own man, and he seems to have been regarded as something of an eccentric in his own community. The problem is not, of course, one for these two historians alone. By what means do anthropologists transmute their field notes (often based on observations made in a single village) into descriptions of a whole culture? On what grounds can they justify the claim that the people with whom they lived represent 'the Nuer' or 'the Balinese'?

All the same, the use of the social microscope can be justified on a number of grounds. The choice of an individual example to be studied in depth may be prompted by the fact that it represents in miniature a situation that the historian or anthropologist already knows (on other

---

[62] Kocka (1984); Medick (1987).

grounds) to be prevalent. In some cases, microhistory is associated with quantitative methods; historical demographers often make case-studies of a single family, or use the computer to simulate the life of an individual within a given family system.

On the other hand, a case may be selected for study precisely because it is exceptional and shows social mechanisms failing to work. It was to discuss this situation that the Italian historian Carlo Poni has coined the phrase 'the exceptional normal'. The tragic fate of the loquacious Menocchio tells us something about the silent majority of his contemporaries. Open conflicts may reveal social tensions which are present all the time but only visible on occasion. Alternatively, microhistorians may focus, like Giovanni Levi, on an individual, an incident or a small community as a privileged place from which to observe the incoherences of large social and cultural systems, the loopholes, the crevices in the structure which allow an individual a little free space, like a plant growing between two rocks.[63]

It should be pointed out, however, that inconsistencies between social norms may not always work to the benefit of the individual. The plant may be crushed between the rocks. As an example of this problem one might turn to a celebrated incident in Japanese history, a social drama which involved only a few people at the time but has been remembered ever since, and represented many times in plays and films, on account of its exemplary or symbolic value.

The story is that of 'the forty-seven *ronin*'. At the beginning of the eighteenth century, two nobles quarrelled at the court of the *shogun*. The first, Asano, considered himself insulted, drew his sword and wounded the other, Kira. As a punishment for drawing his sword in the presence of the *shogun*, Asano was ordered to commit ritual suicide. The samurai in his service therefore became masterless men, or *ronin*. These ex-retainers decided to avenge their master. After waiting long enough to lull suspicion, they attacked Kira's house one night and put him to death. Having done so, they surrendered to the government. For its part, the government faced a dilemma. The retainers had obviously broken the law. On the other hand, they had done just what was required by the informal code of honour among samurai, according to which loyalty to one's lord was one of the highest virtues, and this code of honour was also supported by the government of the *shogun*. The way out of the dilemma was to order them to commit ritual suicide as their master had done, but also to honour their memory.

[63] Levi (1985, 1991).

The appeal of this story to the Japanese, at the time and ever since, is surely related to the way in which it makes manifest (indeed, dramatically so) a latent conflict between fundamental social norms. In other words, it tells us something important about Tokugawa culture. If the microhistorical movement is to escape the law of diminishing returns, its practitioners will need to say more about the wider culture, and to demonstrate the links between small communities and macrohistorical trends.[64]

[64] Hannerz (1986); Sahlins (1988).

3

CENTRAL CONCEPTS

The main purpose of this chapter is to consider the use which historians have made or might make of the conceptual apparatus created by social theorists, or at least – since it is clearly impossible to consider the whole body of concepts in a few pages – of a few of the most important. Some of these concepts, such as 'feudalism' or 'capitalism', are so much part of historical practice that they will not be discussed here. Others, like 'class' or 'social mobility' are familiar to historians, but the various controversies over their use may not be so well known. Yet others, like 'hegemony' or 'reception', are still unfamiliar enough to be regarded as a kind of jargon.

Historians often accuse social theorists of speaking and writing an incomprehensible 'jargon'. British intellectuals are perhaps more prone than most to accuse one another of this sin, thanks to the survival of the tradition of the gentlemanly amateur. In these cases, 'jargon' means little more than the other person's concepts. Let us assume that every divergence from ordinary language is in need of justification, because it makes communication with the general reader more difficult.

All the same, there remains a minimum of technical terms from social theory which historians would be well advised to adopt. Some of these terms have no equivalents in ordinary language, and lacking a word for it, we may fail to notice a particular aspect of social reality. Other terms are defined more precisely than their ordinary-language equivalents, and so enable finer distinctions and a more rigorous analysis.[1]

Another objection to the technical terms of social theory is worth

[1] Erikson (1989).

taking more seriously. A historian may well ask why it should be considered necessary to offer modern substitutes for the concepts used by contemporaries (by the 'actors' as the theorists say) to understand their society. After all, contemporaries knew their society from within. The inhabitants of a seventeenth-century French village doubtless understood that society better than we will ever be able to do. There is no substitute for local knowledge.

Some theorists at least have some sympathy with this point. Anthropologists in particular stress the need to study the ways in which ordinary people experience their society, and the categories or models (in a broad sense of the term 'model') which they employ to make sense of that world of experience. Indeed, it might be suggested that historians have something to learn from the thoroughness with which these scholars reconstruct what Malinowski called 'the native's point of view', the concepts and categories employed in the cultures or subcultures which they study. Unlike traditional historians, they pay as much attention to unofficial categories as to official ones. Their aim is to recover what they call the 'folk models' or 'blueprints' for action without which much of human behaviour would remain unintelligible.[2]

The point, however, is not to replace but rather to supplement folk models with modern ones. Contemporaries do not understand their society perfectly. Later historians have at least the advantages of hindsight and a more global view. At the provincial or the national level, at least, they may even be said to understand the problems of the seventeenth-century French peasantry (say), better than the peasants themselves. In fact it would be difficult to understand French history, let alone European history, if we had to limit ourselves to local categories. As the last chapter pointed out, historians often make general statements about large areas (such as Europe) in particular periods. They also make comparisons. To do so they have created their own concepts: 'absolute monarchy', 'feudalism', 'the Renaissance', and so on.

I should like to suggest that these concepts, although still useful, are not enough, and that historians might be well advised to learn the language – or rather, the languages – of social theory. This chapter offers an introductory phrasebook, or to vary the metaphor, a basic tool-kit suitable for some of the most common breakdowns in historical analysis. The metaphor is in fact somewhat misleading, since concepts are not neutral 'tools'. They tend to come in packages of assumptions which need to be scrutinized with care. Hence the concern in this

[2] Holy and Stuchlik (1981); Geertz (1983), 55–72.

chapter with the original meaning and context of the concepts examined. Since the proof of a concept's value lies in its application, each
term is also discussed with reference to concrete historical problems.

However, the chapter is not addressed to historians alone, but to
social theorists as well. Historians are sometimes accused of stealing
theory without paying for it, of a dependence on theorists which almost
justifies Herbert Spencer's gibe (above, p. 9) about historians as
carriers of bricks for sociologists to make into buildings. On the contrary (so I shall argue), they do have something of value to offer in
return.

Given that the main concepts employed in social theory were created
by students of nineteenth- and twentieth-century Western societies (or
in the case of anthropology, by Western students of what they called
'primitive' or 'tribal' societies), it is extremely likely – to put it mildly –
that these concepts are culture-bound. They are often associated with
theories about social behaviour which are equally culture-bound. Hence
they may require to be adapted, rather than simply 'applied' to other
periods as well as to other parts of the world.

The so-called 'laws' of classical economics, for instance, are not
necessarily universal. Alexander Chayanov argued that the theory of
marginal utility was irrelevant to the peasant family, which would go
on working marginal land, despite decreasing returns, as long as its
needs remained unsatisfied.[3] A similar argument can be found in a book
by a distinguished Polish economic historian, the late Witold Kula.

Kula's *Economic Theory of the Feudal System*, first published in
1962, studied some great estates owned by Polish nobles in the seventeenth century. In this book, an unusually explicit example of the
construction and testing of a historical model, Kula pointed out that the
laws of classical economics did not work in this case. When the price of
rye rose, production fell; and when the price fell, production rose. To
explain the anomaly, Kula emphasized two factors: the aristocratic
mentality and the existence of serfdom. Seventeenth-century Polish
aristocrats were not interested in making ever-increasing profits, but in
receiving a steady income which would enable them to live in the
manner to which they were accustomed. When the price of rye fell, they
needed to sell more of it to maintain their standard of living, and they
presumably asked the overseers to work the serfs harder. When the
price of rye rose, everyone relaxed.[4]

[3] Chayanov (1925); Kerblay (1970).
[4] Kula (1962).

This re-interpretation of Polish economic history is of course extremely controversial, but it is an intellectual tour de force as well as a challenge to traditional assumptions. Einstein did not undermine the Newtonian system, but he showed that it only applies under certain conditions. In a similar manner, Kula has shown that the laws of classical economics may not apply everywhere. He has historicized them. Further examples of this kind of historicization will be discussed in the course of the chapter.

Social Role

One of sociology's most central concepts is that of 'social role', defined in terms of the patterns or norms of behaviour expected from the occupant of a particular position in the social structure.[5] The expectations are often, but not always, those of one's peers. 'Child', for example, is a role defined by the expectations of adults, expectations which have changed a good deal in western Europe since the Middle Ages. The late Philippe Ariès went so far as to suggest that childhood is a modern invention, which according to him originated in seventeenth-century France. In the Middle Ages, he claimed, the seven-year-old, who had reached what the Church called the 'age of reason', was expected to behave as much like an adult as possible. He or she was regarded as a small, weak, inefficient, inexperienced and ignorant adult, but an adult all the same. Given these expectations, what we call 'childhood' must have been very different in the Middle Ages from anything westerners experience today. The conclusions of Ariès are considered by many historians to be somewhat exaggerated, but the suggestion that 'child' is a social role remains a valuable one.[6]

I should like to argue that historians have much to gain by making a greater, a more precise and a more systematic use of the concept of 'role' than they have done so far. Doing so would encourage them to take more seriously forms of behaviour which have generally been discussed in individual or moral rather than social terms and condemned too easily and ethnocentrically.

Royal favourites, for example, have often been regarded as if they were simply evil men who had a bad influence on weak kings such as Edward II of England and Henri III of France. It is more illuminating,

[5] Dahrendorf (1964); Runciman (1983–9), 2, 70–6.
[6] Ariès (1960).

however, to treat 'favourite' as a social role with precise functions in court society (it may be worth adding that the position survived into our own century, as is shown by the career of Philipp Eulenburg at the court of Kaiser Wilhelm II).[7] Rulers, like other people, need friends. Unlike other people, they need unofficial advisers, particularly in societies where the right to give official advice was a monopoly of the aristocracy. They also need some means of bypassing the formal machinery of their own government, at least on occasion. Rulers need someone they can trust, someone independent of the nobles or officials who surround them, someone who can be relied on to be loyal to them because his own position depends entirely on this loyalty, and, not least, someone to take the blame when things go wrong.

A favourite was all these things. Specific favourites, such as Piers Gaveston in the reign of Edward II or the Duke of Buckingham in the reigns of James I and Charles I, may well have been political disasters.[8] They may have been chosen because the ruler was attracted to them – James I wrote to Buckingham as his 'sweet child and wife'. All the same, like the power of eunuchs in the Byzantine and Chinese empires, the power of favourites cannot be explained simply in terms of the weakness of the monarch.[9] There was a place in the court system which needed to be filled by the king's friend and a pattern of behaviour associated with this role.

One problem for favourites is that their role was not viewed in the same way by nobles and ministers as it was by the ruler. Different groups may have incompatible expectations of individuals occupying a particular role, leading to what is known as 'role conflict' or 'role strain'. For example, it has been argued that the *oba*, the sacred ruler of the Yoruba, was surrounded by chiefs who expected him both to assert himself and to accept their decisions.[10] A similar point might be made about the relationship between many European rulers and their nobility. Reverence for the role of king might inhibit open criticism of its holder, on the grounds that 'the king can do no wrong', but it did not prevent attacks on his policies by other means, notably the denunciation of his 'evil councillors'. This recurrent denunciation was at once an indirect way of criticizing the king and an expression of hatred for advisers who (like favourites) were not noble in origin

---

[7] Röhl (1982), 11.
[8] Peck (1990), 48–53.
[9] Coser (1974); Hopkins (1978), 172–96.
[10] Lloyd (1968).

but 'raised from the dust' by the royal favour. The continuity of such criticisms, from the England of Henry I and the twelfth-century chronicler Ordericus Vitalis to the France of Louis XIV and the Duc de Saint-Simon, suggests that the problem was indeed a structural one.[11]

In many societies, from ancient Greece to Elizabethan England, contemporaries have been well aware of social roles. They have viewed the world as a stage on which 'each man in his life plays many parts'. All the same, social theorists have taken these ideas further. A notable figure in this respect was the late Erving Goffman, who was fascinated by what he called the 'dramaturgy' of everyday life.[12] Goffman linked the concept of 'role' to those of 'performance', 'face', 'front regions', 'back regions' and 'personal space', in order to analyse what he called 'the presentation of self' or 'impression management'.

It may seem odd for a historian to turn to Goffman, who based his work on observations of contemporary life, for the most part in the United States, and was not particularly concerned with differences between cultures or change over time. However, I would argue that his approach is even more important for the study of the Mediterranean world of the past than it is for American society in the present.

Goffman's analysis is of obvious relevance to Renaissance Italy, for example. Machiavelli's *Prince* and Castiglione's *Courtier* are, among other things, instructions on making a good impression – *fare bella figura*, as the Italians say – when performing particular social roles. Machiavelli's treatise is very much concerned with 'name' or 'reputation'. Indeed, at one point he goes so far as to say that it is not necessary to possess the qualities of an ideal ruler, only to appear to do so. In this case there is a relatively good fit between the actor's models of social reality and more recent social theory. Goffman's ideas have recently attracted the attention of historians interested in the 'individualism' traditionally associated with the Renaissance man, or the presentation of self in the Renaissance portrait. Portraits, for example, reveal what the artist considered – or what he thought his client considered – the pose, gestures, expression and 'properties' appropriate to the sitter's role, including armour for nobles who never fought and books for bishops who never studied.[13] In this case, reading Goffman has sensitized historians to certain features of Italian society. Unlike Goffman, however, the question of variation is central for them. They

[11] Rosenthal (1967).
[12] Goffman (1958).
[13] Weissman (1985); Burke (1987), 150–67.

want to know whether there was more concern with the presentation of self in certain places or periods or among certain groups or whether the style of presentation changed or varied.

The concept of social role also has its uses for historians of the nineteenth and twentieth centuries. Hitler has been described as a role-player, who 'always appeared more ruthless, more cold-blooded, more certain than he actually was'.[14] It is not difficult to think of more examples, from Mussolini, who is supposed to have left the lights on in his study to give the impression of working into the night, to Churchill, who was well aware of the importance of 'props' such as his famous cigar. At the collective level, the debate over deference in nineteenth-century Britain has been enriched by the suggestion that for at lest some members of the working class, deference, and even respectability, was not a fundamental part of their social identity but simply a role to be played in front of a middle-class audience.[15]

Sex and Gender

A few years ago it would have seemed surprising, if not shocking, to discuss the division between males and females as an example of a division between social roles. If the idea that masculinity and femininity are socially 'constructed' is coming to seem obvious, the change is due in large part to the feminist movement.

In the first chapter I suggested that the relation between history and theory has generally been indirect. Historians have found theories more useful in suggesting questions than suggesting answers. Feminist theory offers a vivid illustration of this generalization. If one examines recent studies of women's history – the work of Natalie Davis, for example, Elizabeth Fox-Genovese, Olwen Hufton, Joan Kelly, or Joan Scott – one finds little or no reference to the work of theorists – from Hélène Cixous (say), to Nancy Chodorow or Elaine Showalter.[16] On the other hand, feminism has made an enormous indirect contribution to the writing of history in the past generation. Like 'history from below', women's history offers a new perspective on the past, the consequences of which are far from having been worked out.

One result of this new perspective, it has been argued, is 'to call into

[14]　Mason (1981), 35.
[15]　Bailey (1978).
[16]　Moi (1987).

question accepted schemes of periodization'.[17] After all, many of these schemes – with the obvious exception of the periods of demographic history – were devised without thinking of women. Women have been virtually 'invisible' to historians in the sense that the importance of their everyday work, their political influence (at all levels of politics), has generally been overlooked, while social mobility has generally been discussed in terms of men alone.[18] In another striking metaphor, women have been described as an example of a 'muted' group, only able (in many times and places) to express their ideas through the language of the dominant males.[19]

The feminist movement and the theories associated with it have encouraged female and male historians alike to ask new questions about the past. About male dominance, for example, in different times and places. Was it reality or myth? To what extent and by what means could it be resisted? In what regions and periods and in what domains – within the family, for example – did women exercise unofficial influence?[20] In an age in which God's fatherhood has become a matter for debate, a medievalist has studied the image of Jesus as mother.[21]

Another set of questions concerns women's work. What kinds of work were performed by women in particular places and times? Has the status of working women declined since the industrial revolution, or even since the sixteenth century?[22] Women's work has often been neglected by male historians, not least because – in a striking example of the problem of 'invisibility' – much of it has gone unrecorded in the official documents, surveys of workers ordered and carried out by male officials. In the city of São Paulo in the early nineteenth century, for example, the activities of many poor working women, black and white – activities such as selling food in the street, for example – can only be recovered by indirect means, notably the judicial records of crimes and disputes which occurred during work.[23]

It has already been suggested that this new perspective on the past is equivalent in importance to that of 'history from below'. One might also say that it runs a similar risk. In compensating for the omissions of traditional history, both new forms of history risk perpetuating a binary

---

[17] Kelly (1984), 19; cf. Scott (1988, 1991).
[18] Bridenthal and Koonz (1977); Scott (1988).
[19] Ardener (1975).
[20] Rogers (1975); Segalen (1980), 155–72.
[21] Bynum (1982), 110–66.
[22] Lewenhak (1980).
[23] Tilly and Scott (1978); Dias (1983).

opposition, between elite and people in one case, male and female in the other. From the point of view adopted in this study, that of 'total history', it would be more useful to focus on changing relations between men and women, on gender boundaries and conceptions of what is properly masculine or feminine. That this change of focus is indeed taking place is suggested by the recent foundation of a journal concerned with *Gender and History* (1989).

If the differences between men and women are cultural rather than natural, if 'man' and 'woman' are social roles, defined and organized differently in different periods, then historians have a good deal of work to do. They need to make explicit what was almost always left implicit at the time, the rules or conventions for being a woman or a man of a particular age-group or social group in a particular region and period. More exactly – since the rules are sometimes contested – they need to describe the 'dominant gender conventions'.[24]

Again, explaining the rise of witch-trials of early modern Europe is or ought to be a problem for historians of gender, given the well-known fact that in most countries the majority of the accused were female. It is a challenge to which there has been curiously little response so far.[25] Again, the history of institutions such as monasteries, regiments, guilds, fraternities, cafés and colleges may be illuminated by considering them as examples of 'male bonding'. So may politics, as long as women were excluded from the 'public sphere' (below, p. 78).[26]

The process of the social or cultural construction of gender is also under historical scrutiny. A striking example is a recent study of 119 Dutch women who lived as men (notably in the army and navy) in early modern Europe, their motives for this change of life and the alternative cultural tradition which made their decisions possible. Maria van Antwerpen, for example, who was actually born in Breda in 1719, was an orphan, taken in but mistreated by her aunt. She entered domestic service, but was dismissed, so she decided to enlist as a soldier. According to her autobiography, she did so because she had heard of other women who had done so and because she was afraid of being forced into prostitution.[27]

Sex has been approached in a similar way, thanks to the bold reconceptualizations of Michel Foucault, who went so far as to suggest

---

[24] Fox-Genovese (1988); cf. Scott (1988), 28–50.
[25] Thomas (1971), 568–9; Levack (1987), 124–30.
[26] Wiesner (1989); Völger and Welck (1990); Landes (1988).
[27] Dekker and Pol (1989), esp. 64–5.

that homosexuality, indeed sexuality itself were modern inventions, a new form of discourse about human relationships. Foucault contrasted this discourse with 'the manner in which sexual activity was problematized by philosophers and doctors' in ancient Greece, ancient Rome and the early Christian centuries, noting for example that classical texts refer to homosexual acts rather than homosexual persons.

Foucault's approach has been widened and deepened in recent studies by anthropologists and classical scholars attempting to reconstitute the rules and assumptions underlying sexual activity in different cultures. For instance, a recent study argues that for the ancient Greeks, pleasure was not mutual, but confined to the dominant partner. As a result, sex was 'symbolic of (or constructed as) zero-sum competition' between 'hard' winners and 'soft' losers. A sexual relationship between men was not shameful in itself, but to play the subordinate or 'female' role put honour at risk.[28]

Family and Kinship

The most obvious example of an institution composed of a set of mutually dependent and complementary roles is surely the family. In the past thirty years or so the history of the family has become one of the most rapidly growing fields of historical research, and has led to a dialogue between historians, sociologists and social anthropologists in which each group has both learned from the others and forced the others to revise some of their assumptions.

In an early sociological classic, *L'organisation de la famille* (1871), Frédéric Le Play distinguished three main types of family. There was the 'patriarchal', now better known as the 'joint' family, where the married sons remain under their father's roof; the 'unstable', now known as the 'nuclear' or 'conjugal' family, which all the children leave on marriage; and in between the two, the type most closely asociated with Le Play, the 'stem family' [*famille souche*], in which only one married son remains with his parents.[29]

The next step was to arrange these three types in a chronological order, and to present the history of the European family as a story of gradual contraction, from the early medieval 'clan' (in the sense of a large group of kin), through the stem family in early modern times

[28] Foucault (1976–84); Ortner and Whitehead (1981); Winkler (1990), esp. 11, 37, 52, 54.
[29] Laslett (1972), 17–23; Casey (1989), 11–14.

to the nuclear family characteristic of industrial society. However, this theory of 'progressive nuclearization', which used to be sociological orthodoxy, has been challenged by historians, notably by Peter Laslett and his colleagues in the Cambridge Group for the Study of Population and Social Structure but also in other countries, such as the Netherlands.[30] The Group offer a slightly different threefold classification to Le Play's, concentrating on the size and composition of the household and distinguishing 'simple', 'extended' and 'multiple' family households. Their best-known finding is that between the sixteenth and the nineteenth centuries, household size in England scarcely varied from a mean of 4.75. They also note that households of this size have long been characteristic of Western Europe and Japan.[31]

The household approach is both precise and relatively easy to document, thanks to the survival of census records, but it does have its dangers. Two of these dangers in particular have been noted by sociologists and anthropologists, in fresh contributions to the dialogue between disciplines.

In the first place, the differences between the households described as 'multiple', 'extended' or 'simple' may – as the Russian Alexander Chayanov had already pointed out in the 1920s – be no more than phases in the developmental cycle of the same domestic group, which expands while the young couple are bringing up their children and contracts again as the children marry and move out.[32]

A second objection to the treatment of household size and composition as an index of family structure brings us back to the problem of the hard and soft data (above, p. 36). What we want to discover is the way in which family relationships are structured in a given place and time, but this structure may not be revealed by the size of the household. The family is not only a residential unit but also – at least on occasion – an economic and a legal unit. Most important of all, it is a moral community, in the sense of a group with which the members identify and with which they are emotionally involved.[33] This multiplicity of functions poses problems because the economic, emotional, residential and other units may not coincide. Hence an index based on co-residence may not tell us what we most need to know about family structure.

[30] Woude (1972), esp. 299–302.
[31] Laslett (1972).
[32] Chayanov (1925); cf. Hammel (1972).
[33] Casey (1989), 14.

For instance, a sociological study of the working class in East London in the 1950s pointed out that relatives who live in separate households may live near one another and see one another virtually every day.[34] In this case a 'conjugal' household coexists with an 'extended' mentality. Historical examples of this coexistence are not hard to find. In Renaissance Florence, for instance, noble kinsmen often lived in neighbouring palaces, met regularly in the family *loggia*, and collaborated closely in economic and political affairs. The history of the patrician family in Florence, or Venice, or Genoa (to go no further afield) cannot be written in terms of the household alone.[35]

Following some of the criticisms summarized above, a revised version of the nuclearization theory was launched by Lawrence Stone in a study concentrating on the upper classes in England between 1500 and 1800. Stone argued that what he calls the 'open lineage family' dominant at the beginning of the period was first replaced by the 'restricted patriarchal nuclear family', and then, in the eighteenth century, by the 'closed' domesticated nuclear family'. However, even this revised version has been questioned by Alan Macfarlane, who suggests that the nuclear family was already in place in the thirteenth and fourteenth centuries.[36]

The controversy over the dating of the nuclear family in England is not a matter of purely antiquarian interest, but reflects different views of social change. On one side, there is the thesis that economic changes, notably the rise of the market and the early industrial revolution, reshape social structures, including those of the family. On the other side stands the argument that social structures are highly resilient, and that the rise of Western Europe in general and of England in particular is to be explained by the 'fit' between pre-existing social structures and capitalism.[37]

Whatever their position on these issues – to be discussed in more detail in the final chapter – historians of the family now work with a more precise vocabulary than they previously did and are able to make finer distinctions than was possible before they concerned themselves with social theory. In return, they have persuaded sociologists to revise some of their original generalizations in this field.

[34] Young and Willmott (1957).
[35] Kent (1977); cf. Heers (1974).
[36] Stone (1977); Macfarlane (1979).
[37] Goode (1963), 10–18; Macfarlane (1986), 322–3.

Community and Identity

In the previous section, the family was described as essentially a 'moral community'. The concept of community has come to play an increasingly important part in historical writing in the past few years. As we have seen (above, p. 40), community studies were already well established in anthropology and sociology by the middle of the century. In the case of history, the tradition of monographs on villages is much older, but these studies were generally made for their own sake, or as an expression of local pride, rather than as a means of understanding the wider society. As already mentioned (p. 39), Le Roy Ladurie's *Montaillou* (1975) adopts a more sociological or anthropological approach, like some older studies which emphasize political and religious differences between the *plaine* and the *bocage*, in other words between arable regions and the more wooded pastoral regions in northwest France.[38]

Community studies of early modern England also reveal cultural contrasts between types of settlement in different environments. The difference between arable and pasture, for example was associated with differences in the extent of literacy and even with religious attitudes or contrasting allegiances in the Civil War. For example, settlements in wooded areas were smaller in scale, more isolated, less literate and more conservative in their attitudes than corn-growing villages.[39] Studies of this kind, emphasizing the relation between the community and its environment, avoid the twin dangers of treating a village as if it were an island and ignoring the relation between analysis at the micro and the macro level.

There is also a case for pursuing this approach in a completely different kind of environment, where the very existence of communities is problematic – in great cities. An older generation of urban sociologists, from Georg Simmel to Louis Wirth, stressed the anonymity and the isolation of individuals in the city. More recently, however, sociologists and anthropologists have come to view the city as a set of communities or 'urban villages'.[40] The challenge to urban historians is to study the construction, maintenance and destruction of such communities.

Recent studies of ritual and symbol may help urban historians re-

[38] Siegfried (1913); Tilly (1964).
[39] Spufford (1974); Underdown (1979).
[40] Simmel (1903); Wirth (1938); Gans (1962); Suttles (1972).

spond to this challenge. For example, the anthropologist Victor Turner, developing an idea of Durkheim's about the importance of moments of 'creative effervescence' for social renewal, coined the term 'communitas' to refer to spontaneous, unstructured social solidarities (his examples ranged from the early Franciscans to the hippies).[41] These solidarities are necessarily impermanent because an informal group either fades away or congeals into a formal institution. All the same, communitas can be revived from time to time, within institutions, thanks to rituals and other means for what has been called 'the symbolic construction of community'.[42] In the early modern city, for example, parishes, wards, guilds and religious fraternities all had their annual rituals, which declined in importance – but did not disappear altogether – when cities grew larger and became more, but not completely, anonymous.

A useful term for what these rituals encourage is collective 'identity', a concept which has become increasingly prominent in a number of disciplines. Is identity single or multiple? What exactly makes for a strong sense of identity? The formation of national identity in particular has stimulated a number of distinguished recent works. The study of such embodiments of identity as national anthems, national flags and national rituals, such as Bastille Day, is no longer dismissed as mere antiquarianism. The power of memory, of imagination and of symbols – notably language – in the construction of communities is increasingly recognized.[43]

On the other hand, the question of the conditions under which national identities were formed, especially in the nineteenth century, has aroused more controversy. For Benedict Anderson, for instance, the important factors in the creation of these 'imagined communities' are the decline of religion and the rise of vernacular languages (encouraged by 'print capitalism'). For Ernest Gellner, the crucial factor is the rise of industrial society, which creates a cultural homogeneity which 'appears on the surface in the form of nationalism'. For his part, Eric Hobsbawm is careful to distinguish the nationalism of governments from the nationalism of the people, and argues that what ordinary people felt about nationality only became a matter of political importance in the late nineteenth century.[44]

The way in which the identity of one group is defined against, or

[41] Durkheim (1912), 469, 475; Turner (1969), 131–65.
[42] Cohen (1985).
[43] Hobsbawn and Ranger (1983); Nora (1984–7).
[44] Anderson (1983); Gellner (1983), 39; Hobsbawm (1990).

by contrast to others – Protestants against Catholics, males against females, northerners against southerners, and so on – has been illuminated in a remarkable recent work of historical anthropology which studies blacks in two continents. West Africans were enslaved and taken to Brazil. When, in the nineteenth century, some of them, or their descendants, were freed, they decided to return to Africa, to Lagos for example, a decision which suggests that they considered themselves as Africans. On their return, however, they were regarded by the local community as outsiders, as Brazilians.[45]

The term 'community', then, is at once useful and problematic. It has to be freed from the intellectual package in which it forms part of the consensual, Durkheimian model of society (above, p. 28). It cannot be assumed that every group is permeated by solidarity; communities have to be constructed and reconstructed. It cannot be assumed that a community is homogeneous in attitudes or free from conflicts – class struggle, for example. The problems of 'class' are the subject of the following section.

Class

Social stratification is an area where historians are especially prone to use technical terms such as 'caste', 'social mobility' and so on, without being aware of the problems associated with them or the distinctions which social theorists have discovered to be necessary. In most if not all societies there are inequalities in the distribution of wealth and other advantages such as status and power. To describe the principles governing this distribution and the social relationships to which these inequalities give rise, it is difficult to do without a model. The actors themselves frequently employ spatial metaphors, whether they speak of the social 'ladder' or 'pyramid', or of 'upper' or 'lower' classes, or describe individuals or groups as looking 'up to' or 'down on' others. Social theorists do the same. 'Social stratification' and 'social structure (base, superstructure)' are metaphors borrowed from geology and architecture.

The best-known model of the social structure is surely that of Karl Marx, despite the fact that his chapter on 'class' in *Capital* consists of no more than a few lines, followed by the tantalizing editorial note

[45] Carneiro (1986).

'here the manuscript breaks off'. Attempts have been made to supply the missing chapter by fitting together fragments from Marx's other writings in the manner of a jigsaw.[46]

For Marx, a class is a social group with a particular function in the process of production. Landowners, capitalists and workers who own nothing but their hands are the three great social classes, corresponding to the three factors of production in classical economics, land, labour and capital. The different functions of these classes give them conflicting interests and make them likely to think and act in different ways. Hence history is the story of class conflict.

The criticism most frequently levelled against this model is also the most unfair: that is simplifies. It is the function of models to simplify in order to make the real world more intelligible. The social historian of nineteenth-century Britain, say, working from official documents such as the census, finds that the population is described by a bewildering number of occupational categories. To make general statements about British society it is necessary to find a way of collapsing these categories into broader ones. Marx provided some broad categories together with an explanation of the criteria for his choice. He offered social history the 'backbone' it has sometimes been accused of lacking.[47] It is true that he emphasized differences between his three classes at the expense of variations within each group, and that he omitted marginal cases, such as the self-employed man, who does not easily fit into his categories, but one expects such simplifications from a model.

It is more worrying that Marx's model is not quite as clear and simple as it looks. Commentators have noted that he used the term 'class' in several different senses.[48] On some occasions he distinguished three classes, the owners of land, capital and labour. On other occasions, however, he distinguished only two classes, the opposite sides in the conflict between exploiters and exploited, oppressors and oppressed. Marx sometimes employs a broad definition of class, according to which Roman slaves and plebeians, medieval serfs and journeymen were all part of the same class, opposed to the patricians, lords and masters. At other times he works with a narrow definition according to which the French peasants were not a class in 1850 because they lacked class consciousness, in other words a sense of solidarity with one another across regional boundaries. They were, according to him,

[46] Dahrendorf (1957), 9–18.
[47] Perkin (1953–4).
[48] Ossowski (1957); Godelier (1984), 245–52.

merely an aggregate of similar but distinct individuals or families, like 'a sack of potatoes'.

The stress on consciousness deserves a little more development. It implies that a class is a community in an almost Durkheimian sense. We therefore have to ask the obvious question, whether or not there have been conflicts within classes as well as between them. For this reason the idea of an autonomous 'fraction' of a class has been introduced into Marxist analyses. The term 'ascribed' or 'imputed' class consciousness has been coined in order to speak of a 'working class' at a time when its members lacked the necessary sense of solidarity. I must confess that I do not find this idea of an unconscious consciousness to be of much use. The language of class 'interests' is surely more explicit and less mis-leading.[49] A recent critic has gone so far as to speak of the 'crisis of the class concept' on the grounds that it is difficult to find social groups with shared intentions.[50]

It is not exactly surprising to find that the historians who have found the class model most useful are those concerned with industrial society, especially in Britain (the society where Marx himself was writing and in which the language of class was used by many contemporaries).[51] Once again, there is an apparent fit between actors' models and historians' models. However, the strengths and weaknesses of a model are made more apparent by stretching it, in other words by attempting to use it outside the area for which it was originally designed. For this reason it may be more illuminating to discuss more controversial attempts to analyse preindustrial societies in class terms.

One well-known example of such an analysis is the one offered by the Soviet historian Boris Porshnev in his study of popular revolts in France in the early seventeenth century. There were a considerable number of such revolts in the towns and the countryside alike, from Normandy to Bordeaux, especially between 1623 and 1648. Porshnev emphasized the conflicts opposing landlords and tenants, masters and journeymen, rulers and ruled, and presented the rebels as men with a conscious aim, to overthrow the ruling class and end the 'feudal' regime which was oppressing them. His book was criticized by French his-torians such as Roland Mousnier and his followers for anachronism precisely because Porshnev insisted on using the term 'class' – in Marx's broad sense – to describe seventeenth-century conflicts. According to

[49] Poulantzas (1968); Lukács (1923), 51.
[50] Reddy (1987), 1–33.
[51] Briggs (1960); Jones (1983).

these historians, the revolts were protests against increases in taxation by the central government, and the conflict which they expressed was that between Paris and the provinces, not the ruling class and the people. At the local level, what these protests revealed were links rather than conflicts between ordinary people and the nobility, urban and rural.[52]

Status

Supposing for the moment that the criticisms summarized above are well founded, and that the class model is not helpful in understanding social protest or indeed the social structure in seventeenth-century France. What model should historians put in its place?

According to the leading critic of Porshnev, Roland Mousnier, the right model to use for this particular analysis is that of the three estates, or three orders: the clergy, the nobility and the rest. This was a model employed by contemporaries themselves, and Mousnier makes considerable use of a treatise on 'Orders and Dignities' by a seventeenth-century French lawyer, Charles Loyseau. The division of society into three was consecrated by the law. In France before the revolution of 1789, the clergy and the nobility were privileged estates, exempt from taxation, for example, while the unprivileged formed the residual 'third estate'. Hence Mousnier's claim that Porshnev was trying to impose on the old regime concepts which apply only to the period after the revolution.

It is worth pointing out that Mousnier does not derive his social theory from seventeenth-century treatises alone. He has also read some sociologists, such as the American Bernard Barber.[53] These sociologists stand in a tradition of which the most distinguished representative is Max Weber. Weber distinguished 'classes', whom he defined as groups of people whose opportunities in life (*Lebenschancen*) were determined by the market situation, from 'estates' or 'status groups' (*Stände*), whose fate was determined by the status or honour (*ständische Ehre*) accorded them by others. The position of the status groups was normally acquired at birth and defined legally, but it was revealed by their 'style of life' (*Lebenstil*). Where Marx defined his classes in terms of production, Weber came near to defining his estates in terms of con-

[52] Porshnev (1948); Mousnier (1967, part 1); Bercé (1974); Pillorget (1975).
[53] Barber (1957); Arriaza (1980).

sumption. In the long run, he suggested, property confers status, although in the short run 'both propertied and propertyless people can belong to the same *Stand*'.[54] It will be clear that Weber derived his concept of 'status group' from the traditional European idea of the three estates, which goes back to the Middle Ages. It will also be clear that he refined the idea and made it more analytical, so that to analyse the seventeenth century in Weberian terms is not quite the circular tour it appears to be.

Weber's model was put forward as an alternative to that of Marx, and Marxists have in their turn answered Weber, pointing out, for example, that values like 'status' are not so much the expression of a general social consensus as values which the dominant class attempts to impose – with greater or less success – on everyone else.[55] One might also argue that some contemporary statements about the structure of a particular society should be taken not as neutral descriptions but as attempts by members of a particular group to justify their privileges. For example, the well-known division of medieval society into the three estates or the three functions of 'those who pray, those who fight, and those who work' looks extremely like a justification of the position of those who do not work. In a brilliant study, the historian Georges Duby, making discreet use of the social theorist Louis Althusser (below, p. 95), has examined the rise of this three-fold division of society in France in the eleventh and twelfth centuries, explaining its success in terms of the social and political situation of the time.[56]

In the case of the debate over seventeenth-century French society, it may be argued that Mousnier has accepted the official view of the system rather too easily. Charles Loyseau, the lawyer on whose description of the social structure Mousnier relied most heavily, was not a disinterested, dispassionate observer. He was not simply describing French society in his time but articulating a view of it from the standpoint of an occupant of a particular position within that society, that of an ennobled magistrate. His view should be compared and contrasted with that of the traditional nobles, who rejected the magistrate's claim to high status, and, if possible, with views of the same society from below.[57]

The debate between Marx and Weber is complicated by the fact that

---

[54] Weber (1948), 186–7.
[55] Parkin (1971), 40–7.
[56] Duby (1978); Althusser (1970).
[57] Cf. Sewell (1974).

the two men were trying to answer different questions about inequality. Marx was especially concerned with power and with conflict, while Weber was interested in values and life-styles. The class model has become associated with a view of society as essentially conflictual, minimizing solidarities, while the model of orders has become associated with a view of society as essentially harmonious, minimizing conflict. There are important insights embodied in both models, but the danger of oversimplification will be obvious.

It may therefore be useful to treat the rival models as complementary rather than contradictory ways of viewing society, each of them throwing some features of the social structure into high relief at the price of obscuring others.[58] The orders model seems most relevant to pre-industrial societies and the class model to industrial ones, but insights may also be gained by using both models against the grain.

Historians of non-European societies are forced to do this in any case, since the rival concepts originated, as we have seen, in a European context. Were Chinese mandarins, for example, a status group or a social class? Is it useful to redefine Indian castes as a kind of status group, or is it better to regard Indian society as a unique form of social structure? The most vigorous supporter of the latter view is the French anthropologist Louis Dumont, who argues that the principles underlying inequalities in Indian society, notably purity, are different from their equivalents in the West. Unfortunately, Dumont goes on to identify the contrast between hierarchical and egalitarian societies with that between India and the West, as if the privileged orders of clergy and nobility had never existed in Europe.[59]

In fact, the concept of purity was sometimes used in order to justify the position of certain social groups in early modern Europe. In Spain in particular, 'purity of blood' (*limpieza de sangre*) was officially essential for high status, but elsewhere, in France for example, the nobility often described their social inferiors as unclean.[60] Such concepts were used – without success – to prevent social mobility.

Social Mobility

Like 'class', social mobility is a term familiar enough to historians, and monographs, conferences and special issues of journals have been

---

[58] Ossowski (1957), 172–93; Burke (1992a).
[59] Dumont (1966, 1977).
[60] Devyver (1973); Jouanna (1976).

devoted to this theme. Less familiar, perhaps, are some of the distinctions drawn by sociologists, at least three of which might usefully be
incorporated into historical practice. The first is between movement up
and down the social ladder; the study of downward mobility has been
unduly neglected. The second distinction is that between mobility
within an individual lifetime ('intragenerational', as the sociologists say)
and mobility spread over several generations ('intergenerational'). The
third distinction is that between individual and group mobility. British
university professors, for example, enjoyed a higher status a century ago
than they do today. On the other hand, certain Indian castes can be
shown to have risen socially over the same period.[61]

This distinction between individual and group mobility was not
drawn with sufficient clarity in the debate over the so-called 'rise of the
gentry'. In a famous article of the 1950s, R. H. Tawney argued that the
English gentry rose in wealth, status and power in the century 1540–
1640.[62] A sharp controversy followed, in which it became clear that
participants sometimes confused the rise of certain individuals from the
yeomanry into the gentry, the rise of other individuals from the gentry
into the peerage, and the rise of the whole gentry relative to other social
groups.

There are two major problems in the history of social mobility –
changes in the rate of mobility and changes in its modes. It has been
remarked that historians of all periods seem to resent the imputation
that 'their' society is closed or immobile. Although a Byzantine emperor
once decreed that all sons should follow the occupation of their fathers,
it is unlikely that any stratified society has ever been in a state of
complete immobility, which would mean that all children, male or
female, enjoyed (or suffered from) the same status as their parents.
There is, incidentally, an important distinction to be drawn between
what one might call the 'visible' mobility of men in patrilineal societies
and the 'invisible' mobility of women through marriages in which they
change their names.

The crucial questions to ask about social mobility in a given society
are surely relative ones. For example: was the rate of social mobility
(upward or downward) in seventeenth-century England higher or lower
than that in seventeenth-century France, seventeenth-century Japan,
or England in an earlier or later period? A comparative, quantitative
approach virtually imposes itself. In the case of twentieth-century

---

[61] Srinivas (1966).
[62] Tawney (1941).

industrial societies, a famous study of this kind concluded that despite the American emphasis on equality of opportunity, the rate of social mobility was no lower in Western Europe than it was in the United States.[63] A comparative study of preindustrial Europe along these lines would be difficult to make, but it would also be extremely illuminating.

One example of these pitfalls is provided by a study of China in the Ming and Qing periods (in other words from 1368 to 1911) which argued that Chinese society was much more open than European society in the same period. The evidence for the unusually high rate of social mobility in China was provided by the lists of successful candidates in the civil service examinations, lists which provided information about the social origins of candidates. However, as a critic was quick to point out, 'data on the social origins of a ruling class do not constitute data on overall amounts of mobility or on the life-chances of lower-class persons'. Why not? Because it is necessary to take account of the relative size of the elite. As elites go, Chinese mandarins formed only a small percentage of the population. Even if access to this elite had been relatively open – and even this is controversial – the life-chances of the sons of merchants, craftsmen, peasants and so on would have remained low.[64]

A second major question to ask about social mobility concerns its modes, in other words the various paths to the summit and the different obstacles in the way of potential climbers (downward mobility probably shows less variation). If the desire to rise in the world is a constant, the mode of rising varies from place to place and changes over time. In China, for example, over a long period (from the end of the sixth century to the beginning of the twentieth), the royal road, or better, the imperial road to the top was provided by the examination system. As Max Weber once remarked, in Western society a stranger would be asked who his father was, but in China he would be asked how many examinations he had passed.[65] Success in examinations was the principal means of entry to the Chinese bureaucracy, and posts in the bureaucracy conferred status, wealth and power. In practice, the system was less meritocratic than in theory, since the children of the poor did not have access to the schools teaching the skills required for success in the examinations. All the same, the Chinese system of recruiting mandarins – which inspired the reform of the British civil service in the

---

[63] Lipset and Bendix (1959).
[64] Ping-Ti (1958–9); Dibble (1960–1).
[65] Weber (1964), ch. 5; Miyazaki (1963).

mid-nineteenth century – was one of the most sophisticated and also, in all probability, one of the most successful attempts at recruitment by merit ever developed by a preindustrial government.[66]

The main rival of imperial China in this respect was the so-called 'tribute of children' (*devshirme*) levied by the ruler of the Ottoman Empire, especially in the fifteenth and sixteenth centuries. In this system the administrative and military elites were both recruited from the Christian subject population. The children were apparently selected on the basis of their abilities and given a thorough education. The 'A-stream', including the brightest boys, joined the 'Inside Service' in the Sultan's household, which might lead to important positions such as Grand Vizier, while the 'B-stream' entered the 'Outside Service' in the armed forces. All the recruits were required to turn Muslim. Their conversion to the dominant religion of the empire had the effect – indeed, the function – of cutting them off from their cultural roots, thus making them more dependent on the sultan. Since Muslims had to bring up their children as Muslim, conversion ensured that the sons of elite members were ineligible for office.[67]

In preindustrial Europe, one of the main avenues of social mobility was the Church. To follow Stendhal's famous typology, careers were more open to talent in 'black', in the Church, than they were in 'scarlet', in the army. The son of a peasant might even end his ecclesiastical career as pope, as Sixtus V did in the later sixteenth century. Leading churchmen might also be employed in high positions in the state. In seventeenth-century Europe, for example, the leading ministers of state included cardinals Richelieu and Mazarin, both of them in the service of the kings of France, cardinal Khlesl, in the service of the Habsburg emperor, and archbishop William Laud, in the service of Charles I. Richelieu came from the lesser nobility, but Khlesl was the son of a baker and Laud the son of a clothier from Reading. For European rulers, one of the advantages of the appointment of Catholic clergy, in particular, as ministers was their inability to produce legitimate children who might claim to succeed them in their posts. In this sense the use of the clergy parallels the Ottoman reliance on the *devshirme* and the employment of eunuchs in high positions in the Roman and Chinese empires. They are all examples of what Ernest Gellner calls 'gelding'.[68]

Another important avenue of social mobility in preindustrial Europe

---

[66]   Sprenkel (1958); Marsh (1961); Wilkinson (1964).
[67]   Parry (1969); Inalcik (1973).
[68]   Gellner (1981), 14–15.

was the law. All over Europe, men trained as lawyers were in demand in the sixteenth and seventeenth centuries to fill posts in the growing state bureaucracies. For this reason, fathers ambitious for their sons sent them to study law, whether they liked it or not (among the sons who refused to follow their fathers' wishes in this respect were Martin Luther and Jean Calvin).[69]

Conspicuous Consumption and Symbolic Capital

Another means of rising socially in early modern Europe was to imitate the style of life of a group higher in the social scale, and to engage in 'conspicuous consumption'. Earlier in the chapter, I discussed Witold Kula's criticism of the laws of classical economics on the ground that they did not account for the actual economic behaviour of some groups, such as the Polish magnates of the seventeenth and eighteenth centuries. These nobles did not fit the conventional model of 'economic man'. They were not interested in profit or thrift but in a steady income to spend on imported luxuries such as French wine, a form of 'conspicuous consumption'. This phrase goes back to the American sociologist Thorstein Veblen at the end of the last century.

The phrase formed part of a theory. Veblen – a passionate egalitarian and a man with a conspicuously simple life-style – argued that the economic behaviour of the elite, the 'leisure class' as he called it, was irrational and wasteful, motivated only by 'emulation'. He applied to preindustrial and industrial societies alike the conclusions reached by the anthropologist Franz Boas in his studies of the Kwakiutl, an Indian people living on the Pacific coast of Canada. The most famous Kwakiutl institution was the 'potlatch', the destruction of goods (notably blankets and copper plates) by the chiefs. The destruction was a way of demonstrating that a given chief had more wealth than his rivals, and thus of humiliating them. It was a means of 'fighting with property'.[70]

More recently, the French sociologist Pierre Bourdieu has pursued this approach to consumption as part of a more general study of the strategies by which people – especially upper- and middle-class French people – distinguish themselves from others. Like Boas and Veblen, he argues that 'economic power is first and foremost the power to distance oneself from economic necessity; that is why it is always marked by the

---

[69] Kagan (1974); Prest (1987).
[70] Veblen (1899); Boas (1966); cf. Codere (1950).

destruction of wealth, conspicuous consumption, waste and all forms of gratuitous luxury'. Apparent waste is actually a means for converting economic capital into political, social, cultural or 'symbolic' capital.[71]

Social historians have increasingly adopted the concept of conspicuous consumption, a notion which informs a number of studies of sixteenth- and seventeenth-century elites in England, Poland, Italy and elsewhere.[72] These studies not only illustrate the theory but elaborate it and qualify it in a number of respects. For example, true to their hermeneutic tradition, historians emphasize that some contemporaries at least knew what was going on and analysed it in terms not unlike Veblen's. In the early modern period, a key concept was 'magnificence', a term which sums up very neatly the conversion of wealth into status and power. Writers of fiction were well aware of the importance of status symbols, especially clothes. The Spanish 'literature of the picaresque' of the sixteenth and seventeenth centuries centres on the attempts of the hero (actually a rogue, or *pícaro*) to pass himself off as a noble by precisely these means. Awareness of the use of symbols in the struggle for high status was not confined to writers of fiction. A seventeenth-century burgomaster of Gdansk even had the motto 'in order to envied' (*pro invidia*) inscribed on the facade of his house. At much the same time, a Florentine writer referred to 'the attempt by the rich to distinguish themselves from others', while a Genoese described the patricians of his city as spending more than they needed 'in order to give pain to those who were unable to do the same and to make them sick at heart'.[73] In a similar spirit a seventeenth-century English writer criticized an English nobleman, one of the Berkeleys, for excessive hospitality, saying that he 'sent all his revenues downe the privy house'.[74]

These last comments are obviously moralizing and satirical. They remind us of the need to distinguish different attitudes to conspicuous consumption within the same society. Historians have shown that in early modern Europe, the view of 'magnificence' as an obligation of the great co-existed with the theory that it exemplified spiritual pride. In practice, conspicuous consumption seems to have varied from region to region (high in Italy, low in the Dutch Republic, for example), as well as from one social group to another. There was also a change over the

---

[71] Bourdieu (1979).
[72] Stone (1965); Bogucka (1989).
[73] Burke (1987), 134–5.
[74] Quoted Stone (1965), 562.

long term, with competitive consumption reaching an apparent peak in the seventeenth century.

Refining the concepts further, we may say that strategies of distinction took different forms, including that of conspicuously refraining from consuming, a 'Protestant Ethic' (as Weber called it) which was not in fact confined to Protestants. This option seems to have been increasingly popular in the eighteenth century, the age of a debate over the harmful consequences of 'luxury'. It is worth noting, however, that a strategy of this kind provided a possible escape from the self-destructive consequences of competitive consumption.

Conspicuous consumption is only one strategy for a social group to show itself superior to another. On the other hand, this particular form of behaviour is much more than such a strategy. One of the dangers of theorizing is reductionism, in other words the propensity to see the world as nothing but illustrations to the theory. In this case, the assumption that consumers simply want to display their wealth and status has been attacked by a British sociologist, Colin Campbell, who suggests that the real reason people buy many luxury objects is to sustain their image of themselves.[75]

The simplest means to correct the propensity to reductionism is to turn to a rival theory. At this point it may therefore be useful to look at conspicuous consumption from another angle, that of exchange or reciprocity.

Reciprocity

As in the previous section, a concrete example provides a convenient starting-point. From Franz Boas's description of the Kwakiutl potlatch we move to Fredrik Barth's account of the Swat Pathans. Like the Kwakiutl chiefs, the *khans* are competitors for status and power. They spend their wealth on gifts and hospitality in order to build up a following. The authority of each *khan* is personal, it is what he can 'wrest' from each of his followers. 'Followers seek those leaders who offer them the greatest advantages and the most security.' In return they offer their services and their loyalty. A large number of followers gives a leader honour (*izat*) and the power to humiliate his rivals. On the other hand, the need to satisfy their followers forces the *khans* to compete with one another. In Pathan society, where honour depends on appear-

[75] Campbell (1987, 1990).

ances, a *khan* with economic problems will not reduce his hospitality and may even increase it, even if he has to sell land in order to feed his visitors and clients. The logic underlying this paradox is summed up in a remark made to Barth by one of the khans: 'Only this constant show of force keeps the vultures at bay.'[76] Barth's case-study combines vivid description with penetrating analysis and it illuminates both the economics and the politics of reciprocity.

In the first place, the Pathans offer one of many examples from preindustrial societies of behaviour which is not rational by the standards of classical economics (cf. pp. 46–7 above). Like Kwakiutl chiefs, the *khans* are not interested in accumulating wealth for its own sake; they spend it on hospitality.

If classical economic theory fails to account for what the Kwakiutl and Pathans actually do, it is clearly in need of modification. The essential modifications were proposed in the 1940s by Karl Polanyi, who – like Kula twenty years later – criticized economists for assuming that their generalizations were universally valid. According to Polanyi, there are three basic systems of economic organization. Only one of them, the market system, is subject to the laws of classical economics. Polanyi called the other two modes of organization the 'reciprocity' and 'redistribution' system.[77]

The system of reciprocity is based on the gift. In a study of the islands of the western Pacific, the anthropologist Bronislaw Malinowski had pointed to the existence of a circular system of exchange. Shell armlets travelled in one direction, shell bracelets in the other. As he pointed out, the exchange had no economic value, but it maintained social solidarities. In his famous essay on the gift, Marcel Mauss generalized from examples of this kind, arguing that this 'archaic form of exchange' had great social and religious significance and that it was based on three unwritten laws; the obligation to give, the obligation to receive and the obligation to repay.[78] There is no such thing as a 'free' gift. Polanyi carried generalization one stage further by making the gift the central feature of the first of his three models of economic systems.

Polanyi's second system is based on redistribution. Where gifts are exchanged between equals, redistribution depends on a social hierarchy. Tribute flows in to the metropolis of an empire and flows out again to the provinces. Leaders like the Pathan *khans* distribute to their

[76] Barth (1959).
[77] Polanyi (1944); cf. Block and Somers (1984).
[78] Malinowski (1922); Mauss (1925); cf. Firth (1967) 8–17.

followers the goods they have taken from outsiders. The followers are not expected to give the goods back at a later time, but to offer some other form of 'counter-prestation', as anthropologists call it.

These ideas have had considerable influence on historians concerned with economic life in preindustrial societies, although they have tended to ignore Polanyi's distinction between reciprocity and redistribution and to contrast two systems, the archaic and the modern. For example, the Russian medievalist Aron Gurevich has studied gift exchange in medieval Scandinavia, drawing on Malinowski and Mauss to analyse the rituals accompanying the gift, the setting (usually a feast), the kinds of object bestowed (swords, rings, and so on), the obligation to reciprocate, and so on. His French colleague Georges Duby has emphasized the functions of gift exchange in the rise of the early medieval economy. Fernand Braudel's ambitious study of material life and capitalism in early modern times also owes a considerable debt to the ideas of Polanyi, who is quoted a number of times in that text.[79]

Whether or not it was originally derived from a reading of Polanyi, E. P. Thompson's influential idea of a 'moral economy' may be located in this tradition. As I suggested earlier, the idea of a moral economy is one of the relatively few examples of a concept coined by a historian and later taken up by practitioners of other disciplines. To be exact, Thompson found the phrase 'The Moral Economy of the Factory System' in Andrew Ure's *Philosophy of Manufactures* (1835), which discussed religion in economic terms, as part of the 'moral machinery' of the system. However, Thompson turned Ure on his head by using the phrase to refer to a moralized economics built on the idea of the just price and enforced in times of dearth by eighteenth-century crowds.[80] Whether these crowds looked back to a golden age in the past, as Thompson suggests, is a matter for debate. What is clear is that studies of other societies, some of them as remote from England as south-east Asia, have found the concept of a 'moral economy' to be fertile.[81]

Patronage and Corruption

From the economic point of view, the Swat Pathans offer a striking example of a redistribution system which has survived into the con-

---

[79] Gurevich (1968); Duby (1973); Braudel (1979), 2, 26, 225, 623.
[80] E. P. Thompson (1963, 359ff; 1971).
[81] Stevenson (1985); Scott (1976).

temporary world (the fieldwork on which Barth's book was based was carried out in the 1950s). The political structure of Pathan society is equally worthy of attention. It is based on patronage.

Patronage may be defined as a political system based on personal relationships between unequals, between leaders (or patrons) and their followers (or clients). Each party has something to offer the other. Clients offer patrons their political support and also their deference, expressed in a variety of symbolic forms (gestures of submission, language of respect, gifts and so on). For their part, patrons offer clients hospitality, jobs and protection. This is how they are able to convert wealth into power.

Although it seems to correspond closely to observed reality, there are difficulties inherent in the notion of a patronage system. Some degree of patronage exists in every society, however 'modern'. In some societies, however, where 'bureaucratic' norms are weak, and 'vertical solidarity' particularly strong, the society may be described as based on the patronage system.[82] Problems remain, however. The assumption that the links between patron and client are fundamental, like the idea of an 'estate society' (discussed above, p. 61), encourages the observer or historian not to notice horizontal solidarities or conflicts between rulers and ruled.[83]

Anthropologists and sociologists have made many analyses of the working of patronage, in the Mediterranean world in particular. Their conclusions have undermined, or relativized, what might be called 'classical' political theory as effectively as Polanyi and others have relativized classical economic theory. They have shown that – like the market in economics – parliamentary democracy and bureaucracy cannot be treated as a universal political model and that alternative systems have their own logic. Such systems cannot be treated as mere 'corruption' or as 'pre-political' forms of organization.[84]

If we look for a moment at England in the fifteenth century, more especially at the East Anglia revealed in the correspondence of the Paston family, we find a society which resembles Swat in certain important respects (despite important differences ranging from the widespread use of firearms to the post-colonial situation). In England too the acquisition of land was one of the major goals for adult males, and the competition for land sometimes took a violent form, as in the case

[82] Johnson and Dandeker (1989).
[83] Silverman (1977); Gilsenan (1977).
[84] Gellner and Waterbury (1977).

of the seizure of John Paston's manor of Gresham by his powerful neighbour Lord Moleyns. In England too the ties between local leaders ('lords' or 'masters'), and their followers (known as 'friends' or 'well-willers'), were fundamental to the organization of society. The small men needed the 'good lordship' of the great. Followers courted leaders not only with deference but with gifts. As a correspondent of the Pastons once remarked, 'men do not lure hawks with empty hands'. On the other hand, leaders needed followers in order to increase their honour or 'worship' (their *izat*, as Pathans would say). Hence they kept open house and offered their followers 'livery', in other words presents of clothes in the colours associated with the lord's family, and worn as a demonstration of loyalty and support. Social behaviour which historians once interpreted as a reaction to the breakdown of central authority during the Wars of the Roses turns out to be an example of a much more general tendency.

The existence of patron–client relationships in political life is not news to some historians. It was indeed in the 1920s that Lewis Namier put forward his argument, shocking at the time, that the Whig and Tory parties were not important in eighteenth-century politics. What really mattered was 'faction', in other words a group of clients around a patron, a group united not by an ideology or a programme but by a common relationship to a leader. In similar fashion, two decades later, J. E. Neale described the Elizabethan political scene in terms of the rivalry between great men (the Earl of Leicester versus the Duke of Norfolk, the Earl of Essex versus the Cecils), each great man surrounded by a network of clients. On one occasion Leicester dressed his men in blue laces to show how numerous they were, while Norfolk countered by dressing his supporters in yellow laces.[85]

In his well-known account of the conspicuous consumption of the Tudor and Stuart peerage, Lawrence Stone described their hospitality, following Veblen, essentially in terms of waste, or the need 'to justify the existence of echoing halls and sumptuous state apartments, and to keep at bay the melancholia and loneliness of a half empty mansion',[86] A reading of Fredrik Barth, or indeed of Marcel Mauss, suggests an alternative explanation. Could the patronage networks described by Neale have existed without the hospitality condemned by Stone? If some peers kept open house when they could ill afford it, they were

[85] Namier (1928); Neale (1948).
[86] Stone (1965), 555.

perhaps acting from the same motives as the *khans* who tried by this means to keep the vultures at bay.[87]

The great value to historians of the anthropological approach to these problems is in its emphasis on the order underlying what often looks – to modern Western observers – like disorder, on the rules of the game and the pressures on all the actors, the leaders no less than the followers, to continue to play their roles. Some recent studies of seventeenth-century French politics have taken advantage of the growing anthropological literature on patronage. They note, for example, how cardinal Richelieu chose his subordinates on personal rather than impersonal grounds; in other words, he did not look for the most able candidate to fill a given post, but offered it to one of his clients, or to use the expressive seventeenth-century phrase, one of his 'creatures'. His method of selection was a long way from the 'bureaucratic' model (above, p. 30). However, it had its rationale. Richelieu might not have survived politically had he not acted in this way. He needed subordinates he could trust, and apart from relatives, he could only trust his creatures, just as princes could only trust their favourites.[88]

Again, Sharon Kettering's study of patrons, clients and what she calls (following the anthropologist Eric Wolf), the 'brokers' between them, argues that patronage networks were parallel and supplementary to official political institutions in seventeenth-century France, and that the social rituals of the gift served political purposes. Here too power depended on exchange. However, Kettering also suggests that the system made a positive contribution to political integration at the price of encouraging conflict and 'corruption'. We are left with the paradox of a system said to favour both stability and conflict (cf. p. 104 below).[89]

The problem of 'corruption', which has surfaced several times in this account, deserves a little more attention. Is the term anything more than a personal judgement, implying a decline of standards from a moral golden age at some point in the past? Is it simply a label used by members of so-called 'bureaucratic' societies to dismiss other ways of organizing political life?

Suppose we define corruption in a relatively detached manner as behaviour deviating from the formal duties of a public role. In what social situations does this kind of behaviour arise or flourish? Or better, in what social situations is it perceived to flourish? If we phrase the

---

[87] Cf. Heal (1990), 57–61.
[88] Ranum (1963).
[89] Wolf (1956); Kettering (1986); cf. Lemarchand (1981).

question in this way, we see that corruption is in part in the eye of
the beholder. The more formally organized the society, the sharper the
distinction between public and private spheres, and the clearer the cases
of corruption will be.

As in the case of the royal or court 'favourite' (discussed above,
p. 47), it is also worth asking whether this corrupt behaviour fulfils a
social function for the public as well as for the officials involved;
whether, for example, it should be seen as a form of pressure-group
activity. This question leads to another. Does corruption take different
forms in different cultures? One might for instance distinguish the
granting of favours by officials to their relatives and friends from the
sale of such favours, in other words the exploitation of office in accordance with the rules of the market. The rise of corruption in the latter
sense seems to be part of the general rise of market society from the
eighteenth century onwards.[90]

A study by the French historian J.-F. Waquet reveals yet another
aspect of the problem. In eighteenth-century Florence some high
officials were put on trial, accused either of embezzlement of public
funds or of accepting presents in return for services rendered to private
individuals. Waquet argues that the political dimension of corruption (which might almost be described as 'stealing' power from one's
superiors), is as important as the economic, and that in this case it
reflects the long-term resistance of patrician officials (who were once
autonomous) to the Grand Dukes who had taken power from them in
the course of the sixteenth and seventeenth centuries.[91]

Power

The discussion of patronage and corruption has led us to the problem
of power. 'Power' is a term so embedded in ordinary language, at least
in the West, that it may seem unproblematic. However, the appearance
of clarity is deceptive, a point which emerges from studies of the idea of
power in other cultures, Java for instance, where it is regarded as a
form of creative energy which competitors can take from one another.[92]
A similar assumption underlies the idea of 'charisma' (above, p. 10;
below, p. 89).

[90] Klaveren (1957); Scott (1969).
[91] Waquet (1984); cf. Litchfield (1986).
[92] Anderson (1990), 20–2.

Whether regarded as energy or not, power is a concept which is often reified. It is easy to assume that one person, group or institution in a given society 'has' this power while everyone else lacks it – the 'ruler', for example, the 'ruling class', or the political 'elite'. As the American political scientist Harold Lasswell once asserted in his usual trenchant style, 'Those who get the most are *elite*; the rest are *mass*.'[93] Historians have often made this assumption.

However, the existence of a power elite in a given society is better regarded as a hypothesis than as an axiom. The problems involved in verifying the hypothesis, indeed in defining the concept, may be illustrated from a well-known controversy over the distribution of power in the United States. Robert Dahl, for example, argued that the 'elite model' can only be tested when decisions are made on issues where there is an observable conflict of interests between different groups in society. This formulation certainly brought more clarity and precision into the discussion. However, Dahl has been criticized not only for his suggestion that the United States was 'pluralist' rather than 'elitist' but also for what has been called his 'one-dimensional' view of power, concentrating on decision-making and ignoring the ways in which a particular group or groups may be able to exclude certain issues or grievances from the political agenda.[94]

From the point of view of a historian of preindustrial Europe, let alone an anthropologist, the general issues raised in this debate seem almost inextricably intertwined with assumptions about officially democratic political systems and the kind of pressure groups they generate. All the same, the effort to separate the two kinds of problem is worth while. For example, when studying the patricians of Venice and Amsterdam in the seventeenth century, I found Dahl's manner of testing the 'elite model' to be a useful one. Some historians have treated seventeenth-century Venice as a 'democracy' of nobles (although they numbered 2,000 in a population of 200,000); others suggest that a small oligarchy within this group exercised power. Dahl's article encouraged me to examine conflicts with particular care. This research strategy did not involve assuming that power is only exercised in situations of conflict, only that conflict makes its distribution more visible. It did not involve assuming that all important issues were discussed in public, still less that they have been recorded in surviving documents.

[93] Lasswell (1936), 13.
[94] Dahl (1958); Bachrach and Baratz (1962); cf. Giddens (1985), 8–9.

What it did do was to turn assumptions into hypotheses which could be tested – at least up to a point.[95]

Dahl's critics were in turn criticized by Steven Lukes for their 'two-dimensional' view, which included manipulation as well as decision-making but ignored a good deal else, including the 'power to prevent people ... from having grievances by shaping their perceptions, cognitions and preferences in such a way that they accept their role in the existing order of things'.[96] Again, Michael Mann has suggested that 'Societies are constituted of multiple overlapping and intersecting sociospatial networks of power'. He goes on to distinguish four sources of power – ideological, economic, military and political.[97] Mann's concern with ideological power and Lukes's concern with 'perceptions and cognitions' both imply that a student of power must examine not only political structures but also political 'culture'.

This term – which entered the discourse of political scientists in the 1950s and that of historians in the 1970s – may be defined as the political knowledge, ideas and sentiments current in a given place and time. It includes 'political socialization', in other words the means by which the knowledge, ideas and sentiments are transmitted from one generation to another.[98] In seventeenth-century England, for example, the fact that children grew up in patriarchal families must have made it easier for them to accept a patriarchal society without questioning it. They were told that obedience to the king was enjoined by the biblical commandment 'Honour thy father' (there was considerably less discussion of mothers).[99]

One implication of this more anthropological approach to power is that the relative success or failure of particular forms of political organization – Western-style democracy, for example – in different regions or periods will remain unintelligible without the study of the wider culture. Another implication of this approach is the need to take symbols seriously, to recognize their power in mobilizing political support. Modern elections, for example, have been studied as a form of ritual which concentrates on personalities rather than issues because this makes them more dramatic and appealing.[100] It would be good to

[95] Burke (1974).
[96] Lukes (1974), 24.
[97] Mann (1986), 1, 518–21.
[98] Almond and Verba (1963), 12–26; Baker (1987).
[99] Schochet (1975).
[100] Edelman (1971); Bennett (1983); Kertzer (1988).

have more studies of elections in earlier periods – in eighteenth-century England, let us say – along these lines.

Some recent studies of the French Revolution, on the other hand, have adopted this point of view, and treat the symbols of the revolution as central rather than peripheral to the movement. Thus the French historian Mona Ozouf has devoted a book to the analysis of revolutionary festivals – the Festival of the Federation, the Festival of the Supreme Being, and so on, paying particular attention to the ways in which the organizers of these events tried to restructure the participants' perceptions of space and time. There was a systematic attempt to create new sacred spaces, such as the Champ de Mars in Paris, for instance, in order to replace traditional Catholic ones. Again, the American historian Lynn Hunt has pointed out that in France in the 1790s, different costumes indicated different politics. She emphasizes the importance of the tricolour cockade, the liberty cap and the liberty tree (a kind of maypole which came to acquire a political meaning) in what theorists call the 'political mobilization' of the people. By May 1792, 60,000 liberty trees had been planted. In ways like these, the ideas and ideals of the revolution penetrated everyday life.[101]

Another cultural approach to politics is the work of Jürgen Habermas on the transformation of what he calls the 'public sphere' (*Öffentlichkeit*) in the eighteenth century. Habermas discusses the invasion of the traditional public sphere, restricted to a small elite, by the bourgeoisie, in other words, 'private people come together as a public', who developed their own institutions such as coffee-houses, theatres and newspapers, especially in large cities.[102] After a time-lag of some twenty years, the concept of the public sphere is entering the discourse of historians.[103]

Ironically enough, one of the historical studies which follows this model most closely in its concepts, methods and organization is one which is critical of Habermas for failing to discuss women. Joan Landes argues that women tried to enter the public sphere in the course of the French Revolution (when the *Declaration of the Rights of Man* was quickly followed by the *Declaration of the Rights of Woman*), but found their way blocked. 'The Republic was constructed against women, not just without them.'[104]

At a more general level, Habermas's account is vulnerable to the

---

[101] Ozouf (1976); Hunt (1984b).
[102] Habermas (1962); cf. Hohendahl (1982).
[103] Crow (1985), 1–22; Dooley (1990), 469–74; Chartier (1991), 32–52.
[104] Landes (1988), esp. 5–12.

criticism that the concept of a 'public sphere' is less clear than it looks and that different periods, different cultures and different social groups (men and women, for example) may well draw the line between public and private in different places. It is the same with 'politics', a term which is widening its meaning to encompass the informal, invisible aspects of the exercise of power. Michel Foucault was one of the first to advocate the study of 'micropolitics', in other words the exercise of power in a variety of small-scale institutions, including prisons, schools, hospitals and even families (above, p. 49). A bold suggestion when he uttered it, this view is now well on the way to becoming orthodox.

Centre and Periphery

Processes of political centralization are a traditional object of study. The concept of 'periphery', on the other hand, became current relatively recently, as a consequence of debates among development economists such as Raúl Prebisch, Paul Baran and André Gunder Frank in the 1950s and 1960s. Following the general lines of Lenin's analysis of imperialism and Marx's analysis of capitalism, these economists argued that the contrast between the prosperity of the industrialized nations and the poverty of the so-called 'underdeveloped' countries were opposite sides of the same coin, an illustration of what Marx called the structural 'contradicitions' in the capitalist system: 'The metropolis expropriates economic surplus from its satellites and appropriates it for its own economic development.' Hence the phrase 'the development of underdevelopment'.[105]

Historians from Poland and Hungary made use of this dependency theory to dissolve an apparent paradox in European history: the fact that the rise of the towns and the decline of serfdom in Western Europe took place at much the same time, during the sixteenth and seventeenth centuries, as the decline of the towns and the rise of the so-called 'second serfdom' in Eastern or 'East–Central' Europe. The American sociologist Immanuel Wallerstein went one step further in his account of the rise of capitalism, combining the theories of Latin American economists and East European historians and arguing that the price of economic development in the West included not only serfdom in the East but also slavery in the New World as part of the new division of labour between the 'core' and the 'periphery'. Changes in what he

---

[105] Baran (1957); Frank (1967).

called the 'semiperiphery', especially Mediterranean Europe, formed
part of the same world system. Spatial concepts thus play a central role
in Wallerstein's restructuring of the Marxist theory of social change
(below, p. 141).[106]

Centre–periphery models have also been employed in other areas,
from politics to culture. For example, the historian William McNeill has
organized a study of the Ottoman Empire around this model. The
effectiveness with which he uses the model to account for a sequence of
changes over several generations makes this an appropriate example to
discuss in more detail.

McNeill comes from Middle West America and taught at Chicago;
his study of what he calls 'Europe's steppe frontier' reveals an obvious
debt to F. J. Turner (above, p. 15). However, he is much more concerned than Turner ever was with the nature of the relation between
centre and periphery. His main thesis is that in the Ottoman Empire
'the centre could sustain organized military power on a large scale for
an extended time only by preying upon peripheral communities'. The
booty thus collected saved the regime from having to oppress the
peasantry in its own central provinces. Conquest paid for itself. In
addition, though McNeill does not lay much stress on this point, the so-
called 'tribute of children' collected from the Christian population of
the conquered provinces encouraged a meritocratic system of administration (above, p. 66).

The empire was therefore geared to continuous conquest. The problem for the Ottomans was that conquest could not be sustained and the
frontier expanded indefinitely. As McNeill argues persuasively, it
was necessary to call a halt to this process of expansion for reasons
which were fundamentally logistic. 'The only effective limit upon the
expansion of Turkish power,' he writes, 'was the distance the sultan's
army could travel from its winter quarters for the campaigning season.'

This limit was reached in the late sixteenth century, a time when the
balance of power between the rival empires, Ottoman and Habsburg,
led to a stalemate. The frontier zone between the empires was naturally
ravaged by both sides, with the result that 'the very operations of the
Turkish field armies tended . . . to create conditions at the extreme range
of their effective radius of action that prevented them from going
further'.

When expansion stopped, the political system began to disintegrate
and even the social structure began to change. The soldiers settled down

[106] Wallerstein (1974); cf. Skocpol (1977), Ragin and Chirot (1984).

on the land and 'the drive toward hereditary succession among the military elite of the empire gathered strength'. One might add that the supply of Christian children available for recruitment into the elite probably dwindled. Taxes replaced plunder as the chief source of revenue, so that the burden on the peasantry increased. Local notables emerged, and the political system became less centralized. In short, the organization of the centre was transformed by changes which began on the periphery.[107]

Theorists and historians from Scandinavia, who often describe themselves as inhabitants of the periphery of Europe, have taken a particular interest in this concept. For instance, the Norwegian political scientist Stein Rokkan has offered a typology of different possible relations between territorial centres and their subject peripheries, examining the degree of 'centre distinctiveness', the degree of 'periphery integration', the strength of 'standardizing agencies', and so on, in the age of the formation of national states in Western Europe.[108]

The intellectual elegance of analyses in terms of a pair of opposed yet complementary concepts is extremely seductive. Using these concepts should encourage the pursuit of a fruitful yet relatively neglected line of historical enquiry. Historians are accustomed to study centralization, but they have scarcely begun to explore the process of 'peripheralization'. An obvious example comes from the history of language; the increasing political centralization of Britain and France in the nineteenth century was accompanied by the spread of English and French and the marginalization or peripheralization of Breton, Welsh, Occitan, Gaelic and so on.[109] There are, of course, counter-movements, movements of linguistic revival in the periphery, including declarations of the independence of provincial or colonial forms of a language, as in the case of American or Australian English.

All these concepts have their value, but also their price. Ambiguity, for instance. The term 'centre' is sometimes used in a literal (geographical) sense, but at other times in a metaphorical (political or economic) sense. As a result, statements like 'the centralization of France was the work of Louis XIV' are much less clear than they may seem at first sight.

Another problem arises from the fact that some analyses, Rokkan's for example, imply a view of society which stresses equilibrium, while

---

[107] McNeill (1964); cf. McNeill (1983).
[108] Rokkan (1975), esp. 565–70.
[109] Certeau, Revel and Julia (1976); Grillo (1989).

others, such as Wallerstein's, emphasize conflicts. In the case of the theorists of underdevelopment, it has been argued that the crucial concept of 'surplus' needs clarification and that insufficient evidence has been provided to demonstrate the economic dependence of the core on the politically dependent periphery.[110] However, these criticisms do not imply that the concepts should be abandoned, only that they should be used with care, making discriminations between different types of centre – political, economic, or even ideological.

For example, the American sociologist Edward Shils has analysed what he calls the 'central value system' of society and the central institutional system which it legitimates. 'It is central because of its intimate connexion with what the society holds to be sacred; it is central because it is espoused by the ruling authorities of the society. These two kinds of centrality are vitally related. Each defines and supports the other.'[111] For example, deference is allocated to individuals according to their distance from the centre of society. In this way Shils links important (or even 'central') themes in the work of Durkheim (on the sacrality of the social order) and Weber (on the phenomenon of charisma).

Of the historical studies which make use of Shils's ideas, the most celebrated is surely that of divine kingship in nineteenth-century Bali by the anthropologist Clifford Geertz. In this study the author stresses what he calls the 'expressive nature' of the Balinese state and the theory of the 'exemplary centre', that is, the idea that the ruler and his court are 'at once a microcosm of the supernatural order . . . and the material embodiment of political order'.[112] The ruler sat immobile during court ceremonies in order 'to project an enormous calm at the centre of an enormous activity'. One of the most vivid illustrations of this enormous activity is the description of an elaborate procession ending in the cremation of a Balinese rajah who died in 1847, in which his concubines jumped into the flames, watched by a crowd of some 50,000 spectators. Yet the territory ruled by the rajah was small and his power limited. 'What was high centralization representationally was enormous dispersion institutionally.'[113]

The notion of a sacred or exemplary centre is equally relevant to Europe. In the seventeenth century, for example, the royal court was viewed as a microcosm of the universe. Planetary rooms in palaces and

[110] McKenzie (1977); Lane (1976).
[111] Shils (1975), 2.
[112] Geertz (1980).
[113] Geertz (1980), 121, 122, 132.

representations of kings as gods emphasized the analogy. Philip IV of Spain, for instance, was known as the 'planet king', and when he made his rare public appearances, he seemed to be as immobile as a statue – or a Balinese rajah. The Versailles of the 'Sun King' Louis XIV makes an even clearer example of an exemplary centre. The king's *lever* (which might be described as 'kingrise' on the analogy of sunrise), was an everyday ritual, like his eating and going to bed. The manners of the courtiers, their clothes and their vocabulary, were imitated in Paris and – after a few years' delay – in the provinces.

However, this imitation of the lifestyle of the courtiers does not imply that everyone in France admired or respected Louis XIV or the system of government he represented. Indeed, it may be argued more generally that Shils, like Durkheim, has overestimated social consensus and underestimated social conflict. By contrast, the Dutch sociologist W. F. Wertheim has emphasized the variety of value systems within the borders of a given society and the 'counterpoint' or clashes between them.[114]

Another way of making this criticism of Shils might be to say that his fascinating analysis of centrality has not been matched by equal attention to the periphery, which appears in his work to be little more than a residual concept, the 'non-centre'. In the words of a perceptive analysis of the historiography of Italian art, 'the periphery is only present as an area of shadow which serves to bring out the radiance of the metropolis'.[115]

A more positive, constructive approach to the periphery might be to analyse it as the frontier has been analysed since the days of F. J. Turner, as a region favouring freedom and equality, a refuge for rebels and heretics. The Ukraine of the sixteenth and seventeenth centuries makes a good example of the frontier as a refuge. In the interstices between two or three powers (the Poles, the Russians and the Turks) an egalitarian community of Cossacks was able to flourish, recruiting its members from runaway serfs. If one takes a detached, global view of society, a periphery of this kind appears as a counterpart (perhaps a necessary counterpart) to the orthodoxy and respect for authority and tradition associated with the centre. It adds a third option ('exit') to the conventional alternatives of protest ('voice') and conformity ('loyalty').[116]

---

[114] Wertheim (1974), 105–20.
[115] Castelnuovo and Ginzburg (1979).
[116] Hirschman (1970).

There seems to be a strong case for analysing the relation between centres and peripheries in cultural as well as in economic and political terms.[117] For example, in the Ottoman Empire of the sixteenth and seventeenth centuries, high culture on the Persian model was predominant in the capital, Istanbul, and in the provincial centres. In frontier regions, on the other hand, what predominated was the popular culture of the warriors, together with the popular and sometimes unorthodox religion of the dervishes.[118] The boundary between Christianity and Islam was in practice extremely permeable. Indeed, it was the site of cultural exchanges, with Muslims visiting Christian shrines and paying reverence to Christian saints and vice versa. Poles and Hungarians learned from the fighting methods of their Turkish opponents (the use of light cavalry, the scimitar, etc) just as American and Canadian frontiersmen learned from those of the Indians. Indeed, it might be argued more generally (as it has been in the case of the French and Spanish Pyrenees) that the men and women on each side of a border have more in common with each other than they have with their respective centres.[119]

Hegemony and Resistance

One of the problems raised by the use of the paired concepts of 'centre' and 'periphery', as we have seen, is the problem of the relation between the two; is it a relation of complementarity or a relation of conflict? A similar problem is raised by the use of the terms 'elite culture' and 'popular culture'. One possibility is to replace the terms 'elite' and 'popular' by those of 'dominant' and 'subordinate' cultures, in order to analyse the relation between the two in terms of 'social control' or 'cultural hegemony'.

'Social control' is the traditional sociological phrase to describe the power which society exercises over individuals via law, education, religion and so on.[120] However, it begs a very large question: who is 'society'? The use of the phrase depends on the acceptance of a view which has already been questioned more than once in these pages; the view that a social consensus exists and that society has a centre. If we

---

[117] Wolf (1969), 278ff.
[118] Inalcik (1973).
[119] Sahlins (1989).
[120] Ross (1901).

were to accept these assumptions, we might define social control as the enforcement of the consensus over norms, and the mechanism for the re-establishment of an equilibrium threatened by social 'deviants'. If, on the other hand, we think of society as composed of conflicting social groups, each with its own values, the phrase 'social control' will appear to be dangerous and misleading.

The concept is most useful in those situations in which the question 'Who is society?' is easiest to answer, in other words in the analysis of face-to-face situations in which a nonconformist confronts the community, as in the case of the factory worker who produces more than his colleagues, the student who tries too hard to please the teacher, or the soldier whose equipment is too clean and tidy (it is ironic but revealing that in all these cases the 'deviant' in the face-to-face situation is the one who is following the official norms).

In the case of early modern Europe, one of the most striking forms of this kind of social control was the charivari. The old man who married a young girl, or the husband who allowed himself to be beaten by his wife were considered to have transgressed the norms of the community. Hence the 'rough music' played outside the window, the satirical verses, or even the mock-procession of the victim through the streets of the neighbourhood. The masks worn by the players and singers hid their individuality and implied that they acted in the name of the community.[121] Despite the small scale of these incidents, however, it is not altogether clear who the community were; everyone in the village or parish, or just the young men who organized the charivari? Did they really express a consensus? Were the older men or the women of the neighbourhood likely to see the incident in the same light as the organizers?

Outside these face-to-face situations, the concept of social control becomes still more slippery. Some historians have used it to describe the activities of eighteenth-century English squires enforcing the game laws against poachers, or nineteenth-century town councils banning popular recreations like the football played in the streets of Derby and other cities on Shrove Tuesday and other festive occasions. The objection to this usage is that the term has become 'a label for what one class does to another', treating the values of the dominant class, squirearchy or bourgeoisie, as if they were the values of society as a whole.[122]

The question whether or not the values of the ruling class are

---

[121] Pitt-Rivers (1954), ch. 11; Davis (1971); Thompson (1972).
[122] Yeo and Yeo (1981); cf. Donajgrodzki (1977), Jones (1983).

accepted by the ruled at a particular place and time is obviously a difficult one to answer. If they are so accepted, why is resistance (not to mention open revolt) so frequent? If they are not accepted, how does the ruling class continue to rule? Does its power depend on coercion or consensus, or is there something in between? That there may be something of this kind was suggested by the Italian Marxist Antonio Gramsci. The term he used was 'hegemony'.

Gramsci's basic idea was that the ruling class did not rule by force (or at any rate not by force alone) but by persuasion. The persuasion was indirect: the subordinate classes learned to see society through their rulers' eyes thanks to their education and also to their place in the system.[123] This concept of cultural hegemony did not attract much attention when Gramsci formulated it, but it has since enjoyed a revival. Indeed, it has been taken out of its original context and used more or less indiscriminately to analyse a much wider range of situations. As a corrective to this inflation or dilution of the concept, it may be useful to ask the following three questions.

1 Is cultural hegemony to be assumed to be a constant factor, or has it only operated in certain places and at certain times? If the latter, what are the conditions and the indicators of its presence?
2 Is the concept purely descriptive, or is it supposed to be explanatory? If the latter, is the explanation proposed one which refers to the conscious strategies of the ruling class (or of groups within it) or to what might be called the latent rationality of their actions?
3 How are we to account for the successful achievement of this hegemony? Can it be established without the collusion or connivance of some at least of the dominated? Can it be resisted with success? Does the ruling class simply impose its values on the subordinate classes, or is there some kind of compromise?

Into this analysis it may be useful to introduce two concepts, 'symbolic violence' and 'negotiation'. The first concept, 'symbolic violence', launched by Pierre Bourdieu, refers to the imposition of the culture of the ruling class on dominated groups, and especially to the process by which these dominated groups are forced to recognize the ruling culture as legitimate and their own culture as illegitimate.[124] Examples range from the history of language, for instance the pressure

---

[123] Femia (1981); Lears (1985).
[124] Bourdieu (1972), 190–7.

on dialect speakers to perceive their own speech as incorrect, to the history of popular healers who were turned into heretics or criminals by being labelled as 'witches' and forced to confess that their activities were literally diabolical.

The term 'negotiation', originally used by sociologists in a literal sense to analyse 'plea bargaining' by lawyers and their clients, has been adapted to discuss the silent process of give and take between doctors and patients or between elites and subordinate groups. Thus an analysis of the British class system has argued that in general the underprivileged do not reject dominant values but 'negotiate or modify them in the light of their own existential conditions'.[125]

Historians too have found the term useful, whether to analyse the redefinition of the values of 'respectability' by the skilled workers of Victorian Edinburgh, or the relation between official and unofficial Catholicism in seventeenth-century Naples. The process by which saints were canonized in the Counter-Reformation Church was the result of such a process of negotiation between the periphery, in other words the region in which the cult of a local hero grew up, and the centre, Rome, where the ecclesiastical lawyers decided whether to accept or reject it.[126]

Alternatively, the subordinate classes – slaves, serfs, proletarians, farm hands and so on – may choose to resist rather than negotiate. The term 'resistance' covers a wide variety of forms of collective action, such as 'pilfering, feigned ignorance . . . foot-dragging . . . sabotage . . . arson, flight', and so on. As for foot-dragging, a remarkably vivid description of the process may be found in the reminiscences of the poet Gyula Illyés, who grew up on a large farm on the Hungarian plain at the beginning of the century. Work for the farm servants was unremitting, long hours on weekdays and Sundays alike. Their reaction – like that of the farm animals – was to perform every action in slow motion. Illyés describes watching Uncle Róka fill his pipe with 'tortoise-like deliberation'. 'He handled the matches as if the matchstick in his hand were the last possible means of making fire and the fate of all mankind depended on it'.[127] This style of behaviour may be seen as a form of resistance to excessive demands by the landowners and the overseers, 'an instinctive defence' as Illyés puts it. One wonders how many serfs and slaves in history have behaved in a similar manner.

---

[125] Strauss (1978), 224–33; Parkin (1971), 92.
[126] Gray (1976), ch. 7; Burke (1987), 48–62.
[127] Scott (1990), 188; Illyés (1967), 126–7.

Not only individual or group actions but cultural forms as well may
be analysed in this way. Indeed, some students of popular culture go so
far as to define it as a culture of resistance to the dominance of official
or elite culture.[128] The strategy adopted is defensive, appropriate to
a position of subordination – subversion rather than confrontation,
guerrilla tactics rather than open warfare – but resistance all the same.

A further refinement has been introduced into this approach by Paul
Willis, author of one of the most striking examples of the ethnography
of the British. His study of working-class boys in school offers a sympathetic and richly detailed account, largely in their own words, of the
resistance of these adolescents to the official ethos of the school and of
their contempt for the 'ear-holes', in other words, the boys who collaborate with the system. However, he goes on to point out that the
refusal to collaborate results in academic 'failure' and entry into a
relatively low-paid, working-class job. In other words, an unintended
consequence of adolescent rebellion in school is the reproduction of
inequality over the generations.[129]

Social Movements

On occasion, of course, everyday resistance turns into open revolt or
into some other form of 'social movement'. This term came into use
among sociologists in the United States in the 1950s. One of the first
historians to use the term was Eric Hobsbawm, whose *Primitive Rebels*
carries the subtitle 'Studies in Archaic Forms of Social Movement in
the Nineteenth and Twentieth Centuries', and ranges from bandits to
believers in the imminence of the millennium.[130] His book was soon
followed by a shelf of studies of millenarian movements in particular,
the joint work of anthropologists, sociologists and historians.

A possible weakness in *Primitive Rebels* is its broad use of the term
'social movement' to include anything from a riot lasting only a few
hours to permanent organizations, from the Carbonari to the Mafia. On
the other hand, the value of Hobsbawm's study, and of the term more
generally is to direct attention to characteristics (such as charismatic
leadership) which are shared by religious and political movements,
previously studied in isolation from each other.

[128] Hall (1981); Sider (1986), 119–28; Certeau (1980); Fiske (1989).
[129] Willis (1977).
[130] Heberle (1951); Hobsbawm (1959).

The concept of 'charisma' was borrowed from the church historians by Max Weber and introduced into political studies. Weber defined charisma as 'a certain quality of an individual personality by virtue of which he is considered extraordinary and treated as endowed with supernatural, superhuman or at least specifically exceptional powers or qualities'.[131] The concept describes rather than explains the magnetism by which a religious or political leader attracts followers and becomes the object of a cult. At the very least, however, the reminder that behaviour of this kind is not uncommon may help remove obstacles to understanding the reverence paid to Luther by the Lutherans, for instance, to Hitler by the Nazis, or to Louis XIV by his courtiers. Indeed, there may be a case for extending the term 'charisma' to refer to all cases in which some people impute supernatural power to others, whether they are saints or witches.[132]

Weber has, however, been criticized for focusing on the qualities of the leader, rather than the expectations of the followers who 'impute' these qualities.[133] It is time to ask whether there are kinds of follower or kinds of organization which are particularly susceptible to charismatic leaders.

Formal organizations have long been studied by sociologists and historians. Research on crowds and riots has also flourished following the discovery of 'history from below'. On the other hand, movements which last more than a few hours but have no permanent organization have been relatively neglected by historians, perhaps because they do not fit either model. These movements are essentially fluid and informal, characterized by 'communitas' (above, p. 57). As a result, they cannot last very long in this form. Some of them wither away. The rest are destroyed, or at least transformed, by their own success. Growth leads to the 'routinization of communitas' – as Victor Turner, adapting Weber's 'routinization of charisma', describes it – or, more prosaically, to the development of new institutions such as the Franciscan Order, the Lutheran Church and the Communist Party. The 'movement' ceases to move.[134]

Later, when successful organizations commission official histories of themselves, these histories often give the impression that these bodies were consciously planned and institutionalized right from the start. It is

[131] Weber (1920), 1, 241; Tucker (1968).
[132] Klaniczay (1990b), 7–9.
[133] Shils (1975), 126–34; Anderson (1990), 78–93.
[134] Turner (1969), 131ff; cf. Touraine (1984).

difficult not to read the present back into the past in this way, but the tendency must be resisted, and the concept of a movement encourages awareness of the fluidity and spontaneity of the moment of foundation, a 'moment' which may last as long as a generation but is bound to give way to the phase of routinization or 'crystallization'.

It has sometimes been suggested that the young are prominent in such movements, precisely because their capacity for spontaneous action has not yet been dulled by routine. Historians of the Reformation in particular have taken up this idea and found evidence to support it, at least in the early phases of the movement, the moment of creativity, protest and martyrdom. Luther himself was in his early thirties when his movement began, and his followers were generally younger than he was (though this pattern was perhaps to be expected, given the high proportion of under-thirties in the population of sixteenth-century Europe).[135]

It may be useful to distinguish two types of social movement, according to whether the movement is essentially initiating a process of change or reacting to changes which are already under way. Needless to say, the distinction is one of degree rather than kind.

Although it is not customary to discuss the German Reformation as a social movement, it may be useful to consider its early years in this way, stressing the importance of collective action to change the existing order by direct rather than by institutional means.[136] In the early 1520s, Luther's movement of reform had not yet congealed into a Church. Luther was of course reacting against what he called the 'abuses' of the old system, but these practices were of long standing and their existence is insufficient to explain why the Reformation happened when it did. The impetus for change came from the side of the reformers.

More common, however, is the 'reactive' type of social movement, especially popular movements of protest against economic or social changes which threaten to destroy a traditional way of life. One of the most remarkable of these movements is surely the rebellion in the backlands of northeastern Brazil in 1896–7. Its charismatic leader was a wandering holy man, Antonio Conselheiro, an ascetic who made his reputation with prophecies of imminent disaster from which Brazil would be saved by the return of King Sebastian (who died fighting in North Africa in 1578). Conselheiro led his followers to an old cattle ranch which soon became a holy place, the town of Canudos. The

---

[135] Spitz (1967); Brigden (1982).
[136] Scribner (1979).

inhabitants of this New Jerusalem defeated no fewer than three military expeditions sent to put down their insurrection. This revolt of the periphery against the centre was, among other things, a reaction against the establishment of the Brazilian Republic by a military coup in 1889. In this sense it was comparable to the Vendée rising in western France in 1793 against the French Revolution.[137] However, the messianic and millenarian elements in this revolt, its atmosphere of religious exaltation, the capacity for guerrilla warfare shown by the *jagunços* ('backwoodsmen' or even 'bandits'), and the vivid first-hand account produced by a brilliant journalist, Euclides da Cunha, combine to give the Canudos affair an aura of its own.

Mentality and Ideology

The political problems of domination and resistance lead us back to the realm of culture, to questions of ethos, mentality or ideology. We have seen that the patron−client system depends on a value-system based on honour. The bureaucracies discussed earlier (p. 30) also depend on a particular ethos, including respect (as some would say, excessive respect) for the formal rules which define this type of administrative system. Again, the hegemony of the ruling class depends on a certain degree of acceptance by the subordinate classes. In each case it is impossible to comprehend the workings of the system without understanding the attitudes and values of the participants.

One might therefore claim with some justice that it is impossible to write social history without introducing the history of ideas, provided that the phrase is understood as the history of everyone's ideas rather than the ideas of the most original thinkers of a given epoch. If historians are going to concern themselves with the attitudes and values of everyone living in a given society, they would be well advised to acquaint themselves with two rival concepts, mentality and ideology.

The history of mentalities is essentially a Durkheimian approach to ideas, although Durkheim himself preferred the term collective representations'. It was developed by Durkheim's follower Lucien Lévy-Bruhl in his study *La mentalité primitive* (1927) and elsewhere.[138] Contemporary sociologists and anthropologists sometimes speak of 'modes of thought', 'belief systems' or 'cognitive maps'.

[137] Cunha (1902); Tilly (1964).
[138] Burke (1986b).

Whatever the term used, the approach differs from conventional intellectual history in at least three features. There is a stress on collective attitudes rather than individual ones; on unspoken assumptions rather than explicit theories, on 'common sense' or what appears to be common sense in a particular culture; and on the structure of belief systems, including a concern with the categories used to interpret experience and methods of proof and persuasion. There is an obvious parallel between these three features of the history of mentalities and the approach of Michel Foucault in *The Order of Things* to what he liked to call the 'archaeology' of systems of thought or 'epistemes'.[139]

An example of the kind of problem which the mentalities approach helps to solve is the medieval ordeal. The fact that in the early Middle Ages guilt or innocence was sometimes determined by an ordeal such as carrying red-hot iron or plunging the suspect's hand into boiling water has long been a stumbling-block to the understanding of the period. As the eighteenth-century Scottish historian William Robertson remarked, 'Among all the whimsical and absurd institutions which owe their existence to the weakness of human reason, this . . . appears to be the most extravagant and preposterous.' In the past few years, however, a series of studies have appeared which take the custom of the ordeal seriously and try to render it more intelligible by investigating the assumptions of the participants. The ancient historian Peter Brown, for example, has suggested that the ordeal functioned as an instrument of consensus. Other historians reject this particular conclusion, but share Brown's concern to replace the ordeal in its cultural context. It may therefore be concluded that the history of mentalities has survived its own trial by ordeal.[140]

A similar problem provoked the pioneering study in the history of mentalities in the 1920s. This was the work of the French historian Marc Bloch, whose admiration for Durkheim has already been discussed (p. 16). Bloch wrote a history of the belief in the virtues of the 'royal touch', in other words the idea that the kings of France and England had the miraculous power to cure sufferers from scrofula (a skin disease) by touching them. This power was a sign of their charisma, a concept which Weber had recently formulated but which Bloch did not know. The belief in the royal touch persisted for many centuries. In England the practice lasted till the reign of Queen Anne (Samuel Johnson was touched by her when he suffered the disease as a

---

[139] Foucault (1966).
[140] Brown (1975); cf. Morris (1975); Radding (1979); Bartlett (1986).

small boy), while in France it lasted till the Revolution and was revived by Charles X in 1825.

Bloch started from the assumption that the kings and queens of England and France did not actually have the power to cure skin disease, and went on to consider why this 'collective illusion', as he called it, was able to persist for so long. He stressed the fact that people expected a miracle. If the symptoms of the disease disappeared, they therefore gave the king the credit. On the other hand, if the symptoms did not disappear, that only showed that the sick person needed to be touched again. Bloch also noted that the propensity to believe something which was contradicted by experience is 'an essential trait of the so-called "primitive" mentality', discussed by Lévy-Bruhl.[141]

In France the mentalities approach became popular with historians in the 1960s and inspired a whole shelf of studies. It was relatively slow to attract the British, however, and when it finally did so it arrived by a somewhat roundabout route. The British anthropologist Edward Evans-Pritchard was inspired by Durkheim and Lévy-Bruhl to study the belief system of the Azande (who live in Central Africa). Evans-Pritchard emphasized the self-confirming character of the Zande poison oracles in a manner reminiscent of Bloch (whom he had read when he was a student of medieval history) on the royal touch. 'In this web of belief,' he wrote, 'every strand depends on every other strand, and a Zande cannot get out of its meshes because it is the only world he knows.'[142] Thanks to Evans-Pritchard and his pupils, a concern with modes of thought and belief systems has come to affect the approach of British historians (notably Keith Thomas and his followers) to subjects such as witchcraft, magic and religion in England in the sixteenth and seventeenth centuries.[143]

The history of mentalities has proved itself to be an extremely fruitful approach to the past and Bloch's book is only one of the masterpieces of the genre. All the same, in the course of solving traditional problems, new problems were created. The most serious of these may be called the problem of immobilization, of the static picture. Historians have proved much more successful at describing mentalities at a particular point in the past than at explaining how, when or why they changed. Foucault's *Order of Things* (1966) also suffers from this weakness, as many critics have pointed out. The weakness is closely associated with one of the

---

[141] Bloch (1924), 421n.
[142] Evans-Pritchard (1937), 194.
[143] Thomas (1971).

great strengths of the approach, the assumption of a belief system in which each part depends on the rest. This assumption allows historians to explain the persistence of a certain mentality over time despite the existence of awkward empirical evidence. The more satisfying the explanation of persistence, however, the harder it is to explain a change of mentality when it eventually does occur.

The lack of concern for changes goes with a lack of concern for difference (let alone conflict). A second major problem raised by the history of mentalities might be called the problem of 'homogenization'. To focus on collective mentalities is to risk ignoring variation at several different levels. In the first place, individuals do not think exactly alike. To this objection one might respond in the words of the French historian Jacques Le Goff, who suggests that the term 'mentality' be used only to describe the beliefs which individuals have in common with the rest of their group.[144] In the second place, the same individual will express himself or herself differently in different communicative situations. If one comes across an apparently paradoxical statement made in another period or another culture, it is necessary to replace it in its social context at a micro level as well as a macro level.[145]

A still more serious problem arises from the fact that historians of mentalities easily slip into assuming the existence of a binary opposition between two belief systems, the 'traditional' and the 'modern', reproducing in different words the distinction made by Lévy-Bruhl between what he called 'prelogical' and 'logical' thought. Modern thought is more abstract, less dependent on context, and more 'open' in the sense that there are a number of competing systems available, with the result that individuals are more easily aware of alternatives to their own beliefs.[146] To demonstrate the problems inherent in such an opposition one might try a simple experiment, that of reading in quick succession two classics in the field, Marcel Granet's *La pensée chinoise* (1934) and Lucien Febvre's *Le problème de l'incroyance* (1942). The characteristics attributed to the traditional Chinese and the sixteenth-century French seem very much alike. They are both defined by contrast to the twentieth-century French intellectual, and the contrast between Them and Us reduces the variety of the 'other' to uniformity. This kind of reduction is the price of structural analysis (below, p. 110).

Some of the difficulties associated with the concept of 'collective

---

[144] Le Goff (1974).
[145] Lloyd (1990), ch. 1.
[146] Horton (1967, 1982); Gellner (1974), 156–8.

mentalities' are avoided by an analysis in terms of 'ideology', an approach to the history of thought built on Marxist foundations and developed by Gramsci and by German 'sociologists of knowledge' such as Karl Mannheim. This development took place between the two world wars, in other words at much the same time as the history of mentalities in France.

'Ideology' is a term with many – too many – definitions. Some people use the term in a pejorative sense – I have beliefs, he (or she) has an ideology. Others treat it as neutral, as a synonym for 'world-view'.[147] A useful distinction between two concepts of ideology was made by Mannheim.[148] The first, which he called the 'total' conception of ideology, suggests that there is an association between a particular set of beliefs or view of the world and a particular social group or class, thus implying that Bloch and Febvre were wrong to discuss the mentality of the medieval or the sixteenth-century French without making social distinctions.

The second, which Mannheim called the 'particular' conception of ideology, is the notion that ideas or representations may be utilized to maintain a particular social or political order. For example, the idea of democracy may be used to 'mystify', to conceal the extent to which power is exercised by a small group. Alternatively, ideas may justify (or as Weber would say, 'legitimate') the system, often by representing the political order as natural rather than cultural – the king, for example (p. 83) as the sun. These conceptions of ideology were elaborated at the end of the 1960s by the social theorists Jürgen Habermas and Louis Althusser. For Habermas, ideology is concerned with communication which is 'systematically distorted' by the exercise of domination, while in Althusser's famous phrase, ideology refers to 'the imaginary [or "imagined"] relationship of individuals to their real conditions of existence.'[149]

The relation, or opposition, between mentalities and ideologies may be in need of clarification.[150] For this purpose it may be useful to return to the example of the royal touch. Marc Bloch's classic study in the history of mentalities treated the belief in the royal touch as if it were 'innocent'. An analysis in terms of ideology, on the other hand, would stress the fact that it was in the interests of the royal regime that

---

[147] Geuss (1981), ch. 1; Thompson (1990), ch. 1.
[148] Mannheim (1936).
[149] Habermas (1968); Althusser (1970).
[150] Vovelle (1982), esp. 1–12.

ordinary people should believe that the king had the power to work miracles. Charisma was not a natural property of the kings of France and England. It was in a sense manufactured, produced by royal robes, rituals and so on.

Although the contrast between mentalities and ideologies is a useful one, attempts to analyse the ways in which ideas sustain political systems have brought difficulties to light, not unlike the difficulties associated with the concept 'hegemony' (above, p. 84). Ideology has often been treated as a kind of 'social cement' holding society together. However, its importance in this respect has been challenged in a series of recent studies which criticize Marxists and Durkheimians alike. These studies suggest, for instance, that the social cohesion of liberal democracy is negative rather than positive; in other words, that it depends not on a consensus over the fundamental values embodied in the regime but rather on a lack of consensus over criticisms of the government.[151]

Communication and Reception

The study of ideology leads on to the study of the means by which ideas are spread, in other words, communication. Coming from the study of politics, Harold Lasswell once defined the objects of such a study in his usual vigorous manner as 'Who says what to whom, and with what effects' (implying that these 'effects' were measurable). Coming from literature, Raymond Williams offered a slightly softer definition, with more emphasis on form (style, genre): 'the institutions and forms in which ideas, information and attitudes are transmitted and received'. Coming from linguistics, Joshua Fishman offered another variation on the theme when he proposed 'the study of who speaks what language to whom and when', emphasizing the propensity of many speakers to switch languages or forms of language in different situations or 'speech domains'. Coming from anthropology, Dell Hymes took an even wider view of the topic, recommending an ethnography of communicative events which would take account not only of messages, senders and receivers but of 'channels', 'codes' and 'settings'.[152]

Inspired by Hymes, Fishman and their colleagues, some historians are working on the social history of language, its changing forms and its

[151]   Mann (1970); Abercrombie (1980); Thompson (1990), 3.
[152]   Lasswell (1936); Williams (1962); Fishman (1965); Hymes (1964).

various functions.[153] For example, language is, like consumption, a means for some social groups to distinguish themselves from others. As an example one might take Thorstein Veblen's assertion that the manner of speaking of the leisure class was necessarily 'cumbrous and out of date', because such usages implied a waste of time and so 'exemption from the use and need of direct and forcible speech'.[154] Sociolinguists have also had much to say about the use of language as a status symbol.

One of the best-known examples is the discussion of upper-class and non-upper-class English usage ('U' and 'non-U') in the 1950s, in which it was claimed that the term 'looking-glass' was U, while 'mirror' was non-U; 'writing-paper' U, 'note-paper' non-U, and so on.[155] In seventeenth-century France, François de Callières, private secretary to Louis XIV, had already pointed out differences between what he called 'bourgeois ways of speaking' (*façons de parler bourgeoises*) and the vocabulary characteristic of the aristocracy.

In these cases, the choice of any particular term appears to be arbitrary, motivated by the desire of the aristocrats to distinguish themselves from the bourgeoisie, who in turn change their speech patterns to resemble the aristocracy, who are therefore constantly compelled to innovate. As for the everyday use by certain aristocracies of a foreign language (French in nineteenth-century Russia, eighteenth-century Prussia, the Netherlands in the seventeenth century, and so on), this was at once a means of distinguishing them from people lower in the social scale and a homage to Paris as centre of civilization. Veblen might have added that communicating in a foreign language with native speakers of one's own language makes conspicuous the leisure of 'leisure classes'.[156]

So far we have been considering the communicators, their intentions and strategies. What of the audiences and their responses? In this area it is the literary theorists who have made the most important contribution, emphasizing the role of the reader and his or her 'horizon of expectations' in the construction of meaning.[157] In similar fashion the French theorist Michel de Certeau (whose interests were too wide to be confined in any one discipline) stressed the creativity of ordinary people in the sphere of consumption, their active reinterpretations of the messages beamed at them and their tactics for adapting the system of

---

[153] Burke and Porter (1987, 1991).
[154] Veblen (1899).
[155] Ross (1954).
[156] Burke and Porter (1987), 1–20.
[157] Jauss (1974); cf. Culler (1980), 31–83 and Holub (1984), 58–63.

material objects to their own needs. A central concept in this discussion is that of 'appropriation', sometimes accompanied by its complementary opposite, the 'recuperation' of objects and meanings by the dominant or official culture. The phrase 'transgressive re-inscription' has been coined to emphasize the way in which one group adopts and adapts, or converts, inverts and subverts the vocabulary of another.[158]

Historians would obviously be ill-advised to take sides on the ultimately metaphysical question currently dividing literary critics, the question whether the 'real' meanings are to be found in the texts or whether they are projected on to the texts. On the other hand, the empirical question of the differences between the message transmitted and the message received by viewers, listeners or readers in different times and places is clearly of historical importance. Luther, for example, once complained that the German peasants misunderstood his teaching when they claimed that serfdom should be abolished because Christ died for all men.

This problem is central to what has become known as the 'history of reading'. In a famous passage of his *Cheese and Worms*, Carlo Ginzburg discussed the mental 'grids' through which the heretical miller Menocchio read certain books and the discrepancies between his reading of the religious literature of the late Middle Ages and the orthodox readings of the inquisitors.[159] Roger Chartier and Robert Darnton have made more systematic explorations of this kind, focusing on eighteenth-century France and examining annotations, the records of lending libraries, the differences between originals and translations and so on in order to reconstruct readers' views of certain texts.[160] Art historians too are increasingly concerned with responses to images. Iconoclasm, for example, whether directed against images of devils or images of saints, has been studied as evidence enabling us to reconstruct the point of view of long-dead spectators.[161]

Orality and Textuality

The definition of the ethnography of communication offered by Dell Hymes (above, p. 96) included the 'channels', in other words the media.

---

[158] Certeau (1980); Fiske (1989), ch. 2; Hebdige (1979), 94; Dollimore (1991), 285–7.
[159] Ginzburg (1976); cf. Foucault (1971), 11.
[160] Chartier (1987); Darnton (1991).
[161] Freedberg (1989), 378–428.

The media theorist Marshall McLuhan made the provocative assertion that 'the medium is the message'. It would be more plausible to claim that the medium – oral, written, or pictorial – is part of the message. Even so, the claim is one which historians have to take into account whenever they examine a piece of evidence.

Oral communication, for example, has its own forms, its own styles. A famous study of rumour argued that in the course of oral transmission, messages are adapted to the needs of the receivers in a process which involves simplification ('levelling'), selection ('sharpening') and the assimilation of the unknown to the known.[162] Albert Lord's equally celebrated study of oral epics in Yugoslavia suggested that the stories were improvised by the singer thanks to the use of prefabricated elements, 'formulae' (set phrases like Homer's 'wine-dark sea') and 'themes' (recurrent episodes such as councils and battles). Another media theorist, Walter Ong, has used studies such as Lord's to generalize about the main features of 'orally based thought and expression', which he describes as additive rather than subordinative, full of redundancy, and so on.[163]

These analyses and debates have had a somewhat delayed impact on historical writing. Historical studies of rumour remain rare, despite the example of Georges Lefebvre, who devoted a whole book to the spread of the so-called 'great fear' of 1789. Lefebvre made a meticulous analysis of the chronology, geography and sociology of the propagation of rumours of an aristocratic plot and of imminent attacks by 'brigands', explaining these 'panics' in terms of the economic, social and political situation of a time when bread was scarce and discontent was turning into revolution.[164] He had less to say about the different versions of these rumours, however, and we are still waiting for someone to analyse either the anxieties of 1789 or the English Protestant fears of a 'Popish Plot' in 1678 in terms of the 'levelling' and 'sharpening' processes described by Allport and Postman (or of other processes if appropriate).

Despite the rise of 'oral history' in the last generation, it is only recently that historians have devoted serious attention to oral tradition as an art form. It is instructive in this respect to compare the first edition of the study of oral tradition by the Belgian anthropologist-historian Jan Vansina, published in 1961, which concentrates almost

---

[162] Allport and Postman (1945).
[163] Lord (1960), esp. 30–98; Ong (1982), 31–77.
[164] Lefebvre (1932); cf. Farge and Revel (1988) and Guha (1983), 259–64.

exclusively on the problem of reliability, with the second edition of 1985, which is more concerned with the forms and genres of communication.[165]

Writing too is increasingly investigated as a medium with special qualities and limitations. Jack Goody, for example, has published a series of studies of the consequences of literacy, claiming that the contrast made by Lévy-Bruhl, Lévi-Strauss and others between two 'mentalities' can be explained in terms of two modes of communication, the oral and the written. For example, it is much easier to rearrange a written list than a memorized one; so in this way writing encourages abstraction. Again, writing promotes the awareness of alternatives which transforms a closed system into an open one. In this sense 'writing restructures consciousness', as Ong puts it.[166]

These arguments have been criticized for overemphasizing the difference between oral and written modes, neglecting the qualities of oral communication and for treating literacy as a neutral technique which can be detached from its context.[167] The criticisms qualify rather than undermine the central thesis, but they also suggest new directions for research, for example on the interaction or 'interface' between the oral and the written.[168] For example, formulae and themes are to be found in written texts as well as in oral performances. Do they take a different form, or are they used in a different way? What is changed when a folktale is written down, especially when it is written down by a member of an elite? Charles Perrault, for example, who published *Little Red Riding Hood* at the end of the seventeenth century, was an intellectual and an official in the service of Louis XIV.[169]

For a historian of Europe, a striking feature of this debate is its contrast between orality and literacy at the expense of a third medium, print. In the case of West Africa, frequently discussed in this context, literacy and print arrived at much the same time, so that their consequences are difficult to disentangle. In the case of Europe, on the other hand, there is a long-standing debate on the print 'revolution'. It used to be discussed simply in terms of the diffusion of books, ideas and movements (especially the Protestant Reformation), but attention has been turning from the message to the medium.

---

[165] Vansina (1961).
[166] Goody (1977); Ong (1982), 78–116.
[167] Finnegan (1973); Street (1984).
[168] Goody (1987).
[169] Soriano (1968).

McLuhan, for example, has claimed that printing was responsible for a shift of emphasis from the auditory to the visual (thanks in part to the increasing use of diagrams), and also for a 'split between heart and head'. The American historian Elizabeth Eisenstein translated McLuhan into academically respectable form in her study of 'the printing press as an agent of change', which emphasized such features of 'print culture' as standardization, preservation and more sophisticated means of information retrieval (alphabetical indexes, for example).[170] In similar fashion, Walter Ong (whose early historical work had inspired McLuhan in the first place), describes the way in which print reinforces writing in bringing about the 'shift from sound to visual space' and encouraging 'a sense of closure', of a definitive text.[171]

The proposition that a document is a text which requires the skills of a literary critic to read it is another challenge to historians, from the so-called 'new historicists', especially Stephen Greenblatt in particular. Whether or not Greenblatt's interpretations of specific Elizabethan documents carry conviction, his general proposition about the rhetoric of documents deserves to be taken very seriously by historians, and it will be discussed in more detail below (p. 126).[172]

Myth

To take the discussion a little further, it may be useful to introduce the term 'myth'. Historians often use the term 'myth' to refer to stories which are not true, in explicit contrast to their own stories, or 'history'. It may be illuminating to compare this usage with that of anthropologists, for example, literary theorists or psychologists.[173]

Malinowski, for example, claimed that myths were – primarily if not exclusively – stories with social functions. A myth, he suggested, is a story about the past which serves, as he put it, as a 'charter' for the present. That is, the story performs the function of justifying some institution in the present and thus of keeping that institution in being. He was probably thinking not only of the stories told by his Trobriand Islanders, but also of Magna Carta, a document which was used to justify a variety of institutions and practices over the centuries. Because

[170] Eisenstein (1979), 43–159.
[171] Ong (1982), 117–38.
[172] Greenblatt (1988).
[173] Cohen (1969).

it was continually misinterpreted, or reinterpreted, the document was always up-to-date. The 'liberties' or privileges of the barons turned into the liberty of the subject. What was important in English history was not so much the text as the 'myth' of Magna Carta.[174] In similar fashion the so-called 'Whig Interpretation of History' current in Britain in the nineteenth and early twentieth centuries, in other words 'the tendency to write on the side of Protestants and Whigs, to praise revolutions provided they have been successful, to emphasize certain principles of progress in the past', functioned as a justification of the contemporary political system.[175]

An alternative definition of myth might be a story which has a moral, for instance the triumph of good over evil, and stereotyped characters who, whether heroes or villains, are larger (or simpler) than life. In this sense one might speak of the 'myth of Louis XIV' or the 'Hitler myth', for example, on the grounds that these rulers were presented in the official media of their day as heroic figures who were virtually omnisci- ent or omnipotent.[176] An alternative myth of Hitler as a diabolical figure was also in circulation. In similar fashion, during the witch-hunts of early modern Europe the common belief that the witches were servants of Satan may be described as a 'myth'.[177] These examples can of course be accommodated by Malinowski's definition. The myth of Hitler justified (or as Max Weber would say, 'legitimated') his rule, and the myth of the witches legitimated the persecution of old women whom posterity believes to have been harmless. All the same, it is illuminating to define myth in terms not only of functions but also of recurrent forms or 'plots' (the meaning of the Greek term *mythos*). Jung would have called them 'archetypes' and explained them as unchanging products of the collective unconscious. A historian is more likely to view them as the products of culture, changing slowly over the long term.[178]

In any case it is important to be aware that oral and written narra- tives, including those which the narrators regard as the unvarnished truth, include elements of archetype, stereotype, or myth. Thus par- ticipants in the Second World War described their experiences by means of images taken (consciously or unconsciously) from accounts of the First. A real event is often remembered – and may have been experi-

---

[174] Malinowski (1926); Thompson (1948), esp. 373–4.
[175] Butterfield (1931), v; cf. Burrow (1981).
[176] Burke (1992b); Kershaw (1989).
[177] Cohn (1970).
[178] Passerini (1990), 58.

enced in the first place – in terms of another event.[179] Heroes are sometimes conflated with one another in a process akin to what Freud, analysing dreams, called 'condensation'. There are occasions when we can observe the process of 'mythification' at work, in a series of accounts of the past which come closer and closer to an archetype.

Some critics – notably Hayden White – would argue that written history is a form of the 'fictions' and 'myths' which have just been discussed. Similar points have been made about the 'textual construction of reality' by sociologists and anthropologists.[180]

[179] Fussell (1975); Samuel and Thompson (1990).
[180] White (1973, 1976); Clifford and Marcus (1986); Atkinson (1990).

4

CENTRAL PROBLEMS

In many cases, some of them illustrated in the previous chapter, we can increase our vocabulary – and, let us hope, the sophistication of our analysis – by borrowing concepts from other disciplines without making radical changes to our own intellectual traditions. Other ideas are more dangerous. They carry a heavier weight of philosophical presuppositions. Hence they resist incorporation into an alien tradition – indeed, they threaten to transform any intellectual system into which they are introduced.

It is with these ideas, or some of them at any rate, that this chapter is concerned. It concentrates on three sets of intellectual conflicts. First, the opposition between the idea of function (or structure) on one side and that of human agency (the 'actors') on the other. Secondly, the tension between the view of culture as mere 'superstructure' and culture as an active force in history (whether it encourages change or continuity). Thirdly, the conflict between the idea that historians, sociologists, anthropologists and others give us 'the facts' about societies in the present or the past, and the view that what they produce is some kind of fiction. The point of the discussion, here as elsewhere in this essay, is to raise problems and explore possibilities, rather than to tell anyone what to do.

Function

'Function' is, or at any rate was, a key concept in social theory. It may well seem a harmless concept, implying only that institutions have their uses. Defined more precisely, however, there is a cutting edge to the idea which makes it at once more interesting and more dangerous. The function of each part of a structure, so the definition goes, is to maintain the whole. To 'maintain' it is to keep it in 'equilibrium' (an influential analogy between the world of nature, from mechanics to biology, and the world of society). What makes the theory both attractive and dangerous is the fact that it is not just descriptive but explanatory as well. The reason for the existence of a particular custom or institution, according to the functionalists, is precisely the contribution it makes to social equilibrium.

The idea of social equilibrium is not completely strange to historians. In the seventeenth and eighteenth centuries, the idea of the 'balance' of power, property and trade' was central to political and economic analysis. When Gibbon, for example, explained the decline and fall of the Roman Empire in terms of its 'immoderate greatness', he was thinking in terms of a balance or see-saw. Many social theorists, however, have treated 'equilibrium' not only as a metaphor to employ occasionally but also as a basic assumption underlying the kinds of question they ask and the kinds of answers they regard as acceptable.

Functionalism is sometimes criticized as a complicated way of saying the obvious. In certain cases, however, functionalist explanations flout common sense rather than confirming it, as in the case of the analysis of the social function of conflict.[1] One of the most brilliant discussions of these issues occurs in a book which deliberately avoids the terms 'structure' and 'function'. The book is explicitly concerned with Africa but it has much wider implications.

The author, the late Max Gluckman, constructed his book round a series of paradoxes. For example, a chapter entitled 'The Peace in the Feud' argued that the feud is not a threat to peace, as common sense might assume. On the contrary, it is an institution with the function of preserving peace and maintaining social cohesion. The point is that individuals often find themselves bound to both sides by ties of blood or friendship, and this conflict of loyalties gives them an interest in keeping the peace. Again, Gluckman argued that 'rebellions, far from destroying the established social order, work so that they even support this order'; that is, their function is to maintain this order by acting as a safety-valve. Yet again, discussing certain Zulu rituals of reversal, the author made the point that the annual lifting of the customary taboos 'serves to emphasize them'.[2]

---

[1] Coser (1956).
[2] Gluckman (1955).

As we have seen (above, p. 13), the functionalist approach dominated sociology and social anthropology from about 1920 to about
1960, so much so that it was described towards the end of this period
not as a mode of analysis among others but as *the* sociological method.[3]
Such a claim would be impossible to sustain in an age in which phenom-
enology, structuralism, hermeneutics and post-structuralism compete
for supremacy. However, it might reasonably be argued that the functionalist tradition still leads a submerged existence in sociology and
anthropology, and even that it continues to exercise an influence all the
more important for being more or less forgotten.

Historians on the other hand, despite the example of Gibbon, have
been slow to adopt this approach. Indeed, it was only in the 1960s,
when the sociologists were becoming unhappy with the idea of a social
function, that a number of practising historians began to experiment
with this kind of explanation.

In his classic study of witchcraft and magic, Keith Thomas, for
instance, argued that 'witch-beliefs served to uphold the traditional
obligations of charity and neighbourliness at a time when other social
and economic forces were conspiring to weaken them' in English village
communities, because the more prosperous villagers feared being cursed
or bewitched by the poorer ones if they turned them away from the
door empty-handed. Alan Macfarlane has also suggested that 'the fear
of the witch acted as a sanction in enforcing neighbourly conduct',
though he is also tempted by an alternative (indeed opposite) functional
explanation, to the effect that witchcraft prosecutions were 'a means of
effecting a deep social change' from a more neighbourly society to a
more individualistic one.[4] The fact that these opposite explanations are
compatible with the same evidence ought to make us uneasy. Functional
explanations are easy to impute and difficult to verify (or falsify).

The appeal of functionalism to historians is that it compensates for
their traditional tendency to explain too much of the past in terms
of the intentions of individuals. An example in which traditional
'intentionalism', as it has been called, has come into open conflict with
functionalism is the historiography of the Third Reich.[5] Attempts to
explain the structures of the National Socialist state and the events
of the period 1933–45 completely in terms of the intentions of the
Führer look increasingly implausible now that research has turned to

---

[3] Davis (1959).
[4] Thomas (1971), 564–6; Macfarlane (1970), 105, 196.
[5] Mason (1981).

the regions, the 'periphery' of the system. There is an increasing tendency to consider political and social pressures on Hitler as well as his
conscious plans and even his unconscious drives. Although this concern
with structures and pressures may not be functionalist in the strict sense
of the term, it serves to illustrate the need for a political history which is
not confined to the actions and thoughts of political leaders.

If it solves problems, functionalism also raises them. One of these
problems may be illustrated from an essay which was discussed in an
earlier chapter, Stone's analysis of the causes of the English Revolution.
According to this essay, economic growth and social change in England
in the century 1529–1629 led to 'disequilibrium' between the social
and political systems. The reaction of one reviewer was to ask, 'When
was there an equilibrium?' and to conclude that the concept could
not be applied to medieval or early modern Europe. In similar fashion,
Edmund Leach once declared that 'Real societies can never be in equilibrium'.[6] These criticisms are a little exaggerated. Pareto, for instance,
did not view societies in terms of a 'perfect' or static equilibrium, but
rather of a 'dynamic' one, defined as 'such a state that if it is artificially
subjected to some modification . . . a reaction at once takes place, tending to restore it to its real, its normal state'.[7]

A historical example which might almost seem to have been invented
to demonstrate the strengths of functionalism is the Venetian Republic
of the sixteenth and seventeenth centuries.[8] Venice was much admired
at the time for the unusual stability of its social and political system.
The Venetians themselves explained this stability, which they claimed
was eternal, in terms of their mixed or 'balanced' constitution, in which
the monarchical element was provided by the Doge, the aristocratic
element by the Senate, and the so-called 'democratic' element by the
Great Council, which was composed of some 2,000 adult male nobles.
In practice, Venice was ruled by an oligarchy of some 200 leading
nobles (known at the time as the *grandi*) who took turns to hold the key
political offices. The idea of the mixed constitution might therefore be
described as an 'ideology', or a 'myth' (in the Malinowskian sense of
that term), serving to keep the system in being.

It is unlikely that the myth was powerful enough to perform this
function by itself, persuading the lesser nobles, the citizens and the
commoners that all was well, but other institutions existed to defuse or,

[6] Stone (1972); Koenigsberger (1974); Leach (1954); cf. Easton (1965), 19–21.
[7] Pareto (1916), section 2068.
[8] Burke (1974).

to stay with our central metaphor, to 'counter-balance' opposition from these quarters. In Venice as in Gluckman's Africa, conflicting loyalties served the cause of social cohesion. The lesser nobles were pulled one way by group solidarity, but they were tugged in the opposite direction by the ties of patronage (discussed above, p. 72) which bound them as individuals to individual *grandi*. Caught in this conflict, they had a stake in compromise.

What about the rest of the population? The most articulate group of commoners who might have challenged the Venetian oligarchy were the citizens, a relatively small group of 2,000–3,000 adult males. They enjoyed certain formal or informal privileges to compensate for their exclusion from the Great Council. Certain offices in the administration were reserved for them alone. Their daughters not infrequently married nobles. Certain religious fraternities were open to nobles and citizens alike. It might be argued that these privileges made the citizens feel that they were close to the nobles and so detached them from the rest of the commoners.

These commoners, about 150,000 of them, were pacified like the populace of ancient Rome by a combination of bread and circuses.[9] Corn was subsidized by the government, which also sponsored splendid public rituals. Carnival, which was unusually elaborate in Venice, was a ritual of reversal in which the authorities could be criticized with more or less impunity, a safety-valve like the Zulu rituals analysed by Gluckman. The fishermen of Venice were allowed to elect their own Doge, who was solemnly received and kissed by the real Doge, a ritual which might be described as serving the function of persuading ordinary people that they participated in a political system from which they were effectively excluded.[10]

There remained the population of the territories subject to Venice, including a substantial part of northern Italy (Padua, Vicenza, Verona, Bergamo and Brescia). The patricians of these cities probably resented their loss of independence but they had opportunities for employment as officers in the Venetian army. As for the ordinary people, in many cases their hostility to their own patricians made them pro-Venetian. One might therefore say that the stability of the system depended on a complex balance of power.

There seems to be an elective affinity between this example of stability and the method of functional analysis. All the same, the example

[9] Veyne (1976).
[10] Cf. Muir (1981).

may serve to illustrate the weaknesses of the method as well as its strengths. For example, there is the problem of change. All the world is not Venice, and the frequent conflicts and crises in the sister-republics of Florence and Genoa – to go no further afield – are difficult to explain in functionalist terms. Even in the Venetian case the system was not eternal. The Republic was abolished in 1797, and even in earlier centuries it passed through a number of crises which led to structural change – the closing of the Great Council to new recruits, the increasing importance of the Council of Ten, the shift from a maritime empire to an empire in northern Italy, and so on.

Change is often the result of conflict, which may remind us that even in its more sophisticated versions the functional approach remains tied to a Durkheimian, consensual model of society. Historians of Italy have effectively recognized this point by coining the phrase the 'myth of Venice' to refer to the image of a stable, balanced society, implying that image was a distorted one. It would indeed be unwise to assume that ordinary people shared all the values of the ruling class or that they were easily manipulated by rituals such as the inauguration of the fishermen's Doge. As we have seen, social stability need not imply consensus. It may depend on prudence or inertia rather than a shared ideology (above, p. 96). It is also assisted by particular types of political and social structure.

To sum up. The concept of 'function' is a useful item in the tool-kit of historians and theorists alike, provided that it is not blunted by indiscriminate use. It carries with it temptations to neglect social change, social conflict and individual motives, but these temptations can be resisted. There is no need to assume that every institution in a given society has a positive function, without any costs ('dysfunctions'). There is no need to assume that a given institution is indispensable to the performance of a given function; in different societies or periods, different institutions may act as functional equivalents, analogues or alternatives.[11] However, functional explanations should not be viewed as replacements for other kinds of historical explanation, which they complement rather than contradict, since they tend to be answers to different questions rather than different answers to the same question.[12] What is being suggested here is not that historians throw intentionalist explanations overboard, but simply that they take on board something for which they have no 'functional equivalent'.

[11] Merton (1948); Runciman (1983–9), 2, 182–265.
[12] Gellner (1968).

Structure

Functional analysis is concerned not with people but with 'structures'. In practice, different approaches to society have utilized different conceptions of structure, of which it may be useful to distinguish at least three. First, the marxian approach, in which the architectural metaphor of 'base' and 'superstructure' is central, and the base or infrastructure tends to be conceived in economic terms. This approach will be analysed in more detail in the following chapter. Secondly, the structural-functionalist approach, discussed above, in which the concept 'structure' is used more generally to refer to a complex of institutions – the family, the state, the legal system and so on.

In the third place, the so-called 'structuralists', from Claude Lévi-Strauss to Roland Barthes (and as some would say, the Michel Foucault of *The Order of Things*), were primarily concerned with structures or systems of thought or culture. The fundamental model or metaphor underlying their thinking was the model of society or culture as a language. Theorists of language – Saussure, Jakobson, Hjelmslev – provided the inspiration for this 'semiotic' or 'semiological' approach to culture as a 'system of signs'. Saussure's famous distinction between 'langue' (the resources of the language) and 'parole' (a specific utterance, selected from these resources) has been generalized into a distinction between 'code' and 'message'. The point which Saussure stresses is that the meaning of a message depends not (or not only) on the intentions of the individual transmitting it, but on the rules which make up the code, in other words its structure.[13]

In similar fashion, inspired by the linguists, Lévi-Strauss wrote a study of the 'elementary structures of kinship', in which he analysed kinship systems as permutations of the same fundamental elements, for example the binary oppositions male/female, father/son and so on. He went on to write a study of myths in which he broke them down into their constitutive units or 'mythemes', arguing that Amerindian myths are transformations of one another and concerned in particular with the binary opposition between nature and culture.[14]

In France in particular, these ideas were taken up and applied, or adapted, in a number of different fields, giving rise to a structuralist literary criticism (in the work of Roland Barthes, for example), a structuralist version of psychoanalysis (Jacques Lacan), and a structuralist

---

[13] Runciman (1969); Lane (1970); Culler (1976).
[14] Lévi-Strauss (1949; 1958, 31–54; 1964–72).

version of Marxism (Louis Althusser). In Russia, there was an independent development, leading from the linguists Roman Jakobson and Nicolai Trubetzkoi to the studies of the folktale by Vladimir Propp and the studies of Russian literature and culture by Juri Lotman. Propp, for example, studied the 'morphology' of the Russian folktale, identifying thirty-one recurrent elements or 'functions' – the hero is prohibited from doing something, the prohibition is ignored, and so on.[15]

What has all this to do with history? Structural history is well known, whether it follows the model of Marx or Braudel, but is there a place for structuralist history as well? It may well seem that an opposition to history is built into the structure of structuralism. Saussure defined his position in opposition to the linguists of his day, whose model of language was evolutionary. His innovation was to suggest that the state of the language at any moment could be explained by the relation between its different elements, without reference to the past. Saussure's was an equilibrium model which deliberately privileged structure (the 'synchronic') over change (the 'diachronic'). In similar fashion, Lévi-Strauss privileged structure over change on the grounds that the societies studied by anthropologists were relatively static – 'cold', as he put it – while complex societies are 'hot'. On occasion, at least, he and other structuralists wrote as if the fundamental categories of culture were timeless.

The opposition between structuralism and history must not be exaggerated. Lévi-Strauss does not ignore history. On the contrary, he has devoted attention to such topics as the comparative history of marriage. Barthes has entered the territory of the historians to offer a structuralist analysis of historical discourse. As for Lotman, he has devoted most of his time to the study of traditional Russian culture.[16] For their part, a few historians were tempted by the structuralist approach in the years of its intellectual dominance, especially in the study of myth. Ancient Greek myths, for example, and medieval saints' lives (which often tell the same stories about different individuals) have been analysed according to the paradigms of Propp and Lévi-Strauss, emphasizing recurrent elements and binary oppositions.[17]

One of the most impressive structural analyses carried out by a historian is a study of another historian, François Hartog's essay on Herodotus, which concentrates on the ways in which Herodotus rep-

---

[15] Propp (1928); Lotman and Uspenskii (1984).
[16] Lévi-Strauss (1958, 1–27; 1983); Barthes (1967); Lotman (1984).
[17] Vernant (1966); Gurevich (1972); Boureau (1984).

resents the 'other', in other words, non-Greeks. The Scythians, for
example, are represented not only as different from but in many
respects as the inverse of the Greeks. Greeks live in cities, for instance,
while the Scythians live in the wilderness. Greeks are civilized, Scythians
are 'barbarians'. However, when Herodotus comes to describe the
attack on the Scythians by the Persians, who also attacked Greece, this
event inverts the inversion and the Scythians appear in a more favourable light. Hartog's work, like that of Roland Barthes and Hayden
White, illustrates the textual strategies of historians and also what
White calls 'the content of the form', its effects on the message.[18]

In the course of working with structuralism, certain problems have
become apparent. Some linguists and literary critics have expressed
their discomfort with an idea of meaning abstracted from the context of
place, time, speaker, hearer and situation.[19] Others – notably Jacques
Derrida and the so-called 'post-structuralists' – are uncomfortable with
structural determinism, as opposed to the free play of meanings on the
part of transmitters and receivers alike, a point which has already been
discussed in the section on communication and will be discussed again
below under the heading of 'culture' (pp. 97, 118).[20]

One of Propp's examples may serve to illustrate some of the difficulties in the structuralist method. He compares two stories, in one
of which a magician gives Ivan a ship which takes him to another
kingdom, while in the other a queen gives Ivan a ring with the same
results. For Propp, these examples illustrate function number 14, 'a
magical object is put at the hero's disposition'. It is indeed difficult to
deny the similarity in the structure of the two episodes. To analyse
stories in this way is surely illuminating. All the same, something significant in a story is lost when an element like a ring or a horse, rich
in associations in many cultures, is reduced to an algebraic x or y.
Historians, like linguists and literary critics, wish to attend to objects
and associations such as these, to the surface of the story as well as the
structure. Hence the *bricolage* I described above is not so much a case
of timidity as of intellectual reservations.

For a strongly expressed example of such reservations we may return
to Jan Vansina, who goes so far as to describe structuralism as a
'fallacy', a method which is 'invalid' because its procedures 'are neither
replicable nor falsifiable'.[21] I would not go so far myself. For one thing,

[18] Hartog (1980).
[19] Bakhtin (1952–3); Hymes (1964).
[20] Culler (1980); Norris (1982).
[21] Vansina (1985), 165.

I do not think that any analysis of texts or oral traditions can be as scientific as Vansina would like it to be. For another, I continue to believe that – although binary oppositions are not the only patterns to be found in culture – an increased sensitivity to such patterns is something we owe to the structuralist movement.

In the past few years, some sociologists have been trying to move beyond the notions of structure associated with the structural-functionalists on one side and the structuralists on the other. Alain Touraine, for example, has called for the 'return of the actor' and suggested that the study of social movements is central to sociology.[22] Anthony Giddens has suggested that the apparent opposition between agency and structure can be resolved or dissolved by concentrating on the role of social actors in the process of 'structuration' (a theme to which the next chapter will return).[23]

Again, Pierre Bourdieu has criticized the approaches of both Durkheim and Lévi-Strauss as too rigid and mechanical. He prefers a more flexible notion of structure as a 'field' or set of fields (the religious field, the literary field, the economic field and so on). Social actors are 'defined by their *relative postitions* in this space', which Bourdieu also describes as a 'field of forces' imposing certain relations on those who enter, 'relations which are not reducible to the intentions of individual agents or even to direct *interactions* between agents'. Interesting attempts have been made to use Bourdieu's concept of a field to analyse the 'birth' of French writers and French intellectuals as self-conscious groups in the seventeenth and nineteenth centuries respectively, revealing in the process the difficulty of defining 'literary' or 'intellectual' space. However, no one has so far tested the value of the approach for historians by embarking upon a more general study structured in this way.[24]

Historians too have been reacting against the notion of structures. The supporters of Marx and Braudel have been accused – not for the first time – of determinism, of leaving the people out of history, and in extreme cases of being 'unhistorical', in the sense of studying static structures at the expense of change over time. Although these charges are generally exaggerated, attempts to combine structural with historical analysis raise problems which demand discussion, notably that of the relation between individual actors and the social system, in other words the problem of determinism versus freedom. It will be

---

[22] Touraine (1984).
[23] Giddens (1979), ch. 2.
[24] Bourdieu (1984), 230; Viala (1985); Charle (1990).

obvious that a problem of this kind, one of the perennial problems of philosophy, is not going to be solved in a brief discussion in a book such as this. All the same, it needs to be raised. The following two sections will view the problem from two angles, from psychology and from culture.

Psychology

So far, psychology has played a somewhat marginal role in this book. The reason for this apparent neglect lies in the relation between psychology and history. In the United States in the 1950s, a new term came into circulation to denote an exciting new approach: 'psychohistory'. The study of the young Luther by the psychoanalyst Erik Erikson led to a lively debate, while the President of the American Historical Association, a respected elder statesman of the profession, surprised his colleagues by telling them that the 'next assignment' for historians was to take psychology more seriously than they had done.[25] Since those days, journals devoted to psychohistory have been founded, and leaders such as Trotsky, Gandhi and Hitler studied from this point of view.[26] All the same, the advertised meeting between history and psychology seems to have been adjourned. Even in the 1990s, it remains the next rather than the current assignment.

One reason for the reluctance of historians to come to grips with psychology – besides the empiricist's resistance to theory – is surely the variety of competing versions – Freudian, neo-Freudian, Jungian, developmental and so on. Another is the obvious difficulty of applying Freud's methods to the dead, of psycho-analysing documents rather than people. Yet another is the fact that the encounter between history and psychology took place at an inauspicious moment, at a time when historians were distancing themselves from 'great men', and focusing on the rest of the population. For them, the important problem was not so much the personality of Hitler, say, as the susceptibility of the German people to his style of leadership.

What then of collective psychology? In the 1920s and 1930s some historians, notably two Frenchmen – Marc Bloch and Lucien Febvre – preached and tried to practise what they called a 'historical psychology' of groups, drawing not on Freud but on French psychologists and philosophers such as Charles Blondel, Henri Wallon and Lucien Lévy-

---

[25] Erikson (1958); Langer (1958).
[26] Wolfenstein (1967); Erikson, E. (1970); Waite (1977).

Bruhl, whose idea of a 'primitive mentality' has already been discussed (p. 91). However, their successors as historians of mentalities have generally turned their attention from psychology to anthropology.

As for the anthropologists and sociologists, they too have kept their distance from psychology. Durkheim defined sociology, the science of society, by contrast to psychology, the science of the individual. In the 1930s and 1940s there were attempts at rapprochement, like the work of the American 'culture and personality' school – Ruth Benedict, for instance – or the synthesis of Weber and Freud offered by Norbert Elias (to be discussed below, p. 140), or the synthesis of Marx and Freud offered by Erich Fromm, or the collective study of the 'authoritarian personality' directed by Theodor Adorno.[27] The relevance of this approach to historians is obvious. If 'basic' personality varies from society to society, it must have varied from one period to another. The work of the culture and personality school – its contrast between 'shame cultures' and 'guilt cultures' for example – underlies the classic study of ancient Greece by E. R. Dodds, who cited both Benedict and Fromm.[28] In general, however, these works had remarkably little impact on historical practice.

In any case, the rapproachement did not last. Anthropologists grew increasingly unhappy with the idea of national character, or 'social character', preferring to work with the more flexible notion of culture. The rise of a historical anthropology centred on this notion of culture has been one of the most fruitful inter-disciplinary developments of recent years. Yet its success should not blind us to the potential of that abandoned project, historical psychology. Psychological theory can be of use to historians in at least three different ways.

In the first place, in freeing them from the 'common-sense' assumptions about human nature, assumptions all the more powerful for being unacknowledged, if not unconscious in the precise Freudian sense of the term. As Peter Gay puts it, 'The professional historian has always been a psychologist – an amateur psychologist.'[29] Theory (more exactly, rival theories) may reveal the rational roots of apparently irrational behaviour and vice versa, thus discouraging historians from assuming too easily that one individual or group acts rationally, while dismissing other individuals or groups as irrational ('fanatical', 'superstitious', and so on).

[27] Benedict (1934); Elias (1939); Fromm (1942); Adorno (1950).
[28] Dodds (1951).
[29] Gay (1985), 6.

In the second place, psychological theory has a contribution to make to the process of source criticism. To make proper use of an autobiography or diary as historical evidence – the memoirs of Saint-Simon for instance – it is necessary, so a distinguished psychoanalyst has suggested, to consider not only the culture in which the text was written and the literary conventions of the genre, but also the age of the author, his or her position in the life-cycle.[30] In similar fashion, a social psychologist has suggested that all of us rewrite our biographies all the time in the manner of the Soviet Encyclopaedia in the age of Stalin. Oral historians too have begun to consider the element of fantasy in the testimonies they collect and the psychological needs underlying such fantasies.[31] Again, a recent book, eclectic in its use of rival theories, from Wilhelm Reich to Giles Deleuze, examines the aggressively misogynist fantasies of members of the Free Corps, ex-soldiers involved in militant right-wing politics in Germany immediately after the First World War.[32]

It is only a short step from daytime fantasies to dreams. The example of psychoanalysts of various schools might encourage historians to utilize a type of source rarely studied, that is, dreams (more exactly, records of dreams). A suitable case for study in this way is that of William Laud, archbishop of Canterbury and, together with his master Charles I, a hammer of the Puritans. Laud appears to be a classic instance of the inferiority complex, since he was a man of low stature, low birth and aggressive behaviour. But how can a historian possibly show that Laud actually felt inferior, anxious or insecure? At this point dreams may have something to tell us. Between 1623 and 1643 Laud recorded thirty dreams in his diary. Two-thirds of these dreams present disasters, or at least embarrassing situations. For example, 'I dreamed marvellously, that the King was offended with me, and would cast me off, and tell me no cause why.' For some psychologists, a dream of a king signifies the dreamer's father. For others, all figures in dreams represent aspects of the dreamer's personality. All the same, in this particular case it is hard to resist the conclusion that Laud was indeed anxious about his relationship with the king, and that the arrogance about which contemporaries complained expressed a fundamental lack of confidence.[33]

[30] Erikson (1968), 701–2.
[31] Samuel and Thompson (1990), 7–8, 55–7, 143–5.
[32] Theweleit (1977).
[33] Burke (1973).

In the third place, psychologists have a contribution to make to the debate on the relation between the individual and society. For example, they have considered the psychology of followers as well as that of leaders – the need for a father-figure, for example. From this perspective, the imputation of charisma discussed above (p. 89) becomes somewhat easier to understand.

Again, some psychologists have discussed the relation between what Georges Devereux called 'psychologistic' and 'sociologistic' accounts of motivation, in other words what ordinary language calls 'public' and private motives. In a study of the Hungarian freedom fighters of 1956, Devereux argued that they often had private reasons for rebellion, but that the public cause allowed them to act out their desires without guilt.[34] In other words, analyses of individual motivation and analyses of the reasons underlying a social movement are complementary rather than contradictory. Freud's famous concept of 'overdetermination' seems to apply here.

Another way in which psychologists have helped redefine the relation between the individual and society is by discussing child-rearing in different cultures, and this discussion too may illuminate historical problems. Noting the contrast between the relatively enterprising political elite of seventeenth-century Amsterdam and the more cautious elite of Venice, I found myself wondering whether it had anything to do with different ways of raising children. It was intriguing to discover fragments of evidence suggesting that Amsterdammers were generally weaned early, Venetians relatively late. In similar fashion Philip Greven's study of colonial America, inspired by Freud and Erikson, distinguishes three basic 'temperaments' and explains their genesis in terms of child-rearing. The 'evangelicals', characterized by hostility to the self, were the product of strict discipline. The 'moderates', whose main characteristic was self-control, had undergone a more moderate discipline, their wills bent rather than broken in childhood. Finally the 'genteel', defined by their self-confidence, had been treated with affection and even indulgence when they were children. Of course these character-types can be found in other cultures too, and comparative studies might add nuances to the picture. So far, however, comparative studies of childhood have not been historical, while historical studies have not been comparative.[35]

These discussions of the relation between individuals and societies

---

[34] Devereux (1959).
[35] Burke (1974); Greven (1977).

occupy a middle ground between conventional assertions of freedom or determinism. They are concerned with the possible 'fit' between public reasons and private motives. They point to social pressures on individuals, which are more or less difficult (rather than impossible) to resist. They note the existence of social constraints, but view them as reducing the area of choice rather than requiring the individual to behave in a certain way. This middle ground between freedom and determinism has also been the arena for recent debates over the nature of culture.

Culture

In the past few years there has been a widespread reaction among social scientists and historians alike against the determinism associated with functional analysis, with Marxism, with quantitative methods and indeed with the idea of a social 'science'. This reaction or revolt has taken place under the banner of 'culture', a term which, like 'function', is linked to a particular style of explanation.

'Culture' is a concept with an embarrassing variety of definitions. In the nineteenth century, the term was generally used to refer to the visual arts, literature, philosophy, natural science and music, while expressing a growing awareness of the ways in which the arts and sciences are shaped by their social milieu.[36] This growing awareness led to the rise of a sociology or social history of culture. This tendency was essentially Marxist or Marxian in the sense of treating art, literature, music and so on as a kind of superstructure, reflecting changes in the economic and social 'base'. A typical example of the genre is the famous *Social History of Art* by Arnold Hauser, which characterizes the art of fifteenth-century Florence, for example, as 'middle-class naturalism', or explains Mannerism as the artistic expression of the economic and political 'crisis' which followed the discovery of America and the invasion of Italy by France in 1492 and 1494 respectively.[37] This approach has been undermined in the last few decades by two parallel and connected developments.

In the first place, the term 'culture' has been widening its meaning as historians, sociologists, literary critics and others have widened their interests. Increasing attention has been given to popular culture, in the

---

[36] Kroeber and Kluckhohn (1952); Williams (1958).
[37] Hauser (1951), 2, 27, 96–9; for criticisms, see Gombrich (1953, 1969).

sense of the attitudes and values of ordinary people and their expression in folk art, folksongs, folktales, festivals and so on.[38] The concern with popular artifacts and performances – the popular equivalents of easel paintings, operas and so on – has in turn been criticized as too narrow. The current tendency is to turn away from the so-called 'opera-house' definition of culture and to use the term in the wide sense long favoured by American anthropologists. A generation ago there was a sharp contrast between British 'social anthropology' and American 'cultural anthropology' in the tradition of Franz Boas and Ruth Benedict. Where the British stressed social institutions, the Americans emphasized 'patterns of culture', in other words 'the symbolic-expressive aspect of human behaviour' or the shared meanings informing the practices of everyday life.[39] The amount of attention devoted on both sides of the Atlantic to Clifford Geertz's *Interpretation of Cultures* (1973), concerned as it is with systems of meanings, suggests that the distinction between the 'hard' British and the 'soft' American schools has now been eroded. So has the distinction between social history and literary history, at least in the work of the 'new historicists', who emphasize what they call the 'poetics of culture', in other words the conventions underlying non-literary as well as literary texts, informal performances as well as formal ones.[40]

In the second place, as the term has widened its meaning, there has been an increasing tendency to think of 'culture' as active rather than passive. The structuralists had of course tried to redress the balance a generation ago, and it might well be argued that Lévi-Strauss, in particular, has turned Marx on his head, in other words returned to Hegel, by suggesting that the really deep structures are not economic and social arrangements but mental categories. However, structuralists and Marxists are now frequently lumped together and rejected as determinists. Instead the emphasis falls on popular resistance to the 'system' and collective creativity.[41] What used to be assumed to be objective, hard social facts like gender or class or community are now assumed to be culturally 'constructed' or 'constituted'.

The studies of the late Michel Foucault on changing Western views of madness and sexuality, and his critique of impoverished conceptions of the 'real' which omit the reality of what is imagined, have been

[38]   Burke (1978); Yeo and Yeo (1981).
[39]   For the 'opera-house' definition, Wagner (1975), 21; for the 'symbolic-expressive', Wuthnow et al. (1984), 3.
[40]   Greenblatt (1988); Stallybrass and White (1986).
[41]   Certeau (1980); Fiske (1989).

extremely influencial in this regard.[42] However, Foucault's work is part of a wider trend. Phenomenologists have long emphasized what is sometimes called the 'social construction of reality'.[43] 'Cultural' Marxists such as Louis Althusser and Maurice Godelier are among the theorists who have stressed the importance of thought and imagination in the production of what we call 'society'.[44] The critical theorist Cornelis Castoriadis has also been influential in this regard. However, the launching of the term *l'imaginaire* probably owes most to the example of Jacques Lacan.[45]

Pierre Bourdieu's critique of Lévi-Strauss and other structuralists on the grounds that the notion of cultural 'rules' implicit in their work is too mechanical, points in the same direction. As an alternative, he has proposed the more flexible concept of 'habitus', derived from Aristotle (via St Thomas Aquinas and the art historian Erwin Panofsky). 'Habitus' is defined as a set of 'schemes enabling agents to generate an infinity of practices adapted to endlessly changing situations'.[46] The essence is a kind of 'regulated improvisation', a phrase reminiscent of the formulae and themes of the oral poets studied by Albert Lord (above, p. 99).

Like Foucault (not to mention the philosopher Merleau-Ponty), Bourdieu undermines the classic distinction between mind and body associated with Descartes and parodied as the doctrine of of the 'ghost in the machine'. The practices he writes about are not easy to classify as 'mental' or 'physical'. For example, the honour of the Kabyle of Algeria, among whom Bourdieu did his fieldwork, is expressed as much in their upright manner of walking as in anything they say. Again, the 'tortoise-like deliberation' developed in conscious or unconscious resistance to the authorities by Hungarian farm workers such as Uncle Róka (described above, p. 87) provides a vivid illustration of what Bourdieu means by 'habitus'.

In the fields of literature and philosophy, or the space between them, a similar assumption of cultural creativity underlies the 'deconstruction' practised by Jacques Derrida and his followers, in other words their distinctive approach to texts – a concern for unravelling their contradictions, directing attention to their ambiguities, and reading them against themselves and their authors. If an interest in binary oppositions

---

[42] Foucault (1961, 1976–84).
[43] Berger and Luckmann (1966).
[44] Althusser (1970); Godelier (1984), 125–75.
[45] Castoriadis (1975).
[46] Bourdieu (1972), 16, 78–87.

was the hall-mark of the structuralist, the post-structuralist may be recognized by a concern to undermine these categories. Hence Derrida's interest in the 'supplement', which at once adds to something and supplants it.[47] This deconstructive trend in particular, but also the others described in the last few paragraphs, is sometimes labelled 'post-structuralism' or even 'postmodernism'.[48]

How have historians reacted to these developments? If we define deconstruction, post-structuralism and related developments in a precise way, there will not be very much to report. For example, explicit discussion of the relation between postmodernism and history has scarcely begun.[49] Although the word 'deconstruction' (in the sense of 'taking to pieces') is increasingly fashionable, only a few historians reveal the inspiration of Derrida in their substantive work.

Joan Scott, for instance, has analysed the relation between women's history and history in terms of the 'logic of the supplement'. H. D. Harootunian has offered a new and controversial way of reading the discourse of 'nativism' (in other words the sense of identity) in Tokugawa Japan, using the notion of 'conceptual schemes as forms of play' as an antidote to the traditional view of ideology as the reflection of society. Again, Timothy Mitchell's study of nineteenth-century Egypt builds on Derrida's concept of difference – 'not a pattern of distinctions or intervals between things, but an always unstable deferring or differing within' – in order to rethink accepted views of the colonial city. Mitchell sustains the paradox that 'To represent itself as modern, the city is dependent upon maintaining the barrier that keeps the other out. This dependence makes the outside, the Oriental ... an integral part of the modern city'.[50] For a balanced assessment of the uses of Derrida for historians, we shall have to wait until at least a few more historians try to work with his theories, or until Derrida answers his own call for the deconstruction of 'historical processes' as well as texts.[51]

Suppose, on the other hand, we adopt a broader definition of the new trends, as an anti-structuralism associated with a diffuse sense of liberty and instability, an awareness of contradiction, fluidity and precariousness, of what Marshall Sahlins calls the 'risk' to categories whenever they are used in the everyday world.[52] A collective response

[47] Derrida (1967, 141–64; 1972); Norris (1982); Culler (1983).
[48] Dews (1987); Harland (1987).
[49] Spivak (1985); Attridge (1987); Joyce (1991); Kelly (1991).
[50] Scott (1991), 49–50; Harootunian (1988), esp. 1–22; Mitchell (1988), 145, 149.
[51] Quoted in Dews (1987), 35.
[52] Sahlins (1985), 149.

on the part of historians now becomes rather more visible. For instance, a shift away from the 'social history of culture' of the kind discussed above, and towards what Rogier Chartier has described as the 'cultural history of society' is increasingly prevalent.[53] The current interest by historians in Geertz's work illustrates both the new importance and the new definition given to culture.[54] So does the lively debate between 'materialists' and 'culturalists' over the explanation of economic growth or decline, exemplified in the controversy over a book about the 'decline of the industrial spirit' in Britain from the late nineteenth century onwards.[55] Historians increasingly recognize the power of the 'imagined', as in the study by Georges Duby on the idea of the 'three orders' of society (above, p. 62), or in recent work on images of a nation or culture.[56] Studies on the social history of language have been concerned not only with the influence of society on language but also with the reverse – for instance, with the importance of opposed terms such as 'middle classes' and 'working classes', in the constitution of social groups.[57] Forms of social organization such as 'tribe' or 'caste', once assumed to be 'social facts', are now viewed as illusions, or at least as collective representations.[58] The spread of the compound 'socio-cultural' also suggests an increasing awareness of the importance of 'culture', and, conversely, of the malleability of 'society'.

For a lively account of the process of cultural construction, we may turn to Simon Schama's study of the Dutch in the seventeenth century, *The Embarrassment of Riches*. Schama is particularly concerned with the ways in which the Dutch, a new nation in this period, forged an identity for themselves. He discusses a wide variety of topics, from cleanliness to smoking and from the cult of the ancient Batavians to the myth of the Dutch Republic as the New Israel, viewing these topics in terms of the construction of identity. For example, following the inter-pretation of Jewish dietary laws by the anthropologist Mary Douglas, Schama suggests that 'to be clean, militantly, was an affirmation of separateness'. In similar fashion, he considers drinking and pipe-smoking as customs 'by which the Dutch recognized their common identity'. 'Constructive drinking', as Douglas would say.[59]

[53] Chartier (1989); cf. Hunt (1989).
[54] Geertz (1973); Walters (1980); Darnton (1984); Levi (1991).
[55] Wiener (1981).
[56] Duby (1978); Anderson (1983); Nora (1984–7); Inden (1990).
[57] Burke and Porter (1987); Corfield (1991).
[58] Southall (1970); Inden (1990).
[59] Schama (1987), 200, 380; Douglas (1966, 1987).

These two shifts in the study of culture have been immensely illuminating, but both of them raise problems which have not yet found a
satisfactory solution. To take the problem of 'construction' first. It
would be difficult to deny the reductionism implicit in some traditional
approaches to culture, Durkheimian as well as Marxist, but the reaction
in the opposite direction may well have gone too far. The current
emphasis on cultural creativity and on culture as an active force in
history needs to be accompanied by some sense of the constraints
within which that creativity operates. Rather than simply replacing the
social history of culture by the cultural history of society we need to
work with the two ideas together and simultaneously, however difficult
this may be. In other words, it is most useful to see the relation between
culture and society in dialectical terms, with both partners at once
active and passive, determining and determined.[60]

In any case, cultural construction should be regarded as a problem
rather than an assumption, a problem deserving analysis in more detail.
How does one construct a new conception of class (say) or gender? And
who is 'one'? How can we explain the acceptance of the innovation? Or
to turn the problem round, is it possible to explain why traditional
conceptions cease to convince certain groups at certain times?

Some of these problems were aired – long before terms like 'post-
modernism' were heard – in the debates about perception among psychologists and art historians which led to E. H. Gombrich's classic
study *Art and Illusion* (1960). Like the cultural historian Aby Warburg
and the Gestalt psychologists, Gombrich emphasized the ways in which
the perceptions of artists and their publics, their visual 'levels of
expectation', are shaped by what he variously calls 'schemata', 'stereotypes', 'models' and 'formulae'. He goes so far as to claim that 'All
representations are grounded on schemata which the artist learns to
use.' The parallel with the discussions of orality and receptions in the
previous chapter will be obvious. However, the schemata may also be
regarded as at once constraints on and aids to cultural construction.
Consequently, Gombrich's explanation of changes in visual schemata is
of great importance. To explain change he introduces the idea of the
'correction' of the schema by artists who note discrepancies between
model and reality. The problem here, as a critic pointed out, is one of
circularity. How can artists check the schemata against reality if their
view of reality is itself a product of the schemata?[61] The same point

[60] Cf. Samuel (1991).
[61] Gombrich (1960); Arnheim (1962).

might be made about stereotyped perceptions of the 'other' – cannibals, witches, Jews, lunatics, homosexuals and so on. As in the case of the study of mentalities (above, p. 93), the better historians explain persistence, the more difficult they make it for themselves to explain change. That stereotypes sooner or later fail to satisfy seems obvious. The reasons still await more profound investigation.

Like the idea of 'construction', the conception of culture as a system of shared meanings also needs to be treated as problematic, especially when we are studying the culture of whole nations. This conception has the defects as well as the merits of the Durkheimian approach, stressing consensus at the expense of conflict. Both defects and merits are visible with particular clarity in Schama's description of Dutch culture in the seventeenth century.

Schama is at his best when discussing the attempts of the Dutch to construct a collective identity by distinguishing themselves from their neighbours. However, the socio-cultural divisions within the republic of the United Provinces – between rich and poor, townspeople and peasants, Calvinists and Catholics, Hollanders and Frisians – are scarcely visible in his work. *The Embarrassment of Riches* is vulnerable to the criticisms recently levelled by Gerald Sider against what he calls 'the anthropological concept of culture' on the grounds that an emphasis on shared values is, to say the least, 'not very effective for understanding class-based societies' and that it needs to be replaced by a stress on cultural conflict.[62]

To this criticism one might reply that the concept of conflict implies that of solidarity, and that Sider has simply replaced one community, the region or nation, with another, the social class, which would not be effective if its members did not share values. So what is to be done? It would clearly be a mistake to look for a universal panacea as if all cultures were equally unified or equally fragmented. All the same, in many cases – in modern history at least – there is much to be said for extending and refining the sociological concept of 'sub-culture', defined as a partially autonomous culture within a larger whole.[63]

Sociologists generally study the more visible sub-cultures, such as ethnic or religious minorities, social deviants and youth groups. Historians too have studied groups such as the Jews in medieval Spain or the beggars in Elizabethan London, but they have not often paid much attention to the relation between the culture of these minorities and that

[62] Sider (1986), 5, 109.
[63] Yinger (1960); Clarke (1974); Tirosh-Rothschild (1990).

of the surrounding society. How sharp are these cultural boundaries? Does a sub-culture include all aspects of the life of its members, or only a part? Is the relation between main culture and sub-culture one of complementarity or conflict? Was there more in common in the sixteenth century between two Jews, one of whom was Italian, or two Italians, one of whom was a Jew? Are occupational sub-cultures generally less autonomous than ethnic or religious sub-cultures? How long can the sub-culture of a new group of immigrants, such as the French Protestants in seventeenth-century London or Amsterdam, remain autonomous? Is it possible to generalize about the process of assimilation (or 'acculturation'), or the resistance to assimilation?

It might reasonably be argued, however, that the most important sub-cultures have rarely been studied as such. These are the cultures of social classes. A contrast between the habits and the habitus of the middle class and the working class emerges from Pierre Bourdieu's well-known study of social distinction, but he does not discuss the importance of this difference compared with (say) the difference between the French and their neighbours.[64] It may well be impossible to measure these differences. To a native of a particular country, the cultural contrasts between different classes may well appear overwhelming, while the outsider notices first what they have in common (as in the case of Schama and the Dutch). All the same, the sub-cultural point of view may well have something of value to add to the historical or sociological study of class.

The last point to make about culture leads us to the study of change. It concerns transmission – in other words, 'tradition' or 'cultural reproduction'. This phrase refers to the tendency of society in general and the educational system in particular to reproduce itself by inculcating in the rising generation the values of the past.[65] Traditions do not persist automatically, out of 'inertia', as historians sometimes put it.[66] They are transmitted as the result of a good deal of hard work by parents, teachers, priests, employers and other agents of socialization. The concept 'cultural reproduction' is useful in drawing attention to the effort involved in running on the spot, in other words keeping a society more or less as it is. The qualification 'more or less' has to be added because, as Sahlins argues, 'every reproduction of culture is an alteration, insofar as in action, the categories by which a present world is

---

[64] Bourdieu (1979).
[65] Bourdieu and Passeron (1970); cf. Althusser (1970).
[66] Moore (1966), 485–7.

orchestrated pick up some new empirical content'.[67] If each generation
reinterprets the norms only slightly in the process of receiving and
retransmitting them, appreciable social changes will take place over the
long term, as we will see in the following chapter.

Facts and Fictions

Historians, like sociologists and anthropologists, used to assume that
they dealt in facts, and that their texts reflected historical reality. This
assumption has crumbled under the assaults of the philosophers –
whether or not they may be said to 'mirror' a broader, deeper change in
mentality.[68] It is now necessary to consider the claim that historians
and ethnographers are as much in the business of fiction as novelists
and poets, in other words that they too are producers of 'literary
artifacts' according to rules of genre and style (whether they are conscious of these rules or not).[69] Recent studies of the 'poetics of ethnography' have described the work of sociologists and anthropologists
as the 'textual construction' of reality, and compared it to the work
of novelists. The work of the exiled Pole Bronislaw Malinowski, for
example, looks increasingly like that of his compatriot Joseph Conrad –
whose stories he read in the field – while the anthropologist Alfred
Métraux has been described as an 'ethnographic surrealist'.[70]

In the case of historians, the main challenger is Hayden White, who
once accused his professional colleagues of living in the nineteenth
century, the age of the system of literary conventions known as 'realism',
and of refusing to experiment with modern forms of representation.
The shock-waves following this pronouncement have not yet died down
(although it was made as long ago as 1966).[71]

White also claims, like the literary theorist Northrop Frye, that
historians – like poets, novelists or playwrights – organize their accounts
of the past around recurrent plots or *mythoi*. For example, 'the Comic
mythos served as the plot structure for most of Ranke's historical
works', in the sense that when writing about the French or English civil
wars, for example, he told a three-part story which moved like a
comedy (or tragicomedy) 'from a condition of apparent peace, through

---

[67] Sahlins (1985), 144.
[68] Rorty (1980).
[69] White (1973, 1976); Brown (1977); Clifford and Marcus (1986).
[70] Clifford (1981, 1986); Atkinson (1990).
[71] White (1966).

the revelation of conflict, to the resolution of the conflict in the establishment of a genuinely peaceful social order'. Ranke's story thus con-
tained an irreducibly fictive or creative element. His documents did not
tell him when to start his story or when to end it.[72] To claim, as Ranke
did – and as many historians still do – to be writing down 'what
actually happened', no more and no less, is to fall victim to what an
anthropologist (neatly turning the historians' use of the term 'myth'
against themselves) has recently called 'the myth of realism'.[73]

In other words, the boundary between fact and fiction, which once
looked firm, has been eroded in our so-called 'postmodern' era. (Alternatively, it is only now that we see that the boundary was always
open.)[74] In this border area we find writers who are attracted by the
idea of the so-called 'non-fiction novel', such as Truman Capote's *In
Cold Blood* (1965), which tells the story of the murder of the Clutter
family, or Norman Mailer's *The Armies of the Night* (1968), about a
protest march to the Pentagon, subtitled 'History as a Novel/The Novel
as History'.[75] We also find novelists who incorporate documents
(decrees, newspaper cuttings and so on) into the text of their story; or
who explore alternative pasts, as in Carlos Fuentes's *Terra Nostra*
(1975); or who build their narrative on the obstacles to the attainment
of historical truth, as Mario Vargas Llosa does in *The Real Life of
Alejandro Mayta* (1984), in which the narrator is trying to reconstruct
the career of a Peruvian revolutionary – perhaps for a novel, perhaps
for a 'very free history of the period', in the face of contradictory
evidence. 'Why try to find out everything that happened?' asks one
informant. 'I wonder if we really know what you call History with
a capital H...or if there's as much make-believe in history as in
novels.'[76]

On the other side, a small group of historians, sociologists and
anthropologists have responded to White's challenge and have been
experimenting with 'creative non-fiction', in other words narrative
techniques learned from novelists or film-makers. The historian Golo
Mann, for example, a son of the novelist Thomas Mann, once wrote a
biography of the seventeenth-century general Albrecht von Wallenstein
which he described as 'an all too true novel', and in which he adapted
the stream-of-consciousness technique to historical purposes, especially

[72] Frye (1960); White (1973), 167, 177.
[73] Tonkin (1990); cf. LaCapra (1985), 15–44.
[74] Hutcheon (1989); Gearhart (1984).
[75] Weber (1980), 73–9, 80–7.
[76] Vargas Llosa (1984), 67.

when evoking the last months of his hero's life, when the general, ill and embittered, appears to have been considering changing sides. Mann's footnotes, however, are more conventional than his text.[77]

Carlo Ginzburg, also the son of a novelist, Natalia Ginzburg, is another historian remarkable for the self-consciously literary way in which he writes, almost to the point of undermining his own criticisms of Hayden White.[78] Again, the anthropologist Richard Price has adapted the device of the multiple viewpoint, used to great effect in novels and films such as William Faulkner's *The Sound and the Fury* (1929) and Akira Kurosawa's *Rashomon* (1950), to an account of eighteenth-century Surinam. Instead of juxtaposing individual accounts, he presents the situation as it was seen through the eyes of three collective agents – the black slaves, the Dutch officials and the Moravian missionaries – and then adds his own comments on the other three texts.[79] In other words, he offers an example of the 'multivocal' or 'polyphonic' account recommended by the Russian critic Mikhail Bakhtin.[80]

It remains a pity that the majority of professional historians (I cannot speak for anthropologists and sociologists) have so far been so reluctant to recognize the poetics of their work, the literary conventions they follow. There is a sense in which it is difficult to deny that historians construct the objects they study, grouping events into movements like 'The Scientific Revolution' or 'The Thirty Years' War', which are only visible by hindsight. A more fundamental question was raised long ago by Kenneth Burke in *The Rhetoric of Motives* (1950), the question whether human action as well as speech and writing does not follow the rules of rhetoric (an idea which informs the dramaturgical perspectives of Erving Goffman and Victor Turner (discussed above, p. 49).

It is equally difficult to deny the role of fiction 'in the archives', as Natalie Davis puts it in a recent book in which she engages with some of the problems raised by the literary critic Stephen Greenblatt (above, p. 101). In this study of sixteenth-century France she is essentially concerned with the place of rhetoric and narrative techniques in the construction of texts such as the depositions of witnesses, the interrogation of suspects, or pleas for pardon, in other words documents which positivist historians have traditionally treated as relatively trustworthy

---

[77] Mann (1971); cf. Mann (1979).
[78] Ginzburg (1976, 1984).
[79] Price (1990).
[80] Bakhtin (1981).

evidence. Davis begins her study with the remark that she was taught like other historians 'to peel away the fictive elements in our documents so that we could get at the hard facts', but goes on the confess her discovery – perhaps a result of the challenge from Greenblatt and White – that the craft of storytelling is itself a historical theme of great interest.[81]

On the other side, it is an equal pity that White and his followers, not to mention the theorists of narrative, have not yet seriously engaged with the question whether history is a literary genre or cluster of genres of its own, whether it has its own forms of narrative and its own rhetoric, and whether the conventions include (as they surely do) rules about the relation of statements to evidence as well as rules of representation. Ranke, for example, was not writing pure fiction. Documents not only supported his narrative, but constrained the narrator not to make statements for which evidence was lacking.

Similar points might be made about sociologists and anthropologists. Whether they use documents or construct their accounts entirely out of interviews, conversations and personal observation, they follow a research strategy which includes criteria of reliability, representativity and so on. What we should be discussing (rather than the old dilemma between fact and fiction, science and art) is therefore the compatibility or conflict between these criteria and different forms of text or rhetoric. However, this middle ground, that of the 'fictions of factual representation' (the mask of impartiality, the claim to inside knowledge, the use of statistics to impress the reader, and so on), is only beginning to be explored in a systematic way.[82]

---

[81] Davis (1979; 1987, esp. 3).
[82] Hexter (1968), 381ff; White (1976); Weber (1980); Siebenschuh (1983); Megill and McCloskey (1987); Rosaldo (1987); Agar (1900).

5

SOCIAL THEORY AND
SOCIAL CHANGE

Time and again in earlier chapters, particular approaches, from functionalism to structuralism, have been criticized because they fail to account for change. How does one account for change? Can it be left to the historians and to their traditional concepts, or do social theorists also have a contribution to make? Is there a theory of social change, or at least a model?

In this chapter I shall approach the problem from two opposite directions. In the first place, by working inwards from general to particular, juxtaposing general models of change to the history of particular societies in order to see how far the models fail to fit historical reality and in what respects they need to be tailored or modified. Historians will be seen engaged in their favourite task of 'splitting', as Hexter calls it (above, p. 23), chipping away at theory like a sculptor attacking a block of marble. It will then be time to turn to the complementary process of 'lumping', building up rather than breaking down and working outwards from the particular to the general. The object of the exercise will be to offer accounts of the process of change in specific societies in the hope that these accounts might help in the construction of a revised general model. A final section will attempt to strike at least a provisional balance and also to offer a few reflections on the problematic relation between events and structures.

It needs to be stressed from the start that the term 'social change' is an ambiguous one. It is sometimes used in a narrow sense, referring to alterations in the social structure (the balance between different social classes, for example), but also in a considerably wider sense which includes political organization, the economy and culture. The emphasis in this chapter will fall on the wider definition.

Like philosophies of history, from which they cannot be completely distinguished, models or theories of social change fall into a number of main types. Some are linear, like Judaeo-Christian philosophies of history, or the 'modernization' model which was so popular among sociologists and developmental economists a generation ago. Others are cyclical, like the classical theories of change revived by Machiavelli and others at the Renaissance, or the ideas of the great fourteenth-century Arab historian Ibn Khaldun, or more recently Oswald Spengler's *Decline of the West* (1918–22) and Arnold Toynbee's *Study of History* (1935–61). Cyclical theories of more limited application include Kondratieff's 'long waves', Juglar's shorter economic cycles, and Vilfredo Pareto's account of the 'circulation of elites', which a few historians have found useful in their work.

It may also be useful to distinguish models which emphasize internal factors in change, and often describe society in terms of organic metaphors such as 'growth', 'evolution' and 'decay', from models which stress external factors and use terms like 'borrowing', 'diffusion' or 'imitation'. The latter tradition is represented by Gabriel Tarde, whose *Laws of Imitation* (1890) involved him in controversy with Durkheim, and Thorstein Veblen, whose study of *Imperial Germany and the Industrial Revolution* (1915) centred on the concept of 'borrowing'. Since diffusionism is often condemned nowadays as a superficial and mechanical theory, it may be worth stressing the fact that in the hands of Tarde and Veblen it was neither. Long before the vogue of reception theory, both men were interested in differences in receptivity to new ideas. Veblen, for example, discussed the special 'propensity to borrow' of the Germans, the Scandinavians and the Japanese. More recently, the diffusion of cultural patterns within a given society has come under close scrutiny. Diffusion from the top downwards has been discussed in some detail by the Indian sociologist M. N. Srinivas, who calls it 'sanskritization', and by the French historian Georges Duby.[1] This problem will resurface later in the chapter (p. 156).

In a relatively brief account, however, it is probably best to begin with a discussion of the two main models currently in use, the conflict model and the evolution model, or for simplicity's sake, Marx and Spencer. Needless to say they will necessarily be presented in a simplified form.

---

[1] Srinivas (1966); Duby (1968).

Spencer's Model

'Spencer' is a convenient label for a model which stresses social evolution, in other words social change which is gradual and cumulative ('evolution' as opposed to 'revolution'), and essentially determined from within ('endogenous' as opposed to 'exogenous'). This endogenous process is often described in terms of 'structural differentiation', in other words a shift from the simple, unspecialized and informal to the complex, specialized and formal, or in Spencer's own words a shift from 'incoherent homogeneity' to 'coherent heterogeneity'.[2] This is, broadly speaking, the model of change employed by both Durkheim and Weber.

Durkheim, who disagreed with Spencer on many issues, followed him in describing social change in essentially evolutionary terms. He emphasized the gradual replacement of simple 'mechanical solidarity' (in other words, the solidarity of the similar) by a more complex 'organic solidarity', the solidarity of the complementary, thanks to the increasing division of labour in society.[3] As for Weber, he tended to avoid the term 'evolution' but all the same he viewed world history as a gradual yet irreversible trend towards more complex and impersonal forms of organization such as bureaucracy (above, p. 24) and capitalism. It is thus not too difficult to make a synthesis of the ideas of Durkheim and Weber on social change, as Talcott Parsons and others have done.[4]

The result is the model of modernization, in which the process of change is viewed as essentially a development from within, and the outside world enters only to provide a stimulus to 'adaptation'. 'Traditional society' and 'modern society' are presented as antithetical types on the following lines.

1   The traditional social hierarchy is based on birth ('ascription) and social mobility is low. The modern hierarchy, by contrast, is based on merit ('achievement') and mobility is high. A society of 'estates' (above, p. 61) has been replaced by a society of 'classes', in which there is greater equality of opportunity. Again, in traditional society, the basic unit is a small group in which everyone knows everyone, a 'community' (*Gemeinschaft*) as Ferdinand Tönnies called it (above,

---

[2] Spencer (1876–85); Sanderson (1990), 10–35.
[3] Durkheim (1893); cf. Lukes (1973), ch. 7.
[4] Parsons (1966).

p. 9). After modernization, the basic unit is a large impersonal 'society' (*Gesellschaft*). In the economic sphere this impersonality takes the form of the market, with its 'invisible hand', as Adam Smith called it, while in the political sphere it takes the form of what Weber called 'bureaucracy'. In short, in Parsons's formula, 'universalism' replaces 'particularism'. Of course face-to-face groups do not disappear, but they adapt to the new situation. In order to act on the wider society they take the form of voluntary associations for specific ends – professions, churches, clubs, political parties and so on.

2 These antithetical modes of social organization are associated with antithetical attitudes (if not 'mentalities' – above, p. 91); attitudes to change, for example. In traditional society, where change is slow, people tend either to be hostile to it or unaware that it has taken place (a phenomenon sometimes described as 'structural amnesia').[5] On the other hand, the members of modern societies, in which change is rapid and constant, are well aware of it, expect it and approve of it. Indeed, actions are justified in the name of 'improvement' or 'progress', while institutions and ideas are condemned as 'out of date'. Humanity – or much of it – has moved from a situation in which 'new' was a term of abuse to one in which it is a recommendation in itself. Since the eighteenth century (among the elites of Western Europe) the future has come to be perceived not as a mere reproduction of the present but as a space for the development of projects and trends.[6]

3 To these basic contrasts, a number of others may be added. The culture of traditional societies is often described as religious, magical and even irrational, while that of modern societies is viewed as secular, rational and scientific. Weber, for example, considered both secularization, or as he called it, the 'disenchantment of the world' (*Entzauberung der Welt*), and the rise of more rational forms of organization – the 'bureaucratization of the world' – to be central characteristics of the modernization process, with the Protestant sense of the 'calling', their 'worldly asceticism' (*innerweltliche Askese*), as a crucial stage in the process. Incidentally, the use of the term 'rational' does not mean that Weber wholeheartedly approved of the process, to which he was in fact profoundly ambivalent.

The parallel between this model of sociocultural change and certain well-known models of economic growth and political development will

[5] Barnes (1947), 52.
[6] Koselleck (1965).

be obvious enough. For example, theorists of economic growth have emphasized the 'take-off' from a preindustrial society viewed as static to an industrial society in which growth is the normal condition. 'Compound interest becomes built, as it were, into its habits and institutional structure.'[7] Theorists of political development have stressed the spread of political participation (or to use a more old-fashioned term, 'democracy') as well as the rise of bureaucracy.

The contrast between traditional and modern societies has been elaborated with the help of contributions from other disciplines. Geographers, for example, have suggested that modernity is associated with changes in conceptions of space, which comes to be treated as abstract or 'emptiable', in the sense of being available for a variety of purposes rather than tied to a particular function.[8] Social psychologists have described the development of a 'modern' personality, a social character characterized by increasing self-control and also by the capacity for empathy with others.[9] Social anthropologists have also contrasted traditional with modern modes of thought (above, pp. 115, 91).

However, social theorists have been feeling increasingly uncomfortable with the assumptions underlying this model, notably its triumphalism and its assumption of teleology.[10] Even in the field of economic history, the idea of progress towards an ever more affluent society has been challenged, and an alternative, ecological model proposed, according to which economic innovation is explained as essentially a reaction to the disappearance of some resource and the consequent need to find a substitute.[11]

Indeed, the evolutionary model has been criticized so severely in the past few years that it is only fair to begin by pointing to its merits. The idea of a sequence of social changes which, if not inevitable, are at least likely to follow one another, is not something for historians to reject out of hand. The idea of 'evolution', with its echoes of Darwin, is not to be dismissed lightly either.[12] W. G. Runciman has argued that 'the process by which societies evolve is analogous, although by no means equivalent, to natural selection', emphasizing what he calls the 'competitive selection of practices'.[13] A good deal of military and economic

[7] Rostow (1958).
[8] Sack (1986).
[9] Elias (1939); Lerner (1958), 47–52.
[10] Tipps (1973).
[11] Wilkinson (1973).
[12] Wertheim (1974); Sanderson (1990), 75–102; Hallpike (1986).
[13] Runciman (1980), 171; Runciman (1983–9), 2, 285–310.

history in particular, areas where the idea of competition is at its clearest, falls into place if it is approached in this way.

Another striking illustration of the merits of the model is Joseph Lee's study of Irish society since the Great Famine of the 1840s. It is organized around the concept of modernization in the hope that this term will 'prove immune to the parochial preoccupations implicit in equally elusive and more emotive concepts like gaelicisation and anglicisation'. In this case, the comparative perspective allows the general to be seen in the particular, and suggests more profound or structural explanations for local changes than local historians had previously given.[14]

For another illustration of the advantages of the model we may turn to Germany. Historians as different in their approach to the past as Thomas Nipperdey and Hans-Ulrich Wehler have discussed changes in German society from the late eighteenth century onwards in terms of modernization. Nipperdey, for example, has explained the growth of voluntary associations in the years around 1800, associations founded for a variety of highly specific aims, as part of the general shift from a traditional 'estate society' to a modern 'class society'.[15]

As for Wehler, he has made his own contribution to theory with his concept of 'defensive modernization', which he uses to characterize the reforms carried out in Prussia and other German states between 1789 and 1815. These agrarian, administrative and military reforms were, according to Wehler, a response to what the ruling class perceived as the threat of the French Revolution and Napoleon.[16]

The idea of defensive modernization is clearly capable of a wider application. The traditional notion of the 'Counter-Reformation' for example, modelled on 'counter-revolution', suggests that the Catholic Church reformed or modernized itself in the mid-sixteenth century as a reaction to the Protestant Reformation. Again, a number of movements for reform in the nineteenth century, the 'Young Turks' in the Ottoman Empire, for example, or the Meiji 'restoration' in Japan, may be seen as responses to the threat posed by the rise of the West.

It is time to turn to the theory's defects. Formulated in industrializing countries in the late nineteenth century, the model was elaborated in the 1950s to account for change in the Third World (the 'underdeveloped' countries, as they were called at the time). It is scarcely surprising to

[14] Lee (1973).
[15] Nipperdey (1972).
[16] Wehler (1987).

find that historians of preindustrial Europe in particular should have found discrepancies between the model and the particular societies they study. They have expressed three kinds of misgiving in particular, concerning the direction, the explanation and the mechanics of social change.

(1) In the first place, widening our horizons beyond the last century or two makes it clear that change is not unilinear, that history is not a 'one-way street'.[17] In other words, society does not always move in the direction of increasing centralization, complexity, specialization and so on. Some adherents of modernization theory, S. N. Eisenstadt for example, are aware of what the latter calls 'regression to decentralization', but the thrust of the theory is in the opposite direction. Regression has not yet received the thorough analysis it surely requires.[18]

An example of a regressive trend which is very well known to historians is that of Europe at the time of the decline of the Roman Empire and the invasions of the 'barbarians' (a category which itself deserves re-examination in the light of historical anthropology). The structural crisis of the Roman Empire in the third century AD was followed by a collapse of central government, a decline of the towns and an increasing tendency to local autonomy at both the economic and the political level. Lombards, Visigoths and other invaders were allowed to live under their own laws, so that a shift from 'universalism' to 'particularism' took place. The attempt by emperors to ensure that sons followed the occupation of their fathers suggests that there was also a shift from achievement to ascription. At the same time, Christianity became the official religion of the Empire following the conversion of the emperor Constantine. The Church became increasingly important in cultural, political and even in economic life, while secular attitudes yielded to otherworldly ones.[19]

In other words, the case of the late Roman Empire illustrates the opposite of the process of 'modernization' in almost every social domain. The completeness of the reversal may be taken as evidence that the different trends are connected, as Spencerians assume, and in that sense support theories of social evolution. All the same, these theories have too often been put forward in a form implying that regressions do not take place. The fact that the terms 'urbanization', 'secularization'

---

[17]   Stone (1977), 666.
[18]   Eisenstadt (1973); Runciman (1983–9), 2, 310–20.
[19]   Brown (1971), 111–12.

and 'structural differentiation' have no opposites in the language of sociology tells us more about the assumptions of sociologists than about the nature of social change.

The very term 'modernization' gives the impression of a linear process. However, intellectual historians are well aware that the word 'modern' – which was, ironically enough, already in use in the Middle Ages – has been filled with very different meanings in different centuries. Even the way in which the concept was used by Ranke and Burckhardt, who both believed that modern history began in the fifteenth century, seems curiously old-fashioned today. Ranke stressed state-building and Burckhardt stressed individualism, but neither of them had anything to say about industrialization. This absence is hardly surprising, since the industrial revolution had not yet penetrated the German-speaking world at the time that Ranke wrote his *Latin and Teutonic Nations* (1828) and Burckhardt his *Civilization of the Renaissance* (1860). However, it means that their modernity is not ours.

The trouble with modernity, in other words, is that it keeps changing. As a result, historians have been forced to coin the self-contradictory term 'early modern' to refer to the period between the end of the Middle Ages and the beginning of the industrial revolution. For similar reasons, some analysts of contemporary society have come to describe it not only as 'postindustrial' and 'late capitalist' but also as 'postmodern'.[20] There may well be good reasons for inventing new concepts to analyse the changes of the past twenty years or so in areas as apparently diverse as the economy and the arts. To a historian, however, and especially to a historian concerned with the long term, the choice of the term 'postmodern' is bound to look like yet another example of the hyperbole to which generations of intellectuals have resorted, from the Renaissance onwards, to persuade others that their period or generation is a special one. The rhetoric of any one generation would sound extremely plausible, were it not for one's memories of their predecessors.

(2) In the second place, historians have doubts about the explanation of social change built into the Spencer model, the assumption that change is essentially internal to the social system, the development of potential, the growth of a branching tree. This might be the case if one could isolate a particular society from the rest of the world, but in practice many instances can be found of social change provoked by encounters

[20] Bell (1976); Habermas (1981); Kolakowski (1986); Harvey (1990).

between cultures. It was to discuss this process that anthropologists, whose very discipline grew up in the context of culture contact, developed their concept of 'acculturation'. The value of the term has been neatly illustrated in a discussion of the ways in which historians unaware of anthropology used to discuss the contacts between Christians and Muslims in Spain. Up to a point they did the same job as the anthropologists while using different terms, but they did have considerably less to say about the mechanisms of change.[21]

Conquests are a particularly dramatic class of encounters between cultures, rarely discussed by social theorists.[22] The Norman Conquest of England in 1066, for example, has been described as 'the classic example in European history of the disruption of a social order by the sudden introduction of an alien military technology'.[23] Outside Europe, the Spanish conquest of Mexico and Peru and the British conquest of India are equally classic examples of social change induced from outside (in each case with the aid of a new military technology). In all these cases traditional elites were pushed aside by newcomers.

The changes at the bottom of the social hierarchy were no less profound, and seem to have been at least in part the result of misunderstanding, a factor in social history which, like ignorance, has not received the attention it deserves. The officials of the East India Company, for example, viewed the Indian social structure through English spectacles, as a system of landlords and tenants. They perceived the *zamindars*, who were more or less tax-collectors, as landlords. The newcomers had the power to turn their perceptions into reality by treating the *zamindars* as landlords. Thus, in a classic case of cultural 'construction' or reconstruction, the misunderstanding of the social structure led to change in the social structure.[24]

Although there is less evidence available in the case of the Norman Conquest, we may suspect that something of the same kind happened in England after 1066. The Normans failed to understand the complex social system of the Anglo-Saxons, in which status was expressed in terms of different amounts of 'wergild', in other words the amount of compensation to be paid to the victim's relatives if the person were to be killed. By failing to understand it, the Normans reduced Anglo-Saxon England to a society of serfs, freemen and knights. Like the

---

[21] Dupront (1965); Glick and Pi-Sunyer (1969).
[22] Foster (1960).
[23] White (1962), 38.
[24] Neale (1957); Cohn (1987), 1–17.

previous example, this one suggests that some groups may be more important than others in the cultural 'constitution' of society (above, p. 122). It also suggests the importance of a relatively brief period of innovation, after which society 'crystallizes' into relatively inflexible structures.

Epidemics illustrate a different kind of penetration from outside. In 1348, for example, the Black Death, carried by rats, invaded Europe from Asia and killed about a third of the population in a short space of time. The consequent manpower shortages led to important long-term changes in the European social structure. The Spanish conquest of the New World was accompanied by the spread of European diseases, such as smallpox, to which the indigenous population was extremely vulnerable. Estimates vary, but it is agreed that several million people, probably the majority of the population, died in the first generations after the conquest of Mexico.[25]

In all these cases, the violent impact of forces external to the society in question makes it inappropriate to discuss them in terms of mere stimuli to adaptation, which is the only function allotted to external factors in the Spencer model.

(3) If we want to understand *why* social change takes place, it may be a good strategy to begin by examining *how* it takes place. Unfortunately, the Spencer model makes little reference to the mechanics of change. This lack of reference encourages the false assumption of unilinearity and gives the process of change the appearance of a smooth and virtually automatic sequence of stages, as if all a society had to do was to step onto the escalator.

An unusually explicit example of what we might call the 'escalator model' is Rostow's study of the stages of economic growth, from the 'traditional society', through the 'take-off', to 'the age of high mass-consumption'. For a contrasting approach we may turn to the economic historian Alexander Gershenkron, and his argument that late industrializers, such as Germany and Russia, diverged from the model of early industrializers, notably Britain. In the later cases, the role of the state was greater and the profit motive was less important. The earlier model was inappropriate for latecomers precisely because they were in a hurry to catch up with their predecessors.[26] Latecomers had both advantages

---

[25] McNeill (1976); Postan (1972); Crosby (1986).
[26] Rostow (1958); Gershenkron (1962), 5–30.

and disadvantages compared with early industrializers, but in both cases their situation was a different one.

The advantages of latecomers were generalized into a theory of change by the Dutch historian Jan Romein, who formulated what he called the law of the 'retarding lead', to the effect that an innovating society was usually 'backward' in the preceding generation. The argument for this leapfrog effect or 'dialectics of progress' is that an innovating society tends to invest too heavily – metaphorically as well as literally – in that particular innovation, and so it fails to adapt when diminishing returns set in.[27] It might be argued that the cultural history of the West illustrates the theory rather well, with the Renaissance occurring in Italy (a culture which had not invested heavily in Gothic or scholasticism, as the French had done), while Romanticism developed in Germany (a culture which had not invested much in the Enlightenment).

In similar fashion, E. A. Wrigley has contrasted the process of social change in Britain and the Netherlands. By the middle of the eighteenth century, the working population of one rural region in the Netherlands, the Veluwe, were already involved in the production of paper and textiles as well as in agriculture. A region which lacked towns and factories was 'modern' in the sense that structural differentiation had taken place and that most adults were literate. In other words, the Veluwe illustrates modernization without industrialization. Conversely, the north of England in the early nineteenth century illustrates industrialization without modernization. Here towns and factories coexisted with illiteracy and a strong sense of community.[28]

The moral of these examples seems to be that we should not be looking for the consequences of industrialization (assuming them to be uniform) but rather for the 'fit' or compatibility between different sociocultural structures and economic growth. The example of Japan points in the same direction, revealing the association of a remarkable economic performance with values and structures very different from those of the West. Hence the search by Weberian sociologists for a functional analogue of the Protestant ethic. One of them, Robert Bellah, found evidence for this-worldly asceticism (including a concept, *tenshoku*, much like that of the 'calling'), but he also drew attention to the 'penetration of the economy by political values' in Japan, in stark contrast to the history of the West.[29]

[27] Romein (1937).
[28] Wrigley (1972–3).
[29] Bellah (1957); 114–17.

In short, social change appears to be multilinear rather than unilinear. There is more than one path to modernity. These paths are not necessarily smooth, as the examples of France after 1789 and Russia after 1917 remind us. For an analysis of social change which emphasizes crisis and revolution, we may turn to Marx's model.

Marx's Model

'Marx', like 'Spencer', is a convenient piece of shorthand which will be used here to refer to a model of social change to which Engels, Lenin, Lukács and Gramsci (among others) all made contributions. In a sentence, it may be described as a model or theory of a sequence of societies ('social formations') which depend on economic systems ('modes of production') and contain internal conflicts ('contradictions) which lead to crisis, revolution and discontinuous change. There are of course ambiguities in the theory, allowing different interpreters to stress the importance of economic, political and cultural forces respectively, and to debate whether the forces of production determine the relations of production or vice versa.[30]

In some respects Marx offers little more than a variety of the modernization model, which can therefore be discussed relatively briefly. Like Spencer, Marx includes the idea of a sequence of forms of society – tribal, slave, feudal, capitalist, socialist and communist. Feudalism and capitalism, the social formations which have been discussed in most detail, are virtually defined – like traditional and modern society – as opposites. Like Spencer, Marx explains social change in fundamentally endogenous terms, emphasizing the internal dynamic of the mode of production.[31] However, in some of its versions at least, the Marx model does stand up to the three main criticisms of Spencer summarized above.

First, there is a place in the model for change in the 'wrong' direction, for example the so-called 'refeudalization' of Spain and Italy and the rise of serfdom in Central and Eastern Europe at the same time as the rise of the bourgeoisie in England and the Dutch Republic. Indeed, some Marxist analyses, as we have seen, notably those of Immanuel Wallerstein, emphasize the interdependence of economic and social development in the centre and the 'development of underdevelopment' on the periphery (above, p. 79).

[30] Cohen (1978); Rigby (1987).
[31] Sanderson (1990), 50–74.

Secondly, there is a place in Marx for exogenous explanations of social change. In the case of the West, this place is generally agreed to have been a subordinate one. In the famous controversy among Marxists of the 1950s over the transition from feudalism to capitalism, Paul Sweezy's explanation of the decline of feudalism in terms of external factors such as the reopening of the Mediterranean and the consequent rise of trade and towns met with a chorus of rejection.[32] On the other hand, Marx himself regarded Asian society as devoid of internal mechanisms of change. Writing about the British in India, he suggested that the function of the conquerors (or as he put it, their 'mission') was to destroy the traditional social framework and thus to make change possible.[33]

Generally speaking, where Spencer presents the process of modernization as a series of parallel developments in different regions, Marx offers a more global account which stresses connections between changes in one society and changes in others. Wallerstein, for example, as we have seen (p. 79), studies not the rise of individual European states or economies but the world-economy, in other words the international system. He emphasizes the exogenetic aspects of change.[34]

Thirdly, Marx is much more concerned than Spencer with the mechanics of social change, especially in the case of the transition from feudalism to capitalism. Change is viewed in essentially dialectical terms. In other words, the emphasis falls on conflict and on consequences which are not only unintended but the very opposite of what was planned or expected. Thus social formations which once unleashed productive forces later 'turn into their fetters', and the bourgeoisie dig their own graves by calling the proletariat into existence.[35]

On the question of unilinear versus multilinear development, Marxists disagree. The tribal-slave-feudal-capitalist-socialist schema is obviously unlinear. However, Marx himself considered this schema to be relevant to European history alone. He did not expect India, or even Russia, to follow the Western path, without making it clear what paths he did expect them to take. Two relatively recent analyses within the Marxist tradition are firmly multilinear. Perry Anderson, for example, emphasizes the variety of possible paths to modernity by choosing the ballistic metaphor of 'trajectory' in preference to that of 'evolution', and

[32] Hilton (1976).
[33] Avineri (1968).
[34] Frank (1967); Wallerstein (1974).
[35] Marx and Engels (1848); cf. Cohen (1978).

describing 'passages' from antiquity to feudalism and 'lineages' of the absolutist state.[36] Again, Barrington Moore distinguishes three main historical routes to the modern world. There is the 'classic' route of bourgeois revolution, as in the cases of England, France and the United States; peasant (rather than proletarian) revolution, in the cases of Russia and China; and conservative revolution, or revolution from above, in the cases of Prussia and Japan.[37]

The emphasis on revolution (discussed above, p. 30) is of course a salient characteristic of Marx's model, in contrast to Spencer's. In one case change is smooth, gradual, and automatic, and the structures evolve as it were by themselves. In the other, change is abrupt, and the old structures are broken in the course of a sequence of dramatic events. In the French Revolution, for example, the abolition of the monarchy and the feudal system, the expropriation of the Church and the aristocrats, the replacement of provinces by departments, and so on, all took place in a relatively short time.

The tension, not to say 'contradiction', in the Marxian system between economic determinism and the collective voluntarism of revolution has often been remarked, and battles have ensued between different schools of interpretation. Marx's model thus raises, even if it does not solve, the problem of the relation between political events and social change, as well as the problem of human agency, summarized in the famous phrase, 'Men make history, but not in circumstances of their own choosing'. Followers of Marx have been divided into 'economic', 'political' and 'cultural' Marxists on the basis of their different interpretations of this epigram.

Despite – or because of – these tensions, the Marx model seems to meet the criticisms of historians better than Spencer's alternative. This is not altogether surprising, since the model is much better known to historians, and many of them have modified it. It is difficult to think of a major contribution to social history (as opposed to historical sociology) which utilizes Spencer as a framework. On the other hand, the Marx model is used in classic studies such as E. P. Thompson's famous *Making of the Working Class* (1963), as in Maurice Agulhon's *The Republic in the Village* (1970), a study of eastern Provence in the first half of the nineteenth century, or Emilio Sereni's *Capitalism in the Countryside* (1947), which deals with Italy in the generation after its unification in 1860.

[36] Anderson (1974a,b); cf. Fulbrook and Skocpol (1984).
[37] Moore (1966); cf. Smith (1984).

It may not be coincidence that these three books, and others which might have been cited, deal with Marx's own century and with the transition which he knew and analysed best, the rise of capitalism. The Marx model is considerably less satisfactory as an interpretation of the old regimes of preindustrial societies. It fails to deal with demographic factors, which may well have been the most important motors of change in these societies (below, p. 153). Nor does it have much to offer in the analysis of social conflict in these societies. In practice, Marxist historians of old regimes use a weak version of the model when what is needed is a modified version. For example, social conflict in seventeenth-century France has been presented as a foreshadowing of the conflicts of the nineteenth century (above, p. 60). It is only relatively recently that Marxist historians have taken serious account of social solidarities other than those of class, and the title of one of Thompson's articles, 'Class Struggle without Class', illustrates not only the author's love of paradox but the difficulty of finding an alternative conceptualization.[38]

A Third Way?

Given the existence of two models of social change, each with its particular strengths and weaknesses, it is worth investigating the possibility of a synthesis. This may appear something like an alchemical wedding, in other words a union of opposites. However, in some respects at least, Marx and Spencer are complementary rather than contradictory.

For example, Alexis de Tocqueville's famous account of the French Revolution, which presents it as a catalyst of changes which had already begun taking place during the old regime (above, p. 7), might be said to mediate between the evolutionary and revolutionary models of change. Again, an examination of the important role played by political clubs during the French Revolution, notably that of the Jacobin Club, suggests that an emphasis on the role of voluntary associations and a stress on discontinuous change are perfectly compatible.

Even E. P. Thompson's *Making of the English Working Class*, which begins with an assault on sociology in general and structural differentiation in particular, includes a fascinating account of the place of trade unions and friendly societies in early nineteenth-century

[38] Hobsbawm (1971); Thompson (1978a).

England, the 'rituals of mutuality' of the Brotherhood of Maltsters, the Unanimous Society and so on, thus lending empirical support to the theory of modernization it sets out to undermine.[39]

There have been other signs of convergence between the two models since the 1960s at least. Jürgen Habermas, for example, draws on both Marx and Weber. Barrington Moore's account of the making of the modern world is fundamentally Marxist in orientation, but incorporates insights from modernization theory, while Moore's former pupil Charles Tilly is a 'modernizer' able to respond to some of the Marxist criticisms of this approach. Wallerstein combines a fundamentally Marxian approach with elements from the evolutionary theory in which he was trained, notably his stress on the importance of competition between states, for profits and for hegemony.

However, a synthesis of Marx and Spencer, even if this were possible, would not deal with all the objections which have been raised in the last few pages. The models actually share serious limitations of perspective. Both of them were developed in order to account for industrialization and its consequences, and they are much less satisfactory in their account of changes before the middle of the eighteenth century. For example, 'traditional society' in Spencer, and 'feudal society' in Marx are essentially residual categories, looking-glass worlds in which the principal characteristics of 'modern' or 'capitalist' society are simply reversed. The use of terms such as 'preindustrial', 'pre-political' and even 'pre-logical' (above, p. 93) is extremely revealing in this respect. Such reversals do not make for a realistic analysis.

Is there a third way, a model or theory of social change which will go beyond both Marx and Spencer? The revival of historical sociology in the 1980s includes a number of attempts to do just this, on the part of Anthony Giddens, for example, Michael Mann and Charles Tilly.[40] These three models have some important features in common, notably their stress on politics and war. Giddens, for example, introduces his volume on *The Nation-State and Violence* with a critique of social evolutionism precisely on the grounds that it stresses economic factors ('allocative resources') at the expense of political ones.[41] Mann, like Ernest Gellner, is particularly interested in the interplay of production, coercion and cognition in human history, but concentrates on the last of these factors. He offers what he calls a 'history of power', in which he

[39] E. P. Thompson (1963), 418–29.
[40] Giddens (1985); Mann (1986); Tilly (1990).
[41] Giddens (1985), 8–9.

suggests that 'The growth of the modern state, as measured by finance, is explained primarily not in domestic terms but in terms of geopolitical relations of violence.'[42] Tilly is concerned with what he calls 'capital' as well as 'coercion', but describes himself as going beyond his predecessors precisely 'by placing the organization of coercion and preparation for war squarely in the middle of the analysis'.[43]

In this respect all three sociologists converge not only with one another (and with Perry Anderson, whose volume on the *Lineages of the Absolutist State* was also concerned with the influence of war), but also with historians of early modern Europe. For some time a group of these historians have been arguing that political centralization in the sixteenth and seventeenth centuries, the age of the Habsburgs and the Bourbons, was little more than a by-product of the demands of war, thus illustrating a general theory dear to German historians early this century, that of 'the primacy of foreign policy'.

The argument runs roughly as follows. The sixteenth and seventeenth centuries were an age of 'military revolution' in which armies grew larger and larger. To pay for these armies, rulers had to squeeze more out of their subjects in taxes. The armies in turn helped to enforce the collection of the taxes, thus setting up what Samuel Finer has called the 'extraction-coercion cycle'.[44] The rise of the centralized state was not so much the result of a plan or a theory (such as 'absolutism') as an unintended consequence of competition for power in the international arena.

The other problem on which historical sociologists have been concentrating their attention is that of the 'rise of the West'. It is doubly relevant to any theory of social change, since the challenge is to explain not only how (and when) the Europeans drew ahead of their economic and military competitors, but also what consequences for the rest of the world followed from the establishment of European hegemony. Max Weber spent much of his working life wrestling with this question. Marxists, such as Wallerstein, have done the same. In their different ways, the economic historian Eric Jones and the sociologist John Hall have recently developed alternative explanations.

Although he discusses politics in some detail, borrowing from the theory of the firm to point out the 'economies of scale' enjoyed by large states, Jones is essentially concerned with economic change in Europe

---

[42] Mann (1986), 490; cf. Gellner (1988).
[43] Tilly (1990), 14.
[44] McNeill (1983); Parker (1988); Finer (1975), 96.

over the very long term. Comparing and contrasting Europe with China and India, he argues that industrialization was 'a growth deeply rooted in the past'. His explanatory emphasis falls on Europe's 'geological, climatic and topographical variety', which produced a 'dispersed portfolio of resources' and a lower vulnerability to natural disasters.[45]

John Hall, for his part, places the emphasis on politics. He suggests that capitalism was unable to develop in what he calls 'capstone' states like the Chinese Empire, in which the government presided over a set of separate societies and viewed links between them, including economic links, as a threat to its power. In China, there was too much state, while in the Islamic world there was too little – governments were too weak or too short-lived to provide the services a commercial society needed. If Adam Smith was right to suggest that the political conditions needed for 'the highest degree of opulence' are simply 'peace, easy taxes and a tolerable administration of justice', then Europe was an example of the golden mean. In Europe, the Church and the Empire neutralized one another, thus allowing a 'multipolar system' of competing states to emerge in which services were provided to merchants without too much interference with their trade.[46]

Historical sociologists have certainly been taking an interest in the history of the preindustrial world in general and early modern Europe in particular. In the first edition of this book, I suggested that the sociologists' debate on social change was based for the most part on nineteenth- and twentieth-century examples, so that a historian of early modern Europe might have something to offer. It might be thought that the change of historical climate in the 1980s has removed the need for the following section, which examines six early modern case-studies of social change. The reason for retaining them is that these six studies suggest yet other ways of going beyond Marx and Spencer.

Six Monographs in Search of a Theory

No model of social change will ever satisfy historians completely because of their professional interest in variety and difference. Hence, as Ronald Dore once put it, 'You can't make sociological omelettes without breaking a few historical eggs.' Jack Hexter's attack on Marxism as a 'prefabricated theory of social change' is really an attack on all

---

[45] Jones (1981); cf. Baechler et al. (1988).
[46] Hall (1985, 1988); Smith quoted in Hall (1986), 154.

models and all theories.[47] Other historians accept the need for models but are unhappy with all the models currently on offer and turn to do-it-yourself constructions. For example, Gareth Stedman Jones has denounced the quest for a 'short-cut theoretical salvation in sociology' on the grounds that 'theoretical work in history is too important to be sub-contracted to others'.[48]

Without going so far as this, either in rejecting the work of sociologists or in expecting historians to produce a theory of their own, I should now like to discuss the possibility of working outwards from monographs. Six monographs have been chosen for discussion in relative detail. Their authors are all interested in theory as well as in history, and it is no accident that the group includes a sociologist (Elias), an anthropologist (Sahlins) and a philosopher (Foucault) or that the three historians all come from the so-called 'Annales school', in which the interdisciplinary approach has become a tradition.

(1) The late Norbert Elias's study of 'the process of civilization' is a book which has had an unusual fate.[49] First published in German in 1939, it was virtually neglected for decades. Only in the 1970s (or in the English-speaking world, in the 1980s) was this study taken as seriously as it deserved, by sociologists and by historians. There is of course something odd about calling Elias's book a 'monograph'. It was intended as a contribution to sociological theory. Like Talcott Parsons, and at much the same time as Parsons, Elias attempted to make a synthesis of the ideas of Weber, Freud and Durkheim.[50]

All the same, Elias was much more interested in history than Parsons and his work is correspondingly rich in concrete detail. His book is a monograph in the sense that it concentrates on certain aspects of social life in Western Europe, especially in the late Middle Ages. Indeed, Elias's second chapter could hardly be more concrete. Divided into sections on 'behaviour at table', 'blowing one's nose', 'spitting' and so on, it argues the case for a major change in behaviour at the Renaissance. New material objects, such as the handkerchief and the fork, came into use at this time, and Elias argues that these objects were instruments of what he calls 'civilization', which he defines as a shift in what he calls the thresholds or 'frontiers' of embarrassment and shame. At a time

---

[47] Hexter (1961), 14–25.
[48] Jones (1976).
[49] Elias (1939), 1, 51–217.
[50] Niestroj (1989).

when the history of material culture and the history of the body are supposed to be new discoveries, it is worth reminding ourselves that Elias's pages on this subject were written in the 1930s.

The picturesque descriptions of medieval noblemen wiping their noses on their sleeves, spitting on the floor, and so on, are not cited for their own sake. The condemnation of such behaviour in treatises on good manners in the fifteenth and sixteenth centuries is supposed to illustrate what Elias calls the 'sociogenesis of Western civilization'. It is also intended to support a general theory of change. This theory may be regarded as a variation of the modernization model, but one which is not vulnerable to the objections which were discussed above.

In the first place, the theory is multilinear. Elias distinguishes what he called 'two main directions in the structural changes of society . . . those tending toward increased differentiation and integration, and those tending toward decreased differentiation and integration'. There is therefore no problem in principle in fitting the decline of the Roman Empire (say) into the model, though Elias might have said more than he did about the conscious rejection of traditional 'civilized' behaviour in certain periods of European history, for example among the Hungarian nobles of the Renaissance, anxious to define their identity by contrast to other nobilities and to establish their claim to descent from the 'barbarian' Huns.[51]

In the second place, Elias is very much concerned with the mechanics of change, the 'how' as well as the 'why'. The most original section of his book is not the vivid description of changes in table manners, which has perhaps attracted a disproportionate share of readers' attention. Elias's own contribution is rather the argument in the second volume to the effect that the rise of self-control (and more generally, of social integration) is to be explained in political terms, that it was an unintended consequence of the monopoly of force associated with the centralized state. The rise of the centralized or 'absolute' state, which turned the nobles from warriors into courtiers, is in turn explained by Elias as an unintended consequence of the competition for power between small states in the Middle Ages.

The work of Elias has become increasingly influential in historical as well as sociological circles in recent years. It is, however, vulnerable to certain criticisms. Unlike Weber, Elias illustrates his theory from European history alone, leaving the reader in doubt about its generality. One wonders whether a similar process of civilization might be identified

[51] Klaniczay (1990a).

in China (say), or in India (both arenas of competition between small states at some periods in their history).

A more serious criticism of Elias is that his central concept, 'civilization', is problematic. If civilization is defined simply in terms of the existence of shame or self-control, then it is difficult to find any society which is not civilized. Indeed, it is impossible to demonstrate that medieval warriors, or the inhabitants of the so-called 'primitive' societies, felt less shame or embarrassment than Westerners, rather than exhibiting these qualities in different situations.[52] On the other hand, if 'civilization' is defined with more precision, a different kind of difficulty arises. How can one chart the rise of civilization in Europe if the standards of civilization were themselves changing? Despite these disagreements, the continuing relevance of Elias's study to any theory of social change will be obvious.

(2) Michel Foucault's *Discipline and Punish* (1975) is another monograph with strong implications for theory. Like an earlier study by the same author, *Madness and Civilization* (1961), it is concerned with Western Europe in the period 1650–1800. Foucault tells the story of a major shift in theories of punishment, from retribution to deterrence, and also in the practice of punishment, from 'spectacle' to 'surveillance'. The author rejects explanations of the abolition of public executions in humanitarian terms, as he had rejected such explanations of the rise of lunatic asylums. Instead, he stresses the rise of what he calls the 'disciplinary society', increasingly visible from the later seventeenth century onwards in barracks, factories and schools no less than in prisons. As a vivid illustration of this new type of society he chooses Jeremy Bentham's famous project for the 'Panopticon', the ideal prison in which one warder can see everything while himself remaining unseen. At times, Foucault seems to be turning modernization theory on its head, writing about the rise of discipline instead of the rise of liberty. All the same, his vision of a repressively bureaucratic society has something important in common with that of Max Weber.[53]

There is obviously no place for the 'process of civilization' in Foucault's account of social change. All that varies is the mode of repression – physical repression in the old regime, psychological repression later. The cooler and more clinical term 'displacement' is substituted for the conventional idea of 'progress'.

[52] Duerr (1988–90).
[53] O'Neill (1986).

Foucault's work has often been criticized by historians, both fairly and unfairly. Literary historians are unhappy with the way he uses literature as a source for the history of mentalities, art historians with his use of art, while traditional historians disapprove on principle of sources which are not official 'documents'. As for *Discipline and Punish*, its conclusions have been said to have 'no base in archival research'.[54] Another criticism of Foucault by historians fastens on his insensitivity to local variation, his tendency to illustrate generalizations about Europe with French examples as if different regions did not have their own time-scales.

If we think of Foucault as offering a simple model of change rather than telling the whole story, these criticisms become virtually irrelevant. However, this redefinition of the author's purpose does not dispose of a third damaging criticism of his work, its failure to discuss the mechanics of change. A leader in the movement which proclaimed the 'death of man', or at least the 'decentring of the subject', Foucault seems to have shrunk from testing the theory by examining the intentions of the reformers of punishment, demonstrating that the new system which resulted had nothing to do with these intentions, and revealing what had really produced it. The task is of course an extremely intractable one, but if someone claims to be sweeping away traditional historical explanations, it is not unreasonable to expect that person to perform it.

In my own view, what is most valuable in Foucault's work in general and in *Discipline and Punish* in particular is the negative rather than the positive side. After his corrosive criticisms of the conventional wisdom, the history of incarceration, sexuality and so on will never be the same again. Nor will the theory of social change, since Foucault has revealed its associations with the belief in progress which he has done so much to undermine. Those who reject his answers are unable to escape his questions.

(3) The late Fernand Braudel did not have to wait half as long for recognition as Norbert Elias. His study of the Mediterranean world in the age of Philip II of Spain made him famous in France as soon as it was published in 1949. It is only relatively recently, however, that the relevance of his work to social theorists has been perceived, at least outside France, where Braudel debated long ago with the sociologist Georges Gurvitch.[55] Yet the point which Braudel was most concerned

---

[54] Spierenburg (1984), 108.
[55] Braudel (1949).

to emphasize in his huge monograph was not an argument about Philip II or even the Mediterranean, but a thesis concerning social change, or as the author himself put it, the nature of time. It was perhaps for this reason that Paul Ricoeur has described Braudel's book as a narrative, despite the author's low opinion of events.[56]

Braudel's central idea is that historical changes take place at different speeds. He distinguishes three such speeds and devotes a section of his book to each. First is the time of 'geohistory', the relation between humans and their environment, 'a history whose passage is almost imperceptible . . . a history of constant repetition, ever-recurring cycles' (Braudel calls this *histoire structurale*). Secondly, the time of 'economic systems, states, societies and civilizations', with its 'slow but perceptible rhythms' (*histoire conjoncturelle*). Thirdly, the fast-moving time of events and individuals, the subject of traditional narrative history (*histoire événementielle*), which Braudel regards as superficial, interesting only for what it reveals about the forces underlying it.

The first or geohistorical part of the book is the most revolutionary, but it is the second part which is most relevant here, concerned as it is with change in economic, political and social structures. For example, Braudel argues that the social distance between the rich and the poor was increasing in the second half of the sixteenth century, in both the western (or Christian) and the eastern (or Muslim) halves of the Mediterranean. 'Society was tending to polarize itself into, on the one hand, a rich and vigorous nobility reconstituted into powerful dynasties owning vast properties, and on the other, the great and growing mass of the poor and disinherited.'

This last passage is reminiscent of Marx, for whom Braudel frequently expressed respect. However, a major difference between their views of early modern Europe needs to be stressed at this point. The rise of the bourgeoisie is central to Marx's account of the period. Braudel, on the contrary, is concerned with what he calls the 'defection' of the bourgeoisie, or their 'bankruptcy' (*faillite de la bourgeoisie*). In the Mediterranean world at least, the merchants of this period often turned their backs on trade, acquired land, behaved like nobles and sometimes went so far as to buy titles. In other words – a paradox for supporters of modernization theory – this period was less modern than the one before it. In fact Braudel tended to think in terms not of progress but of cycles, an alternation of phases of expansion and phases of contraction ('A phases' and 'B phases', to use the language of the French economist

---

[56] Ricoeur (1983–5), 1, 138ff.

François Simiand). If *The Mediterranean* illustrates any sociological theory of change, it is surely that of Pareto, whose theory of the 'circulation of elites' involved the alternation of 'speculators' and 'rentiers'.

For a historian, one of the most obvious and at the same time the most fundamental criticisms of sociological models of change is that they are too shallow, in the sense of placing too much emphasis on the relatively short term, a generation, a mere thirty years or so. Despite its focus on the reign of Philip II (1556–98), Braudel's work is the most important single book to place on the other side of the scale, together with a famous article in which the author made his views on the long term (*la longue durée*) more explicit and tried to open a dialogue with the social sciences (to which the French sociologist Georges Gurvitch responded).[57] Braudel's view of history is open to criticism on a number of grounds. He surely went too far in his dismissal of events, their capacity for subverting structures. His determinism was also carried to considerable lengths. He viewed individuals as prisoners of destiny, their attempts to influence the course of affairs as ultimately futile. He has both inspired his successors and provoked them to react against his model of social change.

(4) The most brilliant of these successors, Emmanuel Le Roy Ladurie, has studied change over more than two centuries in a Mediterranean region in a large monograph which focuses on the peasants of Languedoc. Like Braudel, Le Roy Ladurie is fascinated by geography – he has written on the history of climate.[58] However, his book on Languedoc is closer to what might be called 'ecohistory' than to Braudel's 'geohistory', because its central concern is with the relation between social groups and their physical environment. Le Roy Ladurie places more emphasis on demography than Braudel did. In his model, which owes something to Malthus and Ricardo, something to twentieth-century economics (notably Konradtieff's idea of 'long waves'), and something to contemporary social anthropology, the real motor of social change is population.

Le Roy Ladurie's study of Languedoc focuses on what the author calls 'a great agrarian cycle, lasting from the end of the fifteenth century to the beginning of the eighteenth'. The basic pattern in this period is one of growth leading to decline (which in turn led to recovery). In phase A (to return to Simiand's formulation), in other words the phase

[57] Braudel (1958); Gurvitch (1957, 1964).
[58] Le Roy Ladurie (1966).

of expansion, a population explosion took place, followed by land clearance, the subdivision of farms, a price rise and what Le Roy Ladurie calls 'a victory of profit' at the expense of rent and wages, in other words a victory of the class living from profit, the entrepreneurs. In the seventeenth century, however, agricultural productivity hit a ceiling, and as a result all the main economic and social trends went into reverse, in a classic example of a B-phase. As the population began to press on the means of subsistence it stopped growing (and later in the century, declined), owing to famine, plague, emigration and a later age of marriage. Profit was defeated by rent, the speculator – to return to the language of Pareto – by the rentier. Holdings which had been fragmented were united once more. Looking at the period 1500–1700 as a whole, Le Roy Ladurie suggests that the region functioned as a 'homeostatic ecosystem'.

Although this model of change is fundamentally ecological and demographic, there is a place in it for culture. As the author explains, 'The forces that first deflected the expansion, then checked it and ultimately broke it were not only economic in a narrow sense but also cultural', in a wide sense of the term 'culture' which includes 'the customs, the way of life, the mentality of a people'. Customs of inheritance, for example. The peasants of Languedoc practised 'partible inheritance', in other words the division of the estate among all the children, so that population growth accentuated the fragmentation of properties. As for mentalities, Le Roy Ladurie discusses the spread of literacy and Calvinism in Languedoc with reference to Max Weber's famous thesis about the interdependence of Protestantism and capitalism.

There is also a place in this model for the history of events which Braudel dismissed. Le Roy Ladurie offers the reader vivid vignettes of social conflict and social protest in order to show how contemporaries perceived social change and how they reacted to it. In phase A, for example, we hear about the carnival of Romans in Dauphiné in 1580, during which craftsmen and peasants declared that the elite of their town 'had grown rich at the expense of the poor people' (the author later made this dramatic event the focus of a book-length study in microhistory[59]). In phase B, the phase of contraction, Le Roy Ladurie discusses the revolt of the Vivarais in 1670, under the traditional slogan 'Long live the king, down with the tax-officials' as an example of 'a more instinctive than rational reaction to the rural crisis'. Whether or

[59] Le Roy Ladurie (1979).

not they have much influence on the restructuration of their society, these social agents are deeply involved in the process.

If there is a general lesson to be drawn from the Languedoc book, it is that in preindustrial societies the most important factor in social change is the growth or decline in population. A similar argument was put forward by the late Michael Postan in a study of medieval England which had much to say about the results of the Black Death. This Malthusian model (or 'neo-Malthusian model', as Le Roy Ladurie prefers to call it), has been criticized by some historians, notably by some Marxists, who argue that both Postan and Le Roy Ladurie have underestimated the importance of class conflict in the societies they studied. However, other Marxist historians, especially in France, have revised their own models to take more account of demography.[60]

(5) In his study of Peru after the Spanish conquest, another French historian, Nathan Wachtel, is also concerned with the place of demography in social change. However, the main reason for turning to his monograph at this point is that it deals with change introduced from outside a given society. Wachtel's main theme is the 'crisis provoked by the conquest'. The key terms in his account of social and cultural change between 1530 and 1580 are 'destructuration' (a term he appropriated from the Italian sociologist Vittorio Lanternari), and 'acculturation' (a term taken, as we have seen, from American anthropology).[61]

By 'destructuration' (a term also used by Gurvitch), Wachtel means the snapping of the links between different parts of the traditional social system. Traditional institutions and customs survived the conquest, but the old structure disintegrated. Tribute survived, for example, but without the old system of redistribution by the state of which it had formed a part. Local chiefs also survived, but their relation to the central government was no longer what it had been in the days of the Incas. Traditional religion survived, but it was now an unofficial, indeed a clandestine cult, regarded as 'idolatry' by the Spanish missionaries, who did all they could to uproot it. Specialists in what Bourdieu calls 'symbolic violence' (above, p. 86), the Spanish clergy were in effect missionaries of sociocultural change or restructuration.

Wachtel has a good deal to say about agency as well as about structure. He discusses the responses of the Indians to the changes taking place in their society in terms of 'acculturation', a term which he

[60] Postan (1972); Aston and Philpin (1985); Bois (1976).
[61] Wachtel (1971a); cf. Wachtel (1974); Lanternari (1966); Dupront (1965).

redefines – with the help of Lanternari and Gramsci – as culture contact in a situation in which one culture is dominant and the other sub-ordinate. Some of the Indians accepted the values of their conquerors, while others resisted, like the participants in the millenarian movement of Taqui Ongo in defence of the traditional gods. Some changed in order to remain the same, like the Araucans, who adopted the horse the better to resist the Spaniards, who had introduced the animal to America. Apparent acceptance of Spanish culture sometimes masked the persistence, conscious or unconscious, of traditional mentalities. For example, the chronicler Guaman Poma de Ayala inserted a great deal of information from Western sources into his history of Peru, but the fundamental categories of his thought, such as his conceptions of space and time, remained indigenous.[62]

An important feature of Wachtel's version of acculturation is that it is concerned not only with 'objective' culture contact, but also with what he calls the 'vision of the vanquished', in other words the sub-ordinate's image of the dominant culture. In other words, he is no simple diffusionist. His concern for the political context of culture contact and his interest in the ways in which members of the two cultures perceive one another give the old acculturation model a new, sharp cutting edge, making it explanatory as well as descriptive.

The model is sometimes employed by historians of Western societies. The pioneer in this regard was the American Oscar Handlin, whose book on immigrants to Boston, subtitled 'a study in acculturation', dates back as far as 1941.[63] In similar fashion, Le Roy Ladurie has described the revolt of the Protestants of the Cévennes at the beginning of the eighteenth century (a reaction to the outlawing of Protestantism by Louis XIV) as a protest against 'deculturation'.

Again, Robert Muchembled has discussed the 'acculturation of the rural world' in north-east France at the end of the sixteenth century, noting that the rise in witch-trials coincided with the Counter-Reformation attack on 'idolatry' as well as the spread of literacy. The centre (or the clergy) was trying to change the values of the periphery (or the laity). In this respect the process of socio-cultural change in the Cambrésis resembled that in Peru.

On the other hand, to speak of 'acculturation' assumes that clergy and people belonged to different cultures, an assumption which is surely exaggerated. They may have belonged to different 'sub-cultures' (above,

[62] Wachtel (1971b).
[63] Handlin (1941).

p. 124) with a common frame of reference. The cultural distance between the two may have been increasing, at a time when a greater proportion of the clergy were being educated in seminaries, but this distance is unlikely to have been anything like as great as that between the Spanish clergy and the Indians they were trying to convert. In this sense the use of the term 'acculturation' by historians of Europe is misleading. It might be better to approach the problem of conversion as a case of the 'negotiation' of meanings between groups discussed earlier (p. 87).[64]

(6) Another ingenious variation on the acculturation model is offered by the Chicago anthropologist Marshall Sahlins, in an account which takes its point of departure from the arrival in Hawaii of Captain Cook in 1779. His account may be broken down into four parts or stages, from narrative via interpretation and analysis to general theory.

i   On his visit to Hawaii, Cook received an enthusiastic welcome on the part of some thousands of people, who came to meet him in their canoes. He was escorted to a temple and participated in a ritual in which he was worshipped. A few weeks later he returned to the island, and his reception was much cooler. The Hawaiians committed a series of thefts and in attempting to put a stop to them, Cook was killed. Some years later, however, the new chief Kamehameha decided on a policy of friendship and commercial relations with Britain.

ii   Sahlins interprets Cook's reception (or more exactly, the various accounts of these incidents) with the hypothesis that the Hawaiians saw Cook as an incarnation of their god Lono, since he arrived at the time when the god was expected. He goes on to suggest that the murder as well as the worship of Cook was a ritual act, the slaying of the god. He interprets the pro-British policies of Kamehameha as appropriate for the man who had inherited Cook's charisma, his *mana*.[65]

iii   Sahlins utilizes this interpretation to comment in a more general way on what he calls the interaction between systems and events, making two complementary points. In the first place, the events which took place were 'ordered by culture'. The Hawaiians perceived Cook through the lens of their own cultural tradition and acted accordingly, thus giving the events a distinctive cultural 'signature'. In this respect, Sahlins is close to Braudel's view of events. On the other hand, unlike Braudel, he goes on to suggest that in the process of assimilating these events, of 'reproducing that contact in its own image', Hawaiian culture

[64] Muchembled (1978, 1984); Burke (1982); Wirth (1984).
[65] Sahlins (1985), 104–35.

'changed radically and decisively'. For example, the tension between chiefs and commoners increased because the distinction between the two groups was overlaid by the distinction between European and Hawaiian. The response of the chiefs was to adopt English names such as 'King George' or 'Billy Pitt', as if to make the point that chiefs are to people as Europeans are to Hawaiians – in other words, the dominant partner in the relationship.

iv   Finally, Sahlins moves to a general discussion of social or historical change, noting how every conscious attempt to prevent change or even to adapt to it brought other changes in its train, and concluding that all cultural reproduction involves alteration. Cultural categories are always at risk when they are used to interpret the world.[66]

There are some intriguing analogies between this historical anthropology of a Polynesian island and a recent study of the historical anthropology of a European island, Kirsten Hastrup's study of Iceland. Hastrup too uses her case-study to make general points about structure and change and she too emphasizes the way in which 'strategies of adaptation' contributed to the process of change which they were designed to limit, so that 'the social reactions to disruptive development themselves contributed to disruption'.[67] Her analysis makes much use of the ambiguous notion of 'contradiction', whether in social categories, in society itself, or in the relation between the two.

Juxtaposing the two islands encourages the reader to ask each author questions provoked by the other's work, to take a closer look at contradictions in Hawaiian culture, for example. It also encourages questions about the extent to which it is possible to generalize from the example of these islands. Is Hawaii a privileged or an eccentric example of culture contact? Is culture contact a privileged or an eccentric way of studying social change? Are Sahlins's generalizations about the relation between structures and events valid in contexts as remote from his 'field' as the German Reformation, say, or the French Revolution?

Conclusions

It is clear that the six case-studies have many implications for the study of social change. By way of conclusion I should like to comment on a few of these implications, concentrating on three false dichotomies, the

---

[66] Sahlins (1981; 1985, vii–xvii, 136–56).
[67] Hastrup (1985), 230.

classical binary oppositions between continuity and change, between internal and external factors, and finally between structures and events.

(1) Conceptions of change imply conceptions of continuity. Continuity used to be described in negative terms as mere 'inertia', but the case-studies suggest more positive ways of characterizing it. For example, Elias's concern with table manners implies the importance of child training as part of the process of civilization. Child training is necessary to enable cultural 'reproduction' (above, p. 125), but may also be an effective means of change.

This is perhaps the best place to introduce the idea of a 'generation', an idea which has long fascinated historians and sociologists alike. One reason for the fascination is that the concept seems to reflect our own experience of growing up and defining ourselves collectively in contrast to older people. Another is that it promises to link events to changes in structures via the sense of belonging to a particular age-group; the generation of 1789, for example ('Bliss was it in that dawn to be alive/But to be young was very heaven'), or the Spanish generation of 1898 (which experienced the end of an empire). There have been some interesting discussions of what might be called the theory of the generation, notably Karl Mannheim's emphasis on what he called 'a common location in the social and historical process' in creating a particular world-view or mentality.[68]

The theory has often not been translated into practice, however, and the few case-studies are mainly concerned with the history of art and literature.[69] An interesting exception to the rule is an anthropological study of a small town in Aragon, carried out in the 1960s, which distinguishes three groups – the 'declining', 'controlling' and 'emerging' generations – in terms of reactions to the formative, not to say traumatic, events of the Spanish Civil War. The first group formed their attitudes before the war, the second participated in the fighting, while the third is too young to remember it. Although these contrasts extend well beyond the political sphere, it is tempting to explain them in political terms. The problem is that to assess the importance of the events of 1936–9 in the split between generations we would need to look at a similar town which did not experience the Civil War.[70]

Another reformulation of the concept of continuity has been offered

[68] Mannheim (1952), 276–320.
[69] Pinder (1926); Peyre (1948); Burke (1972), 230–6; Ramsden (1974).
[70] Lisón-Tolosana (1966), 190–201; cf. Spitz (1967).

by Le Roy Ladurie, who discusses what he calls 'history without move-ment' (*histoire immobile*), in other words cyclical movements, economic or demographic, within a given 'homeostatic system'. The obvious question to ask at this point is, What breaks the cycle? In many cases it is the intrusion of an external factor.

(2) This intrusion from outside is particularly clear in the cases dis-cussed by Wachtel and Sahlins. However, as we have seen, their explanations of change in Peru and Hawaii are not given in external terms alone. On the contrary, both authors emphasize the relation or 'fit' between endogenous and exogenous factors, in a similar way to the reception theorists discussed earlier (p. 97). Let us hope that future models of social change will discuss what makes some societies relatively open (or, shall we say, vulnerable) to influences from outside, while others are better able to resist these influences – indeed are unable to do anything else. Braudel devoted some pages of his *Mediterranean* to this problem, though he did not go beyond the antithetical generalizations that 'a living civilization must be able not only to give but to receive and to borrow', while 'a great civilization can also be recognized by its refusal to borrow'. But what is it that determines the 'choice' (and whose choice is it?) between the acceptance or the rejection of foreign invaders, foreign technology, foreign ideas?

Africanists have gone somewhat further in explaining why some peoples – the Ibo, for instance – display remarkable receptivity to change, while others, like the Pakot, show equally remarkable resist-ance. They contrast highly integrated cultures, which tend to be closed, with others which are less integrated and therefore more open.[71]

It also appears that a tradition of receptivity to foreign influence can be built up over time. The Japanese, for example, used to adapt Chinese ideas, practices and institutions long before their encounter with the West. Yet it might be unwise to offer an explanation of this tradition of innovation in terms of the Japanese character, without investigating differences between social groups or indeed between cultural domains.

The sociological concept of 'cultural lag' has largely dropped out of use, condemned as descriptive rather than explanatory.[72] All the same, it does have the advantage of reminding users that different social groups (urban and rural, metropolitan and provincial, and so on) or the

---

[71] Braudel (1949), 2, 764; Ottenberg (1959); Schneider (1959).
[72] Ogburn (1923).

different spheres or domains of a culture (religious, political, economic), do not necessarily change at the same time.

(3) The relation between events and structures has been highlighted in recent social theory, notably in Anthony Giddens's discussion of 'structuration'.[73] The authors of the case-studies see this relation in various ways. For Braudel, events are nothing but froth and foam, affected by changes in the deep structures but having little or no effect on them in return. Le Roy Ladurie describes the responses of the peasants to the economic '*conjoncture*' with much more interest and sympathy than Braudel. Riots and revolts – typical examples of 'reactive' social movements (above, p. 90) – occupy a significant portion of his book. However, he too assumes that events reflect structures rather than changing them.

The destructive and creative functions of events receive more emphasis in the work of Wachtel and Sahlins. In similar fashion, in a review of a study of the peasants in the age of the French Revolution, Le Roy Ladurie refers to the possibility of an event acting as a 'catalyst' or a 'matrix' (*événement-matrice*). Yet the mixture of metaphors seems to betray a certain hesitation on the part of the author.[74]

The idea that crises such as wars and revolutions act as catalysts or accelerators, speeding up social change rather than initiating it, has been explored in more detail by two historians who look at the First World War from opposite sides. Arthur Marwick suggests that the events of 1914–18 encouraged the 'blurring' of social distinctions in Britain, while Jürgen Kocka argues that in Germany, the 'same' events made social distinctions still more sharp.[75] The two societies reacted to the war in opposite ways because their prewar structures were very different. In a similar manner, the financial problems for both sides arising from the protracted wars between Britain and France in the age of Louis XIV seem to have accentuated existing differences between the two states, making the French monarchy still more 'absolute' while leading to a reduction in the power of the British king.[76]

The six case-studies above have little to say about the role which individuals or groups may play in shaping events. Although Sahlins, for

---

[73] Giddens (1979, 1984); Thompson (1984), 148–72; Bryant and Jary (1991).
[74] Le Roy Ladurie (1972).
[75] Marwick (1965); Kocka (1973).
[76] Mousnier (1951).

example, gives the impression that Kamehameha was a leader of considerable ability, he does not discuss the extent of the Hawaiian chief's room for manoeuvre between the structures. Braudel is characteristically the most explicit and the most negative in this respect. The 'hero' of his book, Philip II, is more of an anti-hero, powerless to change the course of history. Suppose, however, that Braudel had chosen to write about Russia in the age of Lenin. Would he have found it so easy to play down the role of the individual in history? A theory of social change surely needs to grapple with this question, and discuss the ways in which the decisions of individuals and small groups influence social development.

Two contrasting examples from the history of Japan may help to illuminate this problem. It is obvious that rulers are no more able to hold back social change than Canute was able to hold back the waves (this was actually the point that the king was making to his courtiers by taking them to the seashore). All the same, rulers have attempted to do this. In seventeenth-century Japan, for instance, at a time when towns were growing and trade expanding, the Tokugawa regime tried to freeze the social structure with a decree that the four main social groups should rank in the following order: samurai, peasants, craftsmen and merchants. As one might have expected, the decree did not prevent wealthy merchants from achieving an unofficial social status higher than many samurai.

On the other hand, the abolition of the samurai by the Meiji regime which replaced that of the Tokugawa in 1868 was a decree with important social consequences. For example, many ex-samurai went into business, a career previously closed to them.[77] Why did the Meiji succeed while the Tokugawa failed? The obvious answer is that one regime tried to resist change, the other to assist it. However, it might be worth exploring the possibility that the Meiji were doing more than assist the inevitable; that their regime was concerned with what might be called the 'management' of social change – not so much giving orders to the waves as diverting the stream in the direction they preferred.

In Giuseppe de Lampedusa's great historical novel *The Leopard* (1958), set in Sicily in the middle of the nineteenth century, one aristocrat remarks to another that 'in order to keep everything as it is we have to change everything'. Some aristocracies (notably the British) seem to have had a talent for this kind of adaptation to new circumstances, for making sacrifices or tactical concessions in the interests of a

[77] Moore (1966), 275–90.

strategy of the survival of the family or the class over the long term. Such activities surely deserve a place in any general theory of social change.

One might also hope that the theory might also specify the types of situation in which a strategy of this kind has a chance of success. Two independent studies of aristocratic behaviour, concerned respectively with nineteenth-century England and twentieth-century Rajasthan, offer remarkably similar accounts of one such situation. Both studies describe a ruling class which was split between an upper group which was more sympathetic to change and a lower group which had more to lose from it. However, in both cases the lower group traditionally looked to the upper group for leadership. In this situation it was very difficult for the group with most to lose to organize resistance to change. Hence the ruling class as a whole followed the 'adaptation' policy of its leaders and social change took place without violence.[78]

If individuals, groups and events have an important place in the process of social change, the form no less than the content of the analysis (whether it is offered by social historians, sociologists or social anthropologists) may be in need of revision. In fact the turn (or return) to narrative has been the object of much recent discussion in all three disciplines. The problem might be posed in the form of a dilemma. The analysis of structures is too static and does not allow either writers or readers to be sufficiently aware of change. On the other hand, traditional historical narrative is unable to accommodate these structures at all. A search is therefore under way for new forms of narrative appropriate for social history.

One might call this the search for a 'braided' narrative, since it interweaves analysis with storytelling.[79] Alternatively, one might speak of 'thick' narrative, on the model of Geertz's 'thick description', on the grounds that the new forms need to be constructed to bear a heavier weight of explanation than the old (concerned as they were with the actions of prominent individuals). The new forms – new for historians at any rate – include stories which present the same events from multiple points of view (p. 128) or deal with the experience of ordinary people at the local level in what might be called 'micronarratives'.[80]

The turn to microhistory was discussed in an earlier chapter (above, p. 38). Sometimes it takes the form of a description, as in Le

---

[78] F. M. L. Thompson (1963); Rudolph and Rudolph (1966).
[79] Fischer (1976).
[80] Burke (1991).

Roy Ladurie's study of the community of Montaillou, but it can also take the form of a story. One of the most dramatic of such stories concerns Martin Guerre. Martin was a peasant from south-western France who ran away from the family farm to serve in the wars with Spain, returning to discover that his place had been taken by an intruder, a man who claimed to be him. The story has been retold by the historian Natalie Davis not only for its dramatic qualities but also to shed light on social structures, including the structure of the family, and on the way in which these structures were experienced in everyday life. In her account the central figure is not so much Martin as his wife, Bertrande de Rols. Abandoned by her husband, she was neither wife nor widow. Davis suggests that Bertrande's decision to recognize the intruder, for whatever reason, as her long-lost husband, was the only honourable way for her to escape from this impossible situation.[81]

The potential of this method for the study of social and cultural structures is only beginning to be worked out. Hence this is not the moment for closure, for a final verdict on the experiment. Like a number of issues explored here, the question of narrative remains open.

Like its predecessor of 1981, this essay is a conscious attempt to occupy the middle ground between what David Hume used to call 'enthusiasm' and 'superstition' – in this case the uncritical zeal for new approaches and the blind devotion to traditional practice. I hope that it will persuade historians to take social theory more seriously than many currently do, and social theorists to take a greater interest in history.

It will be clear by now, if it was not obvious from the start, that empiricists and theorists are not two closeknit groups but two ends of a spectrum. Conceptual borrowing tends to take place from neighbouring disciplines on the theoretical side. Thus historians may borrow from anthropologists, who borrow from linguists, who borrow from mathematicians.

In return, historians, like ethnographers, offer reminders of the complexity and variety of human experience and institutions which theories inevitably simplify. This variety does not imply that theorists are wrong to simplify. As I tried to argue above (p. 28), simplification is their function, their specific contribution to the division of labour between approaches and disciplines. What this variety does suggest, however, is that theory can never be 'applied' to the past.

[81] Davis (1983).

What theory can do, on the other hand, is to suggest new questions for historians to ask about 'their' period, or new answers to familiar questions. Theories too come in an almost infinite variety which poses problems for would-be users. In the first place, there is the problem of choosing between rival theories, generally on the grounds of the more or less close fit between the general theory and the specific problem. There is also the problem of reconciling the theory and its implications with the whole conceptual apparatus of the borrower. This essay may well appear to some of its more philosophical readers to have been an apologia for eclecticism, a charge often levelled (sometimes with justice) against historians who appropriate other people's concepts and theories for use in their own work. So far as this essay is concerned, however, I deny the charge, at least if eclecticism is defined as the attempt to hold inconsistent propositions simultaneously. If, on the other hand, the term means no more than finding ideas in different places, then I am happy to confess to being an eclectic. To be open to new ideas, wherever they come from, and to be capable of adapting them to one's own purposes and of finding ways to test their validity might be said to be the mark of a good historian and a good theorist alike.

BIBLIOGRAPHY

Abercrombie, N., Hill, S. and Turner, B.S. (1980) *The Dominant Ideology Thesis*, London.

Abrams, P. (1980) 'History, Sociology, Historical Sociology', *Past and Present*, 87, 3–16.

Abrams, P. (1982) *Historical Sociology*, Shepton Mallett.

Adorno, T., Frenkel-Brunswick, E. and Levinson, D.J. (1950) *The Authoritarian Personality*, New York.

Agar, M. (1990) 'Text and Fieldwork', *Journal of Contemporary Ethnography*, 19, 73–88.

Allport, G. and Postman, L. (1945) 'The Basic Psychology of Rumour'; rpr. in W. Schramm (ed.), *The Process and Effect of Mass Communication*, Urbana, Ill., 1961, 141–55.

Almond, G. A. and Verba, S. (1963) *The Civic Culture*, Princeton, NJ.

Althusser, L. (1970) 'Ideology and Ideological State Apparatuses'; English trans. in his *Lenin and Philosophy*, London, 1971, 121–73.

Anderson, B. (1983) *Imagined Communities*; rev. edn London, 1991.

Anderson, B. (1990) *Language and Power*, Ithaca, NY.

Anderson, P. (1974a) *Passages from Antiquity to Feudalism*, London.

Anderson, P. (1974b) *Lineages of the Absolutist State*, London.

Anderson, P. (1990) 'A Culture in Contraflow', *New Left Review*, 180, 41–80.

Ardener, E. (1975) 'Belief and the Problem of Women', in S. Ardener (ed.), *Perceiving Women*, London, 1–27.

Ariès, P. (1960) *Centuries of Childhood*; English trans. New York, 1962.

Arnheim, R. (1962) review of Gombrich (1960), *Art Bulletin*, 44, 75–9.

Aron, R. (1965) *Main Currents in Sociological Thought*; 2nd edn Harmondsworth, 1968.

Arriaza, A. (1980) 'Mousnier, Barber and the "Society of Orders"', *Past and Present*, 89, 39–57.

Aston, T. H. and Philpin, C. H. E. (eds) (1985) *The Brenner Debate: Agrarian Class Structure and Economic Development in Preindustrial Europe*, Cambridge.

Atkinson, P. (1990) *The Ethnographic Imagination: Textual Constructions of Reality*, London.

Atsma, H. and Burguière, A. (eds) (1990) *Marc Bloch aujourd'hui*, Paris.

Attridge, D. (1987) *Post-Structuralism and the Question of History*, Cambridge.

Avineri, S. (1968) *Karl Marx on Colonialism*, New York.

Aya, R. (1990) *Rethinking Revolution and Collective Violence*, Amsterdam.

Bachrach, P. and Bratz, M. S. (1962) 'The Two Faces of Power', *American Political Science Review*, 56, 947–52.

Baechler, J., Hall, J. and Mann, M. (eds) (1988) *Europe and the Rise of Capitalism*, Oxford.

Bailey, P. (1978) 'Will the Real Bill Banks Please Stand Up? Towards a Role Analysis of Mid-Victorian Working-Class Respectability', *Journal of Social History*, 12, 336–53.

Baker, A. R. H. and Gregory, D. (eds) (1984) *Explorations in Historical Geography*, Cambridge.

Baker, K. M. (ed.) (1987) *The Political Culture of the Old Regime*, Oxford.

Bakhtin, M. (1952–3) 'The Problem of Speech Genres'; in *Speech Genres and Other Late Essays* (ed. C. Emerson and M. Holquist), Austin, Texas, 1986, 60–102.

Bakhtin, M. (1981) *The Dialogic Imagination*, Manchester.

Baran, P. (1957) *The Political Economy of Growth*, London.

Barber, B. (1957) *Social Stratification*, New York.

Barnes, J. (1947) 'The Collection of Genealogies', *Rhodes–Livingstone Journal*, 5, 48–55.

Barth, F. (1959) *Political Leadership among the Swat Pathans*, London.

Barthes, R. (1967) 'Historical Discourse', in Lane (1970), 145–55.

Bartlett, F. (1986) *Trial by Fire and Water*, Oxford.

Bell, D. (1976) The *Cultural Contradictions of Capitalism*, London.

Bellah, R. J. (1957) *Tokugawa Religion*, Glencoe, Ill.

Bellah, R. J. (1959) 'Durkheim and History', *American Sociological Review*, 24; rpr. in R. A. Nisbet (ed.), *Emile Durkheim*, Englewood Cliffs, NJ, 1965, 153–76.

Bendix, R. (1960) *Max Weber, an Intellectual Portrait*, New York.

Bendix, R. (1967) 'The Comparative Analysis of Historical Change'; rpr. in R. Bendix and G. Roth, *Scholarship and Partisanship*, Berkeley, Ca, 1971, 207–24.

Benedict, R. (1934) *Patterns of Culture*, Boston, Mass.

Bennett, W. L. (1983) 'Culture, Communication and Political Control', in M. J. Aronoff (ed.), *Culture and Political Change*, New Brunswick and London, ch. 3.

Bercé, Y. (1974) *History of Peasant Revolts*; abbr. trans. Cambridge, 1990.
Berger, P. and Luckmann, T. (1966) *The Social Construction of Reality*, New York.
Béteille, A. (1991) *Some Observations on the Comparative Method*, Amsterdam.
Bloch, M. (1924) *The Royal Touch*; English trans. London, 1973.
Bloch, M. (1928) 'A Contribution Towards a Comparative History of European Societies'; rpr. in his *Land and Work in Medieval Europe*, London, 1967, 44–76.
Bloch, M. (1939–40) *Feudal Society*; English trans. London, 1961.
Block, F. and Somers, M. A. (1984) 'Beyond the Economistic Fallacy', in Skocpol (1984), 47–84.
Boas, F. (1966) *Kwakiutl Ethnography* (ed. H. Codere), Chicago and London.
Bogucka, M. (1989) 'Le bourgeois et les investissements culturels', in A. Guarducci, (ed.), *Investimenti e civiltà urbana*, Florence, 571–84.
Bois, G. (1976) *The Crisis of Feudalism*; English trans. Cambridge, 1984.
Bourdieu, P. (1972) *Outlines of a Theory of Practice*; English trans. Cambridge, 1977.
Bourdieu, P. (1979) *Distinction*; English trans. Cambridge, Mass., 1984.
Bourdieu, P. (1984) 'Social Space and the Genesis of Classes', English trans. in his *Language and Symbolic Power*, Cambridge, 1991.
Bourdieu, P. and Passeron, J.-C. (1970) *Reproduction in Education Society and Culture*, London and Beverly Hills, Ca.
Boureau, A. (1984) *La légende dorée: le système narratif de Jacqes de Vorgaine*, Paris.
Braudel, F. (1949) *The Mediterranean and the Mediterranean World in the Age of Philip II*; 2nd edn 1966; English trans. London, 1972–3.
Braudel, F. (1958) 'History and Sociology'; English trans. in his *On History*, Chicago, 1980, 64–82.
Braudel, F. (1979) *Civilization and Capitalism*, 3 vols; English trans. London, 1980–2.
Bridenthal, R. and Koonz, C. (eds) (1977) *Becoming Visible: Women in European History*, Boston, Mass.
Brigden, S. (1982) 'Youth and the English Reformation', *Past and Present 95*, 37–67.
Briggs, A. (1960) 'The Language of Class'; rpr. in his *Collected Essays*, 2 vols, Brighton, 1985, vol. 1, 3–33.
Brown, P. (1971) *The World of Late Antiquity*, London.
Brown, P. (1975) 'Society and the Supernatural', *Daedalus*, 104, 133–47.
Brown, R. (1977) *A Poetic for Sociology*, Cambridge.
Bryant, C. G. A. and Jary, D. (1991) *Giddens' Theory of Structuration: a Critical Appreciation*, London and New York.
Bühler, A. (1965) *Kirche und Staat bei Rudolph Sohm*, Winterthur.
Bulhof, I. N. (1975) 'Johan Huizinga, Ethnographer of the Past', *Clio*, 4, 201–24.

Burckhardt, J. (1860) *Civilisation of the Renaissance in Italy*; English trans. 1875, new edn Harmondsworth, 1990.

Burke, P. (1972) *Culture and Society in Renaissance Italy*; 3rd edn *The Italian Renaissance: Culture and Society*, Cambridge, 1987.

Burke, P. (1973) 'L'histoire sociale des rêves', *Annales E. S. C.*, 28, 239–42.

Burke, P. (1974) *Venice and Amsterdam: a Study of Seventeenth-Century Elites*, London.

Burke, P. (1978) *Popular Culture in Early Modern Europe*, London.

Burke, P. (1982) 'A Question of Acculturation?', in P. Zambelli (ed.) *Scienze, credenze occulte, livelli di cultura*, Florence, 197–204.

Burke, P. (1986a) 'City-States', in Hall (1986), 137–53.

Burke, P. (1986b) 'Strengths and Weaknesses of the History of Mentalities', *History of European Ideas*, 7, 439–51.

Burke, P. (1987) *Historical Anthropology of Early Modern Italy*, Cambridge.

Burke, P. (1988) 'Ranke the Reactionary', *Syracuse Scholar*, 9, 25–30.

Burke, P. (1990) *The French Historical Revolution: The Annales School 1929–89*, Cambridge.

Burke, P. (1991) 'The History of Events and the Revival of Narrative', in P. Burke (ed.), *New Perspectives on Historical Writing*, Cambridge, 233–48.

Burke, P. (1992a) 'The Language of Orders', in Bush (1992), 1–12.

Burke (1992b) *The Fabrication of Louis XIV*, New Haven, Conn., and London.

Burke, P. and Porter, R. (eds) (1987) *The Social History of Language*, Cambridge.

Burke, P. and Porter, R. (eds) (1991) *Language, Self and Society*, Cambridge.

Burrow, J. W. (1965) *Evolution and Society*, Cambridge.

Burrow, J. W. (1981) *A Liberal Descent*, Cambridge.

Bush, M. (ed.) (1992) *Social Orders and Social Classes*, Manchester.

Butterfield, H. (1931) *The Whig Interpretation of History*, London.

Buttimer, A. (1969) 'Social Space in Interdisciplinary Perspective', *Geographical Review*, 59, 417–26.

Bynum, C. W. (1982) *Jesus as Mother*, Berkeley, Ca.

Campbell, C. (1987) *The Romantic Ethic and the Spirit of Modern Consumerism*, Oxford.

Campbell, C. (1990) 'Character and Consumption', *Culture and History*, 7, 37–48.

Carney, T. (1972) *Content Analysis*, London.

Carneiro da Cunha, M. (1986) *Negros, estrangeiros*, São Paulo.

Casey, J. (1989) *The History of the Family*, Oxford.

Castelnuovo, E. and Ginzburg, C. (1979) 'Centre and Periphery'; English trans. in *History of Italian Art*, forthcoming, Cambridge, 1992.

Castoriadis, C. (1975) *The Imaginary Institution of Society*; English trans. Cambridge, 1987.

Certeau, M. de, Revel, J. and Julia, D. (1976) *Une politique de la langue*, Paris.

Certeau, M. de (1980) *The Practice of Everyday Life*; English trans. Berkeley, Ca, 1984.

Chapin, F. S. (1935) *Contemporary American Institutions*, New York.

Charle, C. (1990) *Naissance des 'intellectuels' 1880–1900*, Paris.

Chartier, R. (1987) *The Cultural Uses of Print in Early Modern France*; English trans. Princeton, NJ, 1988.

Chartier, R. (1989) 'From the Social History of Culture to the Cultural History of Society', unpublished paper.

Chartier, R. (1991) *The Cultural Origins of the French Revolution*, Princeton, NJ.

Chayanov, A. V. (1925) *The Theory of the Peasant Economy* (ed. D. Thorner, B. Kerblay and R. E. F. Smith); rpr. Manchester, 1986.

Christaller, W. (1933) *Central Places in Southern Germany*; English trans. Englewood Cliffs, NJ, 1966.

Clarke, D. L. (1968) *Analytical Archaeology*, London.

Clarke, M. (1974) 'On the Concept of Sub-Culture', *British Journal of Sociology*, 25, 428–41.

Clifford, J. (1981) 'On Ethnographic Surrealism'; rpr. in his *The Predicament of Culture*, Cambridge, Mass., 1988, 92–113.

Clifford, J. (1986) 'On Ethnographic Self-Fashioning: Conrad and Malinowski', rpr. in his *The Predicament of Culture*, Cambridge, Mass., 1988, 117–51.

Clifford, J. and Marcus, G. (eds) (1986) *Writing Culture*, Berkeley, Ca.

Codere, H. (1950) *Fighting with property: a Study of Kwakiutl Potlatching and Warfare*, New York.

Cohen, A. P. (1985) *The Symbolic Construction of Community*, Chichester.

Cohen, G. (1978) *Karl Marx's Theory of History*, Oxford.

Cohen, P. S. (1969) 'Theories of Myth', *Man*, 4, 337–53.

Cohn, B. S. (1962) 'An Anthropologist among the Historians'; rpr. in *An Anthropologist among the Historians*, Delhi, 1987, 1–17.

Cohn, N. (1970) 'The Myth of Satan and his Human Servants', in M. Douglas (ed.), *Witchcraft: Confessions and Accusations*, London, 3–16.

Collingwood, R. G. (1935) 'The Historical Imagination'; rpr. in his *The Idea of History*, Oxford, 1946, 231–48.

Comte, A. (1864) *Cours de philosophie positive*, vol. 5, Paris.

Corfield, P. (ed.) (1991) *Language, History and Class*, Oxford.

Coser, L. (1956) *The Functions of Social Conflict*, London.

Coser, L. (1974) *Greedy Institutions*, New York.

Crosby, A. W. (1986) *Ecological Imperialism: the Biological Expansion of Europe 900–1900*, Cambridge.

Crow, T. (1985) *Painters and Public Life in Eighteenth-Century Paris*, New Haven, Conn., and London.

Culler, J. (1976) *Saussure*, London.

Culler, J. (1980) *The Pursuit of Signs*, London.

Culler, J. (1983) *On Deconstruction*, London.

Cunha, E. da (1902) *Rebellion in the Backlands*; English trans. Chicago, 1944.

Dahl, R. A. (1958) 'A Critique of the Ruling Elite Model', *American Political Science Review*, 52, 463–9.

Dahrendorf, R. (1957) *Class and Class Conflict in Industrial Society*; English trans. London, 1959.

Dahrendorf, R. (1964) 'Homo sociologicus', in his *Essays in the Theory of Society*, London, 19–87.

Darnton, R. (1984) *The Great Cat Massacre*, New York.

Darnton, R. (1991) 'History of Reading', in Burke (1991), 140–67.

Davis, K. (1959) 'The Myth of Functional Analysis as a Special Method in Sociology and Anthropology', *American Sociological Review*, 24, 757–72.

Davis, N. Z. (1971) 'The Reasons of Misrule', *Past and Present*, 50, 41–75; rpr. in her *Society and Culture in Early Modern France*, Stanford, Ca, and London, 1975, 97–123.

Davis, N. Z. (1979) 'Les conteurs de Montaillou', *Annales E. S. C.*, 34, 61–73.

Davis, N. Z. (1983) *The Return of Martin Guerre*, Cambridge, Mass.

Davis, N. Z. (1987) *Fiction in the Archives*, Cambridge.

Dekker, R. and Pol, L. van de (1989) *The Tradition of Female Transvestism in Early Modern Europe*, London.

Dening, G. (1971–3) 'History as a Social System', *Historical Studies*, 15, 673–85.

Derrida, J. (1967) *Of Grammatology*; English trans. Baltimore, Md, 1977.

Derrida, J. (1972) *Disseminations*; English trans. Chicago, 1981.

Devereux, G. (1959) 'Two Types of Modal Personality Model'; rpr. in N. J. Smelser and W. T. Smelser (eds), *Psychology and the Social Sciences*, New York, 1963, 22–32.

Devyver, A. (1973) *Le sang épuré: les préjugés de race chez les gentilshommes français de l'ancien régime*, Brussels.

Dews, P. (1987) *Logics of Distintegration*, London.

Dias, M.-O. Leite da Silva (1983) *Daily Life and Power in São Paulo in the Nineteenth Century*; English trans. Cambridge, 1992.

Dibble, V. K. (1960–1) 'The Comparative Study of Social Mobility', *Comparative Studies in Society and History*, 3, 315–19.

Dilthey, W. (1883) *Einleitung in der Geisteswissensachaften*, Leipzig.

Dodds, E. R. (1951) *The Greeks and the Irrational*, Berkeley, Ca.

Dollimore, J. (1991) *Sexual Dissidence*, Oxford.

Donajgrodzki, A. D. (ed.) (1977) *Social Control in Nineteenth-Century Britain*, London.

Dooley, B. (1990) 'From Literary Criticism to Systems Theory in Early Modern Journalism History', *Journal of the History of Ideas*, 51, 461–86.

Douglas, M. (1966) *Purity and Danger*, London.

Douglas, M. (ed.) (1987) *Constructive Drinking*, Cambridge/Paris.

Duby, G. (1968) 'The Diffusion of Cultural Patterns in Feudal Society', *Past and Present*, 39, 1–10.

Duby, G. (1973) *The Early Growth of the European Economy*; English trans. London, 1974.

Duby, G. (1978) *The Three Orders*; English trans. Chicago, 1980.

Duerr, H.-P. (1988–90) *Der Mythos von der Zivilisationsprozess*, Frankfurt.

Dumont, L. (1966) *Homo Hierarchicus*; English trans. London, 1972.

Dumont, L. (1977) *From Mandeville to Marx*, Chicago.

Dupront, A. (1965) 'De l'acculturation', 12th International Congress of Historical Sciences, Rapports, 1, 7–36; revised and enlarged as *L'acculturazione*, Turin, 1966.

Durkheim, E. (1893) *The Divison of Labour in Society*; English trans. 1933, rpr. Glencoe, Ill., 1964.

Durkheim, E. (1895) *Suicide*, English trans., London.

Durkheim, E. (1912) *Elementary Forms of the Religious Life*; English trans. 1915, rpr. New York, 1961.

Easton, D. (1965) *A Systems Analysis of Political Life*, New York.

Edelman, M. (1971) *Politics as Symbolic Action*, Chicago.

Eisenstadt, S. N. (1973) *Tradition, Change and Modernity*, New York.

Eisenstein, E. (1979) *The Printing Press as an Agent of Change*, Cambridge.

Elias, N. (1939) *The Civilizing Process*; English trans., 2 vols, Oxford, 1981–2.

Elias, N. (1987) 'The Retreat of Sociology into the Present', *Theory, Culture and Society*, 4, 223–47.

Elton, G. (1967) *The Practice of History*, London.

Erikson, E. (1958) *Young Man Luther*, New York.

Erikson, E. (1968) 'On the Nature of Psychohistorical Evidence', *Daedalus*, 695–730.

Erikson, E. (1970) *Gandhi's Truth*, London.

Erikson, K. (1970) 'Sociology and the Historical Perspective', *The American Sociologist*, 5.

Erikson, K. (1989) 'Sociological Prose', *Yale Review*, 78, 525–38.

Evans-Pritchard (1937) *Witchcraft, Oracles and Magic among the Azande*, Oxford.

Farge, A. and Revel, J. (1988) *The Rules of Rebellion*; English trans. Cambridge, 1991.

Femia, J. V. (1981) *Gramsci's Political Thought*, Oxford.

Finer, S. (1975) 'State- and Nation-Building in Europe: the Role of the Military', in Tilly (1975), 84–163.

Finnegan, R. (1973) 'Literacy versus Non-Literacy: the Great Divide', in R. Horton and R. Finnegan (eds), London, *Modes of Thought*, 112–44.

Firth, R. (ed.) (1967) *Themes in Economic Anthropology*, London.

Fischer, D. H. (1976) 'The Braided Narrative: Substance and Form in Social History', in A. Fletcher (ed.), *The Literature of Fact*, New York, 109–34.

Fishman, J. (1965) 'Who Speaks What Language to Whom and When', *La Linguistique*, 2, 67–88.

Fiske, J. (1989) *Understanding Popular Culture*, London.

Foster, G. (1960) *Culture and Conquest*, Chicago.

Foucault, M. (1961) *Madness and Civilization*; abbr. English trans. New York, 1965.

Foucault, M. (1966) *The Order of Things*; English trans. London, 1970.

Foucault, M. (1971) *L'ordre du discours*, Paris.

Foucault, M. (1975) *Discipline and Punish*; English trans. Harmondsworth, 1979.

Foucault, M. (1976–84) *History of Sexuality*; English trans. Harmondsworth, 1984–8.

Foucault, M. (1980) *Power/Knowledge* (ed. C. Gordon), London.

Fox-Genovese, E. (1988) *Within the Plantation Household*, Chapel Hill, NC.

Frank, A. Gunder (1967) *Capitalism and Underdevelopment in Latin America*, revised edn, Harmondsworth.

Freedberg, D. (1989) *The Power of Images*, Chicago.

Freyre, G. (1959) *Order and Progress*; English trans. New York, 1970.

Fromm, E. (1942) *The Fear of Freedom*, New York.

Frye, N. (1960) 'New Directions for Old'; rpr. in his *Fales of Identity*, New York, 1963, 52–66.

Fulbrook, M. and Skocpol, T. (1984) 'Destined Pathways: the Historical Sociology of Perry Anderson', in Skocpol (1984), 170–210.

Furet, F. and Ozouf, J. (1977) *Reading and Writing: Literacy in France from Calvin to Jules Ferry*; English trans. Cambridge, 1982.

Fussell, P. (1975) *The Great War and Modern Memory*, Oxford.

Gans, H. (1962) *The Urban Villagers: Group and Class in the Life of Italo-Americans*, New York.

Gay, P. (1985) *Freud for Historians*, New York.

Gearhart, S. (1984) *The Open Boundary of History and Fiction*, Princeton, NJ.

Geertz, C. (1973) *The Interpretation of Cultures*, New York.

Geertz, C. (1980) *Negara*, Princeton, NJ.

Geertz, C. (1983) *Local Knowledge*, New York.

Geertz, H. (1975) 'An Anthropology of Religion and Magic', *Journal of Interdisciplinary History*, 6, 71–89.

Gellner, E. (1968) 'Time and Theory in Social Anthropology'; rpr. in his *Cause and Meaning in the Social Sciences*, London, 1973, 88–106.

Gellner, E. (1974) *Legitimation of Belief*, Cambridge.

Gellner, E. (1981) *Muslim Society*, Cambridge.

Gellner, E. (1983) *Nations and Nationalism*, London.

Gellner, E. (1988) *Plough, Sword and Book*, London.

Gellner, E. and Waterbury, J. (eds) (1977) *Patrons and Clients in Mediterranean Societies*, London.

Gershenkron, A. (1962) *Economic Backwardness in Historical Perspective*, Cambridge, Mass.

Geuss, R. (1981) *The Idea of a Critical Theory*, Cambridge.

Giddens, A. (1979) *Central Problems in Social Theory*, London.

Giddens, A. (1984) *The Constitution of Society*, Cambridge.

Giddens, A. (1985) *The Nation-State and Violence*, Cambridge.

Giglioli, P. P. (ed.) (1972) *Language in Social Context*, Harmondsworth.

Gilbert, F. (1965) 'The Professionalization of History in the Nineteenth

Century', and 'The Professional Historian in Twentieth-Century Industrial Society, in J. Higham, L. Krieger and F. Gilbert (eds), *History*, Englewood Cliffs, NJ, 320–58.

Gilbert, F. (1975) 'Introduction' to Hintze (1975), 3–30.

Gilsenan, M. (1977) 'Against Patron-Client Relations', in Gellner and Waterbury (1977), 167–83.

Ginzburg, C. (1976) *Cheese and Worms*; English trans. London, 1980.

Ginzburg, C. (1984) 'Prove e possibilità', conclusion to the Italian translation of Davis (1983), 131–54.

Glick, T. F. and Pi-Sunyer, O. (1969) 'Acculturation as an Explanatory Concept in Spanish History', *Comparative Studies* in *Society and History*, 11, 136–54.

Gluckman, M. (1955) *Custom and Conflict in Africa*, Oxford.

Godelier, M. (1984) *The Mental and the Material*; English trans. London, 1986.

Goffman, E. (1958) *The Presentation of Self in Everyday Life*, New York.

Gombrich, E. H. (1953) 'The Social History of Art'; rpr. in his *Meditations on a Hobby Horse*, London, 1963, 86–94.

Gombrich, E. H. (1960) *Art and Illusion*, London.

Gombrich, E. H. (1969) *In Search of Cultural History*, Oxford.

Goode, W. J. (1963) *World Revolution and Family Patterns*, Glencoe, Ill.

Goody, J. (1969) 'Economy and Feudalism in Africa', *Economic History Review*, 22, 393–405.

Goody, J. (1977)*The Domestication of the Savage Mind*, Cambridge.

Goody, J. (1983) *The Development of the Family and Marriage in Europe*, Cambridge.

Goody, J. (1987) *The Interface between the Written and the Oral*, Cambridge.

Gray, R. Q. (1976) *The Labour Aristocracy in Victorian Edinburgh*, Oxford.

Greenblatt, S. (1988) *Shakespearian Negotiations*, Berkeley, Ca.

Greven, P. (1977) *The Protestant Temperament*, New York.

Grew, R. (1990) 'On the Current State of Comparative Studies', in Atsma and Burguière (1990), 323–34.

Grillo, R. (1989) *Dominant Languages*, Cambridge.

Guha, R. (1983) *Elementary Aspects of Peasant Insurgency*, Delhi.

Guha, R. and Spivak, G. C. (eds) (1988) *Selected Subaltern Studies*, New York.

Gurevich, A. Y. (1968) 'Wealth and Gift-Bestowal among the Ancient Scandinavians', *Scandinavica*, 7, 126–38.

Gurevich, A. Y. (1972) *Categories of Medieval Culture*; English trans. London, 1980.

Gurr, T. R. (1970) *Why Men Rebel*, Princeton, NJ.

Gurvitch, G. (1957) 'Continuité et discontinuité en histoire et en sociologie', *Annales E. S. C.*, 16, 73–84.

Gurvitch, G. (1964) *The Spectrum of Social Time*, Dordrecht.

Habermas, J. (1962) *Strukturwandel der Öffentlichkeit*; English trans. *The Structural Transformation of the Public Sphere*, Cambridge, 1989.

Habermas, J. (1968) *Knowledge and Human Interests*; English trans. Boston, Mass, 1971.

Habermas, J. (1981) 'Modernity v Postmodernity'; rpr. in H. Foster (eds.), *Postmodern Culture*, New York, 1983.

Hägerstrand, T. (1953) *Innovation Diffusion as a Spatial Process*; English trans. Chicago, 1967.

Hajnal, J. (1965) 'European Marriage Patterns in Perspective', in D. V. Glass and D. C. E. Eversley (eds), *Population in History*, London, 101–43.

Hall, J. A. (1985) *Powers and Liberties*, Oxford.

Hall, J. A. (ed.) (1986) *States in History*, Oxford.

Hall, J. A. (1988) 'States and Societies: the Miracle in Comparative Perspective', in Baechler et al. (1988), 20–38.

Hall, S. (1981) 'Notes on Deconstructing the Popular', in R. Samuel and G. Stedman Jores (eds), *Culture, Ideology and Politics*, London, 227–40.

Hallpike, C. R. (1986) *The Principles of Social Evolution*, Oxford.

Hamilton, G. G. (1984) 'Configurations in History: the Historical Sociology of S. N. Eisenstadt', in Skocpol (1984), 85–128.

Hammel, E. A. (1972) 'The Zadruga as Process', in Laslett (1972), 335–74.

Handlin, O. (1941) *Boston's Immigrants: a Study in Acculturation*, Cambridge, Mass.

Hansen, B. (1952) *Österlen*, Stockholm.

Hannerz, B. (1986) 'Theory in Anthropology: Small is Beautiful?', *Comparative Studies in Society and History*, 28, 362–7.

Harland, R. (1987) *Superstructuralism*, London.

Harootunian, H. D. (1988) *Things Seen and Unseen: Discourse and Ideology in Tokugawa Nativism*, Chicago.

Hartog, F. (1980) The *Mirror of Herodotus*; English trans. Berkeley, Ca, 1988.

Harvey, D. (1990) *The Condition of Postmodernity*, Oxford.

Hastrup, K. (1985) *Culture and History in Medieval Iceland*, Oxford.

Hauser, A. (1951) *A Social History of Art*, 2 vols, London.

Hawthorn, G. (1976) *Enlightenment and Despair*; rev. edn Cambridge, 1987.

Heal, F. (1990) *Hospitality in Early Modern England*, Oxford.

Hebdige, M. (1979) *Sub-Culture: the Meaning of Style*, London.

Heberle, R. (1951) *Social Movements*, New York.

Heckscher, E. (1931) *Mercantilism*; English trans., 2 vols, London, 1935.

Heers, J. (1974) *Family Clans in the Middle Ages*; English trans. Amsterdam, 1977.

Henry, L. (1956) *Anciens familles genevoises*, Paris.

Hexter, J. H. (1961) *Reappraisals in History*, London.

Hexter, J. H. (1968) 'The Rhetoric of History', *International Encyclopaedia of the Social Sciences* (ed. D. Sills), New York, vol. 6, 368–93.

Hexter, J. H. (1979) *On Historians*, Cambridge, Mass.

Hicks, J. (1969) *Theory of Economic History*, Oxford.

Hilton, R. H. (ed.) (1976) *The Transition from Feudalism to Capitalism*, London.

Himmelfarb, G. (1987) *The New History and the Old*, Cambridge, Mass.

Hintze, O. (1975) *Historical Essays* (ed. F. Gilbert), New York.

Hirschman, A. (1970) *Exit, Voice and Loyalty*, Cambridge, Mass.

Hobsbawm, E. (1959) *Primitive Rebels*; 3rd edn Manchester, 1971.

Hobsbawm, E. (1971) 'Class Consciousness in History', in I. Mészaros (ed.), *Aspects of History and Class Consciousness*, London, 5–19.

Hobsbawm, E. J. (1990) *Nations and Nationalism since 1780*, Cambridge.

Hobsbawm, E. and Ranger, T. (eds) (1983) *The Invention of Tradition*, Cambridge.

Hohendahl, P. (1982) *The Institution of Criticism*, Ithaca, NY.

Holub, R. C. (1984) *Reception Theory*, London.

Holy, L. and Stuchlik, M. (eds) (1981) *The Structure of Folk Models*, London.

Hopkins, K. (1978) *Conquerors and Slaves*, Cambridge.

Horton, R. (1967) 'African Traditional Thought and Western Science', *Africa*, 37, 50–71, 155–87.

Horton, R. (1982) 'Tradition and Modernity Revisited', in M. Hollis and S. Lukes (eds), *Rationality and Relativism*, Oxford, 201–60.

Hunt, L. (1984a) 'Charles Tilly's Collective Action', in Skocpol (1984), 244–75.

Hunt, L. (1984b) *Politics Culture and Class in the French Revolution*, Berkeley, Ca.

Hunt, L. (1989) 'History, Culture and Text', in L. Hunt (ed.), *The New Cultural History*, Berkeley and Los Angeles, Ca, 1–22.

Hutcheon, L. (1989) *The Politics of Postmodernism*, London.

Hymes, D. (1964) 'Toward Ethnographies of Communication'; rpr. in Giglioli (1972), 21–44.

Illyés, G. (1967) *People of the Puszta*, Budapest.

Inalcik, H. (1973) *The Ottoman Empire*, London.

Inden, R. (1990) *Imagining India*, Oxford.

Jarvie, I. C. (1964) *The Revolution in Anthropology*, London.

Jauss, H.-R. (1974) *Toward an Aesthetic of Reception*; English trans. Minneapolis, 1982.

Johnson, T. and Dandeker, C. (1989) 'Patronage: Relation and System', in A. Wallace-Hadrill (ed.), *Patronage in Ancient Society*, London, 219–42.

Jones, E. L. (1981) *The European Miracle: Environments, Economies and Geopolitics in the History of Europe and Asia*; rev. edn Cambridge, 1988.

Jones, G. S. (1976) 'From Historical Sociology to Theoretical History', *British Journal of Sociology*, 27, 295–305.

Jones, G. S. (1983) *Languages of Class*, Cambridge.

Jouanna, A. (1976) *L'Idée de race en France*, 3 vols, Lille-Paris.

Joyce, P. (1991) 'History and Post-Modernism', *Past and Present*, 133, 204–9.

Kagan, R. (1974) *Students and Society in Early Modern Spain*, Baltimore, Md.

Kaye, H. J. and McClelland, K. (1990) *E. P. Thompson: Critical Perspectives*, Cambridge.

Kelly, C. (1991) 'History and Post-Modernism', *Past and Present*, 133, 209–13.

Kelly, J. (1984) *Women, History and Theory*, Chicago.

Kemp, T. (1978) *Historical Patterns of Industrialisation*, London.

Kent, F. W. (1977) *Household and Lineage in Renaissance Florence*, Princeton, NJ.

Kerblay, B. (1970) 'Chayanov and the Theory of Peasantry as a Special Type of Economy', in Shanin (1971), 150–9.

Kershaw, I. (1989) *The Hitler Myth*, Oxford.

Kertzer, D. I. (1988) *Ritual, Politics and Power*, New Haven, Conn.

Kettering, S. (1986) *Patrons, Brokers and Clients in Seventeenth-Century France*, New York.

Kindleberger, C. P. (1990) *Historical Economics: Art or Science?* New York.

Klaniczay, G. (1990a) 'Daily Life and Elites in the Later Middle Ages', in F. Glatz (ed.), *Environment and Society in Hungary*, Budapest, 75–90.

Klaniczay, G. (1990b) *The Uses of Supernatural Power*, Cambridge.

Klaveren, J. van (1957) 'Fiscalism, Mercantilism and Corruption'; English trans. in D. C. Coleman (ed.), *Revisions in Mercantilism*, London, 140–61.

Knudsen, J. (1988) *Justus Möser and the German Enlightenment*, Cambridge.

Kocka, J. (1973) *Klassengesellschaft im Krieg*, Berlin.

Kocka, J. (1984) 'Historisch-Anthropologisch Fragestellungen – ein Defizit der Historische Sozialwissenschaft?', in H. S. Süssmuth (ed.), *Historiche Anthropologie*, Götingen, 73–83.

Koenigsberger, H. G. (1974) review of Stone (1972), *Journal of Modern History*, 46, 99–106.

Kolakowski, L. (1986) 'Modernity on Endless Trial', *Encounter*, March, 8–12.

Koselleck, R. (1965) 'Modernity and the Planes of Historicity'; rpr. in *Futures Past*, Cambridge, Mass., 1985, 3–20.

Kosminsky, E. A. (1935) *Studies in the Agrarian History of England*; English trans. Oxford, 1956.

Kroeber, A. L. and Kluckhohn, C. (1952) *Culture: a Critical Review of Concepts and Definitions*; rpr. New York, 1963.

Kula, W. (1962) *Economic Theory of the Feudal System*; English trans. London, 1976.

LaCapra, D. (1985) *History and Criticism*, Ithaca, NY, and London.

Landes, J. B. (1988) *Women and the Public Sphere in the Age of the French Revolution*, Ithaca, NY.

Lane, F. C. (1976) 'Economic Growth in Wallerstein's Social Systems', *Comparative Studies in Society and History*, 18, 517–32.

Lane, M. (ed.) (1970) *Structuralism*, London.

Langer, W. L. (1958) 'The Next Assignment', American Historical Review, 63, 283–304.

Lanternari, V. (1966) 'Désintégration culturelle et processus d'acculturation', *Cahiers Internationaux de Sociologie*, 41, 117–32.

Laslett, P. (ed.) (1972) *Household and Family in Past Time*, Cambridge.

Lasswell, H. (1936) *Politics: who gets what, when, how*; rpr. New York, 1958.

Leach, E. (1954) *Political Systems of Highland Burma*, London.

Leach, E. (1965) 'Frazer and Malinowski', *Encounter*, September, 24–36.

Lears, T. J. (1985) 'The Concept of Cultural Hegemony: Problems and Possibilities', *American Historical Review*, 90, 567–93.

Le Bras, G. (1955–6) *Etudes de sociologie religieuse*, 2 vols, Paris.

Lee, J. J. (1973) *The Modernisation of Irish Society, 1848–1918*, Dublin.

Lefebvre, G. (1932) *La grande peur de 1789*, Paris.

Le Goff, J. (1974) 'Les mentalités, in J. Le Goff and P. Nora (eds), *Faire de l'histoire*, 3 vols, Paris, vol. 3, 76–90.

Lemarchand, R. (1981) 'Comparative Political Clientelism', in S. N. Eisenstadt and R. Lemarchand (eds), *Political Clientelism, Patronage and Development*, Beverly Hills, Ca, 7–32.

Lerner, D. (1958) *The Passing of Traditional Society: Modernizing the Middle East*, Glencoe, Ill.

Le Roy Ladurie, E. (1966) *The Peasants of Languedoc*; abbr. English trans. Urbana, Ill, 1974.

Le Roy Ladurie, E. (1972) 'The Event and the Long Term in Social History'; rpr. in *The Territory of the Historian*, English trans. Hassocks, 1979, 111–32.

Le Roy Ladurie, E. (1975) *Montaillou*; English trans. Harmondsworth, 1980.

Le Roy Ladurie, E. (1979) *Carnival*; English trans. London, 1980.

Levack, B. P. (1987) *The Witch-Hunt in Early Modern Europe*, London.

Levi, G. (1985) *Inheriting Power*; English trans. Chicago, 1988.

Levi, G. (1991) 'Microhistory', in P. Burke (ed.), *New Perspectives in Historical Writing*, Cambridge, 93–113.

Lévi-Strauss, C. (1949) *Elementary Structures of Kinship*; English trans., London, 1969.

Lévi-Strauss, C. (1958) *Structural Anthropology*; English trans. London, 1968.

Lévi-Strauss, C. (1964–72) *Mythologiques*, 4 vols, Paris; English trans. of vols 1–2 as *Introduction to A Science of Mythology*, London, 1969–73.

Lévi-Strauss, C. (1983) 'Histoire et ethnologie', *Annales E. S. C.*, 38, 1217–31.

Lewenhak, S. (1980) *Women and Work*, London.

Leys, C. (1959) 'Models, Theories and the Theory of Political Parties', *Political Studies*, 7, 127–46.

Lipset, S. M. and Bendix, R. (1959) *Social Mobility in Industrial Society*, Berkeley, Ca.

Lison-Tolosana, C. (1966) *Belmonte de los Caballeros*; rpr. Princeton, NJ, 1983.

Litchfield, R. B. (1986) *Emergence of a Bureaucracy: the Florentine Patricians 1530–1790*, Princeton, NJ.

Lloyd, G. E. R. (1990) *Demystifying Mentalities*, Cambridge.

Lloyd, P. C. (1968) 'Conflict Theory and Yoruba Kingdoms', in I. M. Lewis (ed.), *History and Social Anthropology*, 25–58.

Lord, A. B. (1960) *The Singer of Tales*, Cambridge, Mass.

Lotman, J. (1984) 'The Poetics of Everyday Behaviour in Russian Eighteenth-Century Culture', in Lotman and Uspenskii (1984), 231–56.

Lotman, J. and Uspenskii, B. A. (1984) *The Semiotics of Russian Culture* (ed. A. Shukman), Ann Arbor, Mich.

Lukács, G. (1923) *History and Class Consciousness*; English trans. London, 1971.

Lukes, S. (1973) *Emile Durkheim*, London.

Lukes, S. (1974) *Power: a Radical View*, London.

Lukes, S. (1977) 'Political Ritual and Social Integration', in his *Essays in Social Theory*, London.

Macfarlane, A. D. (1970) *Witchcraft in Tudor and Stuart England*, London.

Macfarlane, A. D. (1979) *Origins of English Individualism*, Oxford.

Macfarlane, A. D. (1986) *Marriage and Love in England 1300–1840*, Oxford.

Macfarlane, A. D. (1987) *The Culture of Capitalism*, Oxford.

McKenzie, N. (1977) 'Centre and Periphery', *Acta Sociologica*, 20, 55–74.

McNeill, W. H. (1964) *Europe's Steppe Frontier*, Chicago.

McNeill, W. H. (1976) *Plagues and Peoples*, London.

McNeill, W. H. (1983) *The Great Frontier*, Princeton, NJ.

Maitland, F. W. (1897) *Domesday Book and Beyond*, London.

Malinowski, B. (1922) *Argonauts of the Western Pacific*, London.

Malinowski, B. (1926) 'Myth in Primitive Psychology'; rpr. in his *Magic Science and Religion*, New York, 1954, 93–148.

Malinowski, B. (1945) *The Dynamics of Culture Change*, New Haven, Conn.

Man, P. de (1986) *The Resistance to Theory*, Manchester.

Mann, G. (1971) *Wallenstein*; English trans. London, 1976.

Mann, G. (1979) 'Plädoyer für die historische Erzählung', in J. Kocka and T. Nipperdey (eds), *Theorie und Erzählung in der Geschichte*, Munich, 40–56.

Mann, M. (1970) 'The Social Cohesion of Liberal Democracy', *American Sociological Review*, 35, 423–37.

Mann, M. (1986) *The Sources of Social Power*, Cambridge.

Mannheim, K. (1936) *Ideology and Utopia*, London.

Mannheim, K. (1952) 'The Problem of Generation', in *Essays on the Sociology of Knowledge*, London, 276–320.

Marsh, R. M. (1961) *The Mandarins: the Circulation of Elites in China, 1600–1900*, Glencoe, Ill.

Marwick, A. (1965) *The Deluge: British Society and the First World War*, London.

Marx, K. and Engels, F. (1848) *The Communist Manifesto*; English trans. London, 1948.

Mason, T. (1981) 'Intention and Explanation: a Current Controversy about the Interpretation of National Socialism', in G. Hirschfeld and L. Kettenacker (eds), *Der Führer-Staat*, Stuttgart, 23–40.

Matthews, F. H. (1977) *Quest for American Sociology: Robert Park and the Chicago School*, Montreal and London.

Mauss, M. (1925) *The Gift*; English trans. London, 1954.

Medick, H. (1987) 'Missionaries in the Rowboat? Ethnological Ways of Knowing as a Challenge to Social History', *Comparative Studies in Society and History*, 29, 76–98.

Meek, R. (1976) *Social Science and the Ignoble Savage*, Cambridge.

Megill, A. and McCloskey, D. N. (1987) 'The Rhetoric of History', in J. S. Nelson, A. Megill and D. N. McCloskey (eds), *The Rhetoric of the Human Sciences*, Madison, Wis., 221–38.

Merton, R. (1948) 'Manifest and Latent Functions'; rpr. in his *Social Theory and Social Structure*, New York, 1968, 19–82.

Milo, D. S. (1990) 'Pour une histoire expérimentale, ou la gaie histoire', *Annales E. S. C.*, 717–34.

Mitchell, T. (1988) *Colonising Egypt*, Cambridge.

Miyazaki, I. (1963) *China's Examination Hell*; English trans. New York and Tokyo, 1976.

Moi, T. (ed.) (1987) *French Feminist Thought*, Oxford.

Momigliano, A. (1970) 'The Ancient City'; rpr. in his *Essays on Ancient and Modern Historiography*, Oxford, 1977, 325–40.

Mommsen, W. J. (1974) *The Age of Bureaucracy*, Oxford.

Moore, B. (1966) *Social Origins of Dictatorship and Democracy*, Boston, Mass.

Morris, C. (1975) 'Judicium Dei', in D. Baker (ed.), *Church, Society and Politics*, Oxford, 95–111.

Moses, J. A. (1975) *The Politics of Illusion: the Fischer Controversy in Modern German Historiography*, Santa Lucia, Ca.

Mousnier, R. (1951) 'L'évolution des finances publiques en France et en Angleterre', *Revue Historique*, 205, 1–23.

Mousnier, R. (1967) *Peasant Uprisings*; English trans. London, 1971.

Muchembled, R. (1978) *Elite Culture and Popular Culture in Early Modern France*; English trans. Baton Rouge, La, 1985.

Muchembled, R. (1984) 'Lay Judges and the Acculturation of the Masses', in K. von Greyerz (ed.), *Religion and Society in Early Modern Europe*, London, 56–65.

Muir, E. (1981) *Civic Ritual in Renaissance Venice*, Princeton, NJ.

Mukhia, H. (1980–1) 'Was there Feudalism in Indian History?', *Journal of Peasant Studies*, 8, 273–93.

Namier, L. (1928) *The Structure of Politics at the Accession of George III*, London.

Neale, J. E. (1948) 'The Elizabethan Political Scene'; rpr. in his *Essays in Elizabethan History*, London, 1958, 59–84.

Neale, W. C. (1957) 'Reciprocity and Redistribution in the Indian Village', in Polanyi (1944), 218–35.

Needham, R. (1975) 'Polythetic Classification', *Man*, 10, 349–69.

Niestroj, B. (1989) 'Norbert Elias', *Journal of Historical Sociology*, 2, 136–60.

Nipperdey, T. (1972) 'Verein als soziale Struktur in Deutschland'; rpr. in his *Gesellschaft, Kultur, Theorie*, Göttingen, 1976, 174–205.

Nisbet, R. (1966) *The Sociological Tradition*, New York.

Nisbet, R. (1969) *Social Change and History*, New York.

Nora, P. (ed.) (1984–7) *Les Lieux de mémoire*, 4 vols, Paris.

Norris, C. (1982) *Deconstruction: Theory and Practice*, London.

Ogburn, W. (1923) 'Cultural Lag'; rpr. in his *On Culture and Social Change*, Chicago, 1964.

Ohnuki-Tierney, E. (ed.) (1990) *Culture through Time*, Stanford, Ca.

O'Neill, J. (1986) 'The Disciplinary Society', *British Journal of Sociology*, 37, 42–60.

Ong, W. (1982) *Orality and Literacy*, London.

Ortner, S. and Whitehead, H. (eds) (1981) *Sexual Meanings*, Cambridge.

Ossowski, S. (1957) *Class Structure in the Social Consciousness*; English trans. London, 1963.

Ottenberg, H. (1959) 'Ibo Receptivity to Change' in W. R. Bascom and M. J. Herskovits (eds), *Continuity and Change in African Cultures*, Chicago, 130–43.

Ozouf, M. (1976) *Festivals and the French Revolution*; English trans. Cambridge, Mass., 1988.

Pareto, V. (1916) *The Mind and Society*; English trans. London, 1935.

Park, R. E. (1916) 'The City'; rpr. in *Human Communications*, Glencoe, Ill., 1952, 13–51.

Parker, G. (1988) *The Military Revolution*, Cambridge.

Parkin, F. (1971) *Class Inequality and Political Order*, London.

Parry, V. J. (1969) 'Elite Elements in the Ottoman Empire', in R. Wilkinson (ed.), *Governing Elites*, New York, 59–73.

Parsons, T. (1966) *Societies*, Englewood Cliffs, NJ.

Passerini, L. (1990) 'Mythbiography in Oral History', in Samuel and Thompson (1990), 49–60.

Peck, L. (1990) *Court Patronage and Corruption in Early Stuart England*, Boston, Mass.

Peel, J. D. Y. (1971) *Herbert Spencer: the Evolution of a Sociologist*, London.

Perkin, H. (1953–4) 'What is Social History?', *Bulletin of the John Rylands Library*, 36, 56–74.

Peyre, H. (1948) *Les générations littéraires*, Paris.

Phelan, J. L. (1967) The *Kingdom of Quito in the Seventeenth Century*, Madison, Wis.

Pillorget, R. (1975) *Les mouvements insurrectionels de Provence entre 1596 et 1715*, Paris.

Pinder, W. (1926) *Das Problem der Generation in der Kunstgeschichte Europas*, Berlin.

Ping-Ti, H. (1958–9) 'Aspects of Social Mobility in China', *Comparative Studies in Society and History*, 1, 330–59.

Pintner, W. M. and Rowney, D. K. (eds) (1980) *Russian Officialdom*, Chapel Hill, NC.

Pitt-Rivers, E. (1954) *The People of the Sierra*, London.

Pocock, J. G. A. (1981) 'Gibbon and the Shepherds', *History of European Ideas*, 2, 193–202.

Polanyi, K. (1944) *The Great Transformation*; rev. edn, Boston, 1957.

Pollock, F. and Maitland, F. W. (1895) *History of English Law Before the Time of Edward I*, 2 vols, London.

Pollock, L. (1983) *Forgotten Children*, Cambridge.

Porshnev, B. (1948) *Les soulèvements populaires en France 1623–48*; French trans. Paris, 1963.

Postan, M. M. (1972) *The Medieval Economy and Society*, London.

Poulantzas, N. (1968) *Classes in Contemporary Capitalism*; English trans. London, 1975.

Prest, W. (ed.) (1987) *The Professions in Early Modern England*, London.

Price, R. (1990) *Alabi's World*, Baltimore, Md.

Propp, V. (1928) *Morphology of the Folktale*; English trans., 2nd edn, Austin, Tex., 1968.

Radding, C. M. (1979) 'Superstition to Science', *American Historical Review*, 84, 945–69.

Ragin, C. and Chirot, D. (1984) 'The World System of Immanuel Wallerstein', in Skocpol (1984), 276–312.

Ramsden, H. (1974) *The 1898 Movement in Spain*, Manchester.

Ranum, O. (1963) *Richelieu and the Councillors of Louis XIII*, Oxford.

Reddy, W. (1987) *Money and Liberty in Modern Europe*, Cambridge.

Rhodes, R. C. (1978) 'Emile Durkheim and the Historical Thought of Marc Bloch', *Theory and Society*, 5, 45–73.

Ricoeur, P. (1983–5) *Time and Narrative*; English trans. New York, 1984–8.

Rigby, S. H. (1987) *Marxism and History*, Manchester.

Riggs, F. (1959) 'Agraria and Industria: toward a Typology of Comparative Administration', in W. J. Siffin (ed.), *Toward the Comparative Study of Public Administration*, Bloomington, Ind., 23–110.

Robin, R. (1970) *La société française en 1789: Semur-en-Auxois*, Paris.

Robinson, J. H. (1912) *The New History*, New York.

Röhl, J. C. G. (1982) 'Introduction', to J. C. G. Röhl and N. Sombart (eds), *Kaiser Wilhelm II*, Cambridge.

Rogers, S. (1975) 'The Myth of Male Dominance', *American Ethnologist* 2, 727–57.

Rokkan, S. (1975) 'Dimensions of State Formation and Nation-Building', in Tilly (1975), 562–600.

Romein, J. (1937) 'De dialektiek van de vooruitgang', in *Het onvoltooid verleden*, Amsterdam, 9–64.

Rorty, R. (1980) *Philosophy and the Mirror of Nature*, Princeton, NJ.

Rosaldo, R. (1986) 'From the Door of his Tent', in Clifford and Marcus (1986), 77–97.

Rosaldo, R. (1987) 'Where Objectivity Lies: the Rhetoric of Anthropology', in J. S. Nelson, A. Megill and D. McCloskey (eds), *The Rhetoric of the Human Sciences*, Madison, Wis., 87–110.

Rosenthal, J. (1967) 'The King's Wicked Advisers', *Political Science Quarterly*, 82, 595–618.

Ross, A. S. C. (1954) 'Linguistic Class-Indicators in Present-Day English', *Neuphilologische Mitteilungen*, 55, 20–56.

Ross, E. A. (1901) *Social Control*, New York.

Rostow, W. W. (1958) *The Stages of Economic Growth*, Cambridge.

Roth, G. (1976) 'History and Sociology in the Work of Max Weber', *British Journal of Sociology*, 27, 306–16.

Rudolph, L. I. and Rudolph, S. H. (1966) 'The Political Modernization of an Indian Feudal Order', *Journal of Social Issues*, 4, 93–126.

Runciman, W. G. (1969) 'What is Structuralism?', *British Journal of Sociology*, 20, 253–64.

Runciman, W. G. (1980) 'Comparative Sociology or Narrative History? A Note on the Methodology of Perry Anderson', *Archives européennes de sociologie*, 21, 162–78.

Runciman, W. G. (1983–9) *A Treatise on Social Theory*, 2 vols, Cambridge.

Sack, R. D. (1986) *Human Territoriality: its theory and history*, Cambridge.

Sahlins, M. (1981) *Historical Metaphors and Mythical Realities*, Ann Arbor, Mich.

Sahlins, M. (1985) *Islands of History*, Chicago.

Sahlins, M. (1988) 'Cosmologies of Capitalism', *Proceedings of the British Academy*, 74, 1–52.

Sahlins, P. (1989) *Boundaries: the Making of France and Spain in the Pyrenees*, Berkeley and Los Angeles, Ca.

Samuel, R. (1991) 'Reading the Signs', *History Workshop*, 32, 88–101.

Samuel, R. and Thompson, P. (eds) (1990) The *Myths We Live By*, London.

Sanderson, S. K. (1990) *Social Evolutionism: a Critical History*, Oxford.

Schama, S. (1987) *The Embarrassment of Riches*, London.

Schneider, H. K. (1959) 'Pakot Resistance to Change', in W. R. Bascom and M. J. Herskovits (eds), Continuity and Change in African Cultures, Chicago, 144–67.

Schochet, G. (1975) *Patriarchalism in Political Thought*, Oxford.

Schofield, R. S. (1968) 'The Measurement of Literacy in Preindustrial England', in J. Goody (ed.), *Literacy in Traditional Societies*, Cambridge.

Scott, J. C. (1969) 'The Analysis of Corruption in Developing Nations', *Comparative Studies in Society and History*, 11, 315–41.

Scott, J. C. (1976) *The Moral Economy of the Peasant*, New Haven, Conn.

Scott, J. C. (1990) *Domination and the Arts of Resistance: Hidden Transcripts*, New Haven, Conn. and London.

Scott, J. W. (1988) *Gender and the Politics of History*, New York, 1988.

Scott, J. W. (1991) 'Women's History', in Burke (1991), 42–66.

Scribner (1979) 'The Reformation as a Social Movement', in W. J. Mommsen (ed.), *Stadtbürgertum und Adel in der Reformation*, Stuttgart, 49–79.

Segalen, M. (1980) *Love and Power in the Peasant Family*; English trans. Cambridge, 1983.

Sewell, W. H. (1967) 'Marc Bloch and the Logic of Comparative History', *History and Theory*, 6, 208–18.

Sewell, W. H. (1974) 'Etat, Corps and Ordre', in Wehler (1987), 49–66.

Shanin, T. (ed.) (1971) *Peasants and Peasant Societies*, Harmondsworth.

Shils, E. (1975) *Center and Periphery*, Chicago/London.

Sider, G. (1986) *Culture and Class in Anthropology and History*, Cambridge.

Siebenschuh, W. R. (1983) *Fictional Techniques and Factual Works*, Athens, Ga.

Siegfried, A. (1913) *Tableau politique de la France de l'Ouest sous la troisième république*, Paris.

Silverman, S. (1977) 'Patronage as Myth', in Gellner and Waterbury (1977), 7–19.

Simiand, F. (1903) 'Méthode historique et science sociale'; English trans. *Review*, 9 (1985–6), 163–213.

Simmel, G. (1903) 'The Metropolis and Mental Life'; trans. in P. K. Hatt and A. J. Reiss (eds), *Cities and Society*, Glencoe, Ill., 1957, 635–46.

Skocpol, T. (1977) review of Wallerstein (1974), *American Journal of Sociology*, 82, 1075–90.

Skocpol, T. (1979) *States and Revolutions*, Cambridge.

Skocpol, T. (ed.) (1984) *Vision and Method in Historical Sociology*, Cambridge.

Smelser, N. J. (1959) *Social Change in the Industrial Revolution*, London.

Smith, D. (1984) 'Discovering Facts and Values: the Historical Sociology of Barrington Moore', in Skocpol (1984), 313–55.

Smith, D. (1991) The *Rise of Historical Sociology*, Cambridge.

Sombart, W. (1906) *Warum gibt es in den Vereinigten Staaten keinen Sozialismus?* Tübingen.

Sombart, W. (1929) 'Economic Theory and Economic History', *Economic History Review*, 1–19.

Soriano, M. (1968) *Les contes de Perrault: culture savante et traditions populaires*, Paris.

Southall, A. W. (1970) 'The Illusion of Tribe', in P. W. Gutkind (ed.), *The Passing of Tribal Man in Africa*, Leiden, 28–50.

Spencer, H. (1876–85) *The Principles of Sociology*, 4 vols, London.

Spencer, H. (1904) *An Autobiography*, London.

Spierenburg, P. (1984) *The Spectacle of Suffering*, Cambridge.

Spitz, L. W. (1967) 'The Third Generation of German Renaissance Humanists', in A. R. Lewis (ed.), *Aspects of the Renaissance*, Austin, Tex., 105–21.

Spivak, G. C. (1985) 'Deconstructing Historiography'; rpr. in R. Guha (ed.), *Slected Subaltern Studies*, New York, 1988, 3–32.

Sprenkel, O. van der (1958) *The Chinese Civil Service*, Canberra.

Spufford, M. (1974) *Contrasting Communities: English Villagers in the Sixteenth and Seventeenth Centuries*, Cambridge.

Srinivas, M. N. (1966) *Social Change in Modern India*, Berkeley and Los Angeles, Ca.

Stallybrass, P. and White, A. (1986) *The Politics and Poetics of Transgression*, London.

Steinberg, H.-J. (1971) 'Karl Lamprecht', in H.-U. Wehler (ed.), *Deutsche Historiker*, 1, Göttingen, 58–68.

Stevenson, J. (1985) 'The Moral Economy of the English Crowd: Myth and Reality', in A. Fletcher and J. Stevenson (eds), *Order and Disorder in Early Modern England*, Cambridge.

Stocking, G. (1983) 'The Ethnographer's Magic: Fieldwork in British Anthropology from Tylor to Malinowski', in G. Stocking (ed.), *Observers Observed*, Madison, Wis., 70–120.

Stone, L. (1965) *The Crisis of the English Aristocracy, 1558–1641*, Oxford.

Stone, L. (1971) 'Prosopography', *Daedalus*, 46–73; rpr. in *The Past and the Present Revisited*, London, 1987.

Stone, L. (1972) *The Causes of the English Revolution*, London.

Stone, L. (1977) *The Family, Sex and Marriage in England 1500–1800*, London.

Strauss, A. (1978) *Negotiations*, San Francisco, Ca.

Street, B. S. (1984) *Literacy in Theory and Practice*, Cambridge.

Suttles, G. D. (1972) *The Social Construction of Communities*, Chicago.

Tawney, R. H. (1941) 'The Rise of the Gentry', *Economic History Review*, 11, 1–38.

Temin, P. (ed.) (1972) *The New Economic History*, Harmondsworth.

Theweleit, C. (1977) *Male Fantasies*; English trans., 2 vols, Cambridge, 1987–8.

Thomas, K. V. (1971) *Religion and the Decline of Magic*, London.

Thompson, E. P. (1963) *The Making of the English Working Class*, London.

Thompson, E. P. (1971) 'The Moral Economy of the Crowd', *Past and Present*, 50, 76–136.

Thompson, E. P. (1972) 'Rough Music', *Annales E. S. C.*, 27, 285–310.

Thompson, E. P. (1978a) 'Class Struggle without Class', *Journal of Social History*, 3, 133–65.

Thompson, E. P. (1978b) *The Poverty of Theory*, London.

Thompson, F. (1948) *The Myth of Magna Carta*, New York.

Thompson, F. M. L. (1963) *English Landed Society in the Nineteenth Century*, London.

Thompson, J. B. (1984) *Studies in the Theory of Ideology*, Cambridge.

Thompson, J. B. (1990) *Ideology and Modern Culture*, Cambridge.

Thompson, P. (1975) *The Edwardians*, London.

Thorner, D. (1956) 'Feudalism in India', in R. Coulborn (ed.), Feudalism in History, Princeton, NJ, 133–50.

Tilly, C. (1964) *The Vendée*, London.

Tilly, C. (ed.) (1975) The *Formation of National States in Western Europe*, Princeton, NJ.

Tilly, C. (1990) *Coercion, Capital and European States 990–1990*, Oxford.

Tilly, L. and Scott, J. W. (1978) *Women, Work and Family*, New York.

Tipps, D. C. (1973) 'Modernisation Theory and the Comparative Study of Societies', *Comparative Studies in Society and History*, 15, 199–224.

Tirosh-Rothschild, H. (1990) 'Jewish Culture in Renaissance Italy', *Italia*, 9, 63–96.

Tonkin, E. (1990) 'History and the Myth of Realism', in Samuel and Thompson (1990), 25–35.

Touraine, A. (1984) *The Return to the Actor*; English trans. Minneapolis, 1988.

Toynbee, A. (1935–61) *A Study of History*, 13 vols, London.

Trevelyan, G. M. (1942) *English Social History*, London.

Trimberger, E. K. (1984) 'Edward Thompson', in Skocopl (1984), 211–43.

Tucker, R. C. (1968) 'The Theory of Charismatic Leadership', *Daedalus*, 731–56.

Turner, F. J. (1893) 'The Significance of the Frontier in American History'; rpr. in *The Frontier in American History*, rpr. Huntington, W. Va, 1976, 1–38.

Turner, V. (1969) *The Ritual Process*, London.

Turner, V. (1974) *Dramas, Fields and Metaphors*, Ithaca, NY.

Underdown, D. (1979) 'The Chalk and the Cheese', *Past and Present*, 85, 25–48.

Vansina, J. (1961) *Oral Tradition*; English trans. London, 1965.

Vansina, J. (1985) *Oral Tradition as History*; Madison, Wis.

Vargas Llosa, M. (1984) *The Real Life of Alejandro Mayta*; English trans. London, 1987.

Veblen, T. (1899) *Theory of the Leisure Class*, New York.

Veblen, T. (1915) *Imperial Germany and the Industrial Revolution*; new edn London, 1939.

Vernant, J.-P. (1966) *Myth and Thought among the Greeks*; English trans. London, 1983.

Veyne, P. (1976) *Bread and Circuses*; abridged English trans. 1990.

Viala, A. (1985) *Naissance de l'écrivain: sociologie de la littérature à l'âge classique*, Paris.

Vinogradoff, P. (1892) *Villeinage in England*, Oxford.

Völger, G. and Welck, K. von (eds) (1990) *Männerbande, Männerbunde*, Cologne.

Vovelle, M. (1973) *Piété baroque et déchristianisation en Provence*, Paris.

Vovelle, M. (1982) *Ideologies and Mentalities*; English trans. Cambridge, 1991.

Wachtel, N. (1971a) *The Vision of the Vanquished*; English trans. Hassocks, 1977.

Wachtel, N. (1971b) 'Pensée sauvage et acculturation', *Annales E. S. C.*, 26, 793–840.

Wachtel, N. (1974) 'L'acculuration', in J. Le Goff and P. Nora (eds) *Faire de l'historie*, vol. 1, Paris, 124–46.

Wachter, K. W., Hammel, E. A. and Laslett, P. (eds) (1978) *Statistical Studies of Historical Social Structure*, Cambridge.

Wagner, R. (1975) *The Invention of Culture*; rev. edn, Chicago, 1981.

Waite, R. G. L. (1977) *The Psychopathic God: Adolf Hitler*, New York.

Wallerstein, I. (1974) *The Modern World-System*, New York.

Walters, R. G. (1980) 'Signs of the Times: Clifford Geertz and Historians', *Social Research*, 47, 537–56.

Waquet, J.-C. (1984) *Corruption*; English trans. Cambridge, 1991.

Weber, M. (1920) *Economy and Society*; English trans., 3 vols, New York, 1968.

Weber, M. (1948) *From Max Weber* (ed. H. Gerth), London.

Weber, M. (1964) *The Religion of China*, English trans. London and New York.

Weber, R. (1980) *The Literature of Fact: Literary Nonfiction in American Writing*, Athens, Ohio.

Wehler, H.-U. (1987) *Deutsche Gesellschaftsgeschichte*, vol. 1 (*1700–1815*), Munich.

Weissman, R. F. E. (1985) 'Reconstructing Renaissance Sociology: the Chicago School and the Study of Renaissance Society', in R. C. Trexler (ed.), *Persons in Groups*, Binghamton, NY, 39–46.

Wertheim, W. F. (1974) *Evolution and Revolution*, Harmondsworth.

White, H. V. (1966) 'The Burden of History'; rpr. in his *Tropics of Discourse*, Baltimore, Md, 1978, 27–50.

White, H. V. (1973) *Metahistory*, Baltimore, Md.

White, H. V. (1976) 'The Fictions of Factual Representation'; rpr. in his *Tropics of Discourse*, Baltimore, Md, 1978, 121–34.

White, L. (1962) *Medieval Technology and Social Change*, Oxford.

Wiener, M. (1981) *English Culture and the Decline of the Industrial Spirit*, Cambridge.

Wiesner, M. (1989) 'Guilds, Male Bonding and Women's Work in Early Modern Germany', *Gender and History*, 1, 125–37.

Wilkinson, R. (1964) *The Prefects: British Leadership and the Public School Tradition*, London.

Wilkinson, R. G. (1973) *Poverty and Progress: an Ecological Model of Economic Development*, London.

Williams, R. (1958) *Culture and Society*, London.

Williams, R. (1962) *Communications*, Harmondsworth.

Willis, P. (1977) *Learning to Labour*, London.

Windelband, W. (1894) *Geschichte und Naturwissenschaft*, Berlin.

Winkler, J. J. (1990) *The Constraints of Desire: the Anthropology of Sex and Gender in Ancient Greece*, London.

Wirth, L. (1938) 'Urbanism as a Way of Life'; rpr. in P. K. Hatt and A. J. Reiss (eds), *Cities and Society*, Glencoe, Ill., 1957, 46–63.

Wirth, J. (1984) 'Against the Acculuration Thesis', in K. von Greyerz (ed.) *Religion and Society in Early Modern Europe*, London, 66–78.

Wolf, E. (1956) 'Aspects of Group Relations in a Complex Society'; rpr. in Shanin (1971), 50–66.

Wolf, E. (1969) *Peasant Wars of the Twentieth Century*, London.

Wolf, E. (1982) *Europe and the People without History*, Berkeley, Ca.

Wolfenstein, E. V. (1967) *The Revolutionary Personality: Lenin, Trotsky, Gandhi*, Princeton, NJ.

Wootton, B. (1959) *Social Science and Social Pathology*, London.

Woude, A. M. van der (1972) 'The Household in the United Provinces', in Laslett (1972), 299–318.

Wrigley, E. A. (1972–3) 'The Process of Modernization and the Industrial Revolution in England', *Journal of Interdisciplinary History*, 3, 225–59.

Wuthnow, R., Hunter, J. P. and Bergeson, A. (1984) *Cultural Analysis*, London.

Wyatt-Brown, B. (1982) *Southern Honor*, New York.

Yeo, E. and Yeo, S. (eds) (1981) *Popular Culture and Class Conflict 1590–1914*, Brighton, 128–54.

Yinger, J. M. (1960) 'Contra-Culture and Sub-Culture', American Sociological Review, 25, 625–35.

Young, M. and Willmott, P. (1957) *Family and Kinship in East London*, London.

INDEX